IS THE QURAN THE WORD OF GOD?

Is Islam the One True Faith?

Edward D. Andrews

IS THE QURAN THE WORD OF GOD?

Is Islam the One True Faith?

Edward D. Andrews

Christian Publishing House

Cambridge, Ohio

CHRISTIAN PUBLISHING HOUSE

FOUNDED 2005

IS THE QURAN THE WORD OF GOD?: Is Islam the One True Faith? by Edward D. Andrews

ISBN-13: **978-1-945757-49-5**

ISBN-10: **1-945757-49-3**

Table of Contents

Edward D. Andrews

Preface

For generations, devout Muslims have maintained that the Quran stands as God's final revelation, crowning earlier Scriptures and concluding all prophetic messages with the prophet Muhammad in the seventh century C.E. Many readers, including those of other faiths, remain captivated by the Quran's majestic language and emphasis on complete devotion to the Almighty. Yet questions remain for countless individuals who revere the Bible as Jehovah's written Word. Does the Quran truly continue the lineage of Abraham, Moses, and Jesus? Does it confirm or alter the core doctrines of Scripture? Does it enrich the biblical message, or does it depart from the pattern God established through the Hebrew prophets and the Christian apostles?

The central title of this book—Is the Quran the Word of God?: Is Islam the One True Faith?—frames the investigative thrust that unites all the chapters to come. It also poses a formidable challenge to each reader. If there is one sovereign Creator, as both Christians and Muslims affirm, can these two sacred texts genuinely coexist as two halves of the same revelation? Or, alternatively, does one text preserve the fullness of God's truth while the other diverges from it?

This volume addresses that tension by assessing the foundational claims behind the rise of Islam and the composition of the Quran, weighing them carefully against the historical, prophetic, and theological record enshrined in the Hebrew Scriptures and the Christian Greek Scriptures. The contents illustrate the uncompromising stance of a conservative Bible scholar: a commitment to the objective, historical-grammatical method of interpretation, a refusal of modern skepticism that denies Scripture's inspiration, and a reliance on the internal consistency and external confirmations that buttress the Bible as God's unbroken revelation.

Examining Islam in Light of Biblical Revelation

Both Islam and biblical Christianity proclaim a single sovereign God who created the universe. Yet from that common foundation spring divergent teachings—about the nature of Jesus, the path of salvation, the reliability of older Scriptures, and the place of subsequent revelations. For many centuries, readers of Scripture have debated whether the seventh-century message recited by Muhammad expands or replaces the biblical record. Conservative Christians, guided by texts such as Jude 3, generally hold that "the faith" was delivered in its completeness through Jesus and his apostles, leaving no room for a latter-day message to override or correct it.

Throughout these chapters, the authors invite you to probe the Quran's claim to confirm earlier revelation, discovering in the process where it maintains partial continuity and where it diverges from essential biblical tenets. In some Islamic apologetic traditions, the Quran is presented as a "seal" of prophecy, rectifying what is believed to be the corruption or misinterpretation of the Bible. However, many centuries of manuscript evidence demonstrate that the Bible's text remains stable and uncorrupted, while the content of Scripture stands at odds with key teachings of the Quran. The result is a fundamental discrepancy. If the Quran were a direct extension of the Bible, the continuity would be readily visible; but the chapters within this book systematically uncover how the messages differ—sometimes irreconcilably—on doctrines such as God's personal name, man's condition in death, the ransom sacrifice of Christ, and the final authority of the biblical canon.

Why Comparisons Are Necessary

The earliest Christians in the first century faced controversies from Jewish religious leaders, pagan philosophers, and political authorities. Yet they relied on prophecy, miracles, and the apostolic teachings to confirm the authenticity of the new covenant. When Islam emerged centuries later, it contended that a fresh prophet had arisen to unify believers under a final dispensation. This demands an analysis of whether the biblical pattern, from Moses to Christ, left room for such a prophet. The Gospels' record of Jesus' words, especially those in John 14–16 about a coming helper, have sometimes been reinterpreted by Muslim polemicists to mean Muhammad. But a close reading shows those promises were specifically directed to the apostles of the first century as they awaited the Holy Spirit's guidance. To the Christian, the question of authenticity also concerns whether God

7

consistently provided miraculous signs to authenticate major revelations. Moses parted the Red Sea, Jesus performed healings and rose from the dead, the apostles spoke in tongues, but Muhammad offered no parallel wonders—pointing instead to the Quran's literary quality. By measuring these claims against biblical precedent, believers can judge for themselves which stands on surer ground.

The chapters ahead systematically explore these claims. They do not merely pit the Bible against the Quran in a polemical sense; rather, they examine whether the Quran's message truly weaves into the biblical tapestry or diverges from it. If the God of Scripture declared that "He is not a God of confusion" (1 Corinthians 14:33), can a new text that arrives six centuries after Christ, refutes the cross, and denies the biblical portrayal of Jesus be in harmony with that same God's revealed will? Through historical evidence, textual analysis, and logical reasoning, each chapter marshals arguments either to confirm or challenge the Quran's central claims.

Structure of This Book

In its layout, this book sets the stage with an introductory overview of Islam's emergence (INTRODUCTION to Islam) and then moves on to evaluate the Quran's literary and doctrinal credentials.

CHAPTER 1 (Is the Quran a Literary Miracle?) explores the claim that the beauty and power of the Quran's Arabic text constitute a miracle. Many Muslims maintain that an "illiterate" Muhammad could not produce such a refined composition. Yet from a biblical vantage point, divine authority has historically rested on fulfilled prophecy and confirmed miracles, not rhetorical brilliance alone. The chapter asks whether purely literary excellence can suffice as evidence of inspiration.

CHAPTER 2 (Is There Evidence That the Quran Is the Third Installment of the Inspired, Inerrant Word of God?) probes whether the Quran merges seamlessly with the Hebrew and Greek Scriptures. The text references earlier revelations but also modifies or negates central doctrines, such as Jesus' crucifixion. The consistent biblical pattern calls for harmony and inerrancy, so the chapter inquires whether the Quran complements or contradicts the biblical faith once for all delivered.

CHAPTER 3 (Is the Quran Harmonious and Consistent?) weighs the internal coherence of the Quran's suras. Repetitions and abrogations—wherein later verses override earlier ones—abound in the text. This pattern stands in marked contrast to the biblical tradition, which though spanning over a millennium, shows remarkable continuity from Genesis to Revelation. Does the presence of abrogation indicate a dynamic, human-driven adaptation rather than a once-for-all divine revelation?

CHAPTER 4 (Is the Quran from God or Man?) addresses how biblical prophets were authenticated by supernatural signs. In the case of Islam, the text itself is offered as proof of its source. Does that approach meet biblical standards? The chapter also highlights the role of prophecy in Scripture—where God repeatedly gave predictions centuries in advance, accurately fulfilled in history—and questions whether the Quran demonstrates comparable predictive proof.

CHAPTER 5 (Is Islamic Teaching Rooted in Genuine Divine Revelation or Merely Human Tradition?) confronts the overlap between what the Quran calls revelations and the large body of hadith, or traditions about Muhammad's words and deeds. The biblical worldview underscores abiding by God's Word, but how do we address man-made traditions that overshadow or reinterpret fundamental truths? The complexity of Islamic jurisprudence based on hadith stands in tension with the simpler moral laws revealed in Scripture.

CHAPTER 6 (Are Islamic Jihads Truly of Divine Origin or Driven by Human Ambition?) examines the concept of jihad in Islamic history, comparing it with the new covenant ethic of love, nonviolence, and the spiritual warfare waged by Christians (Ephesians 6:12). Whereas Old Testament Israel had at times engaged in divine warfare under direct commands, Christianity's founder Jesus parted ways with such physical battles. The discussion clarifies whether the expansion of Islam by the sword can align with the righteous character of Jehovah God as known in Scripture.

CHAPTER 7 (Does Sharia Law Reflect Divine Righteousness or Merely Human Ambition?) delves into the extensive code of conduct known as Sharia, derived from the Quran and the Hadith. Since the biblical new covenant replaced Mosaic legislation with a spiritual law "written on hearts" (2 Corinthians 3:3), can a rigid religious code that merges religion and state truly represent the final pattern God intended? The chapter underscores how imposing laws from above can differ from the biblical stress on voluntary worship.

CHAPTER 8 (Does Islam's Modern Worldview and Radical Elements Align With Scriptural Truth?) offers insight into contemporary expressions of Islam, including fundamentalist stances that sometimes justify aggression. The biblical approach to governance and moral change is typically from within hearts, culminating in a spiritual kingdom not of this world. So the question arises: do certain radical elements reflect a continuity with the biblical ethic, or do they reveal a departure from the path established in Scripture?

CHAPTER 9 (Does Radical Islamic Eschatology Clash With Scriptural End-Times Hope?) addresses how Islam interprets the end of days, foreseeing a final conflict involving the Mahdi and Jesus, who subdues unbelievers in a global domain. The Bible, by contrast, presents Christ returning in glory for a final separation of righteous and wicked—no human warfare needed to launch that divine intervention (Matthew 24:30, 31). This divergence in eschatological vision can be profound.

CHAPTER 10 (Does Archaeological Discovery Confirm the Inspired Record?) explores the role of archaeology in supporting biblical authenticity. Over many decades, excavations in Bible lands have corroborated chronological and historical details recounted in Scripture, strengthening the Christian's confidence in the biblical text. By comparing these results with any parallel support for the Quran's historical references, the book highlights how the Bible repeatedly stands vindicated by external evidences.

CHAPTER 11 (Can the Bible Alone Be Trusted as the One Complete Revelation?) focuses on the biblical tradition of reliability—from original manuscripts to thousands of extant copies that preserve a stable text. If Scripture truly endured by God's providence, then the possibility of an entirely new revelation that supersedes it becomes questionable. The chapter counters the charge that the Bible was corrupted, showing how the textual record proves remarkable fidelity over the centuries, in contrast to the later claims that the older revelations needed correction by the Quran.

CHAPTER 12 (How Should We Share Our Faith in Christ With Muslims?) completes the volume with practical guidance on evangelizing in a spirit of gentleness and respect. Christians are called to present biblical truths patiently, addressing sensitive points and seeking common ground where possible, all the while affirming the centrality of Christ's atoning sacrifice and his exclusive role as Mediator (John 14:6). This concluding segment reminds believers that "the slave of the Lord does not need to fight but to be gentle toward all" (2 Timothy 2:24, 25).

Placing Our Confidence in Scripture

Central to all these chapters is the unshakable premise that Scripture alone is God's complete self-revelation for humankind, culminating in the new covenant ratified by Jesus' blood. The command in Revelation 22:18, 19, not to add or remove words from the book, testifies to the completeness of divine revelation. While the Quran claims to be the final word from God, a careful reading shows how it diverges from the biblical portrait in multiple doctrinal areas. This book calls the reader to consider whether God would indeed "change horses midstream," so to speak, by establishing yet another unverified prophet centuries after the apostolic age.

Throughout these pages, the authors remain mindful that many sincere Muslims hold devout convictions about their faith. The purpose here is not to demean individuals but to evaluate the textual and theological claims of the Quran. For the Christian, abiding by the new covenant's emphasis on love (John 13:34), it is paramount to approach discussions with Muslims graciously, contentiously refusing only false doctrines while always holding open the door for honest conversation. This balanced approach acknowledges the sincerity of Muslim worshipers but distinguishes sincerity from truth, recalling that "the word of Jehovah endures forever" (1 Peter 1:25). As Jesus prayed, "Sanctify them by means of the truth; your word is truth" (John 17:17).

The real question is which text fully embodies that truth: the older Scriptures culminating in the Greek New Testament, or the later composition known as the Quran?

Preparing for Such a Study

Readers of this volume should be ready to engage with historical data, scriptural quotations, analyses of Arabic expressions, and expositions of biblical prophecy. While the book does not claim to be an exhaustive encyclopedia of Islam's complexities, it aims to provide a thorough evangelical viewpoint grounded in biblical scholarship. Each chapter addresses specific allegations or arguments, drawing from the moral, doctrinal, historical, and archaeological vantage points that a conservative Christian might emphasize. The final goal is not merely to compare academic theories but to fortify believers with a coherent defense of scriptural authority and to help them see how to share the gospel of Christ with Muslims in a way that respects them as persons made in God's image.

Indeed, from the earliest days of the church, Christians have encountered diverse philosophies and rival claims to revelation. The apostle Paul once debated philosophers in Athens (Acts 17:22-34), adjusting his language to reason from a vantage the Greek crowd could grasp. Similarly, believers today adapt to new settings, such as outreach to Muslim neighbors or co-workers. This book arms them with the knowledge to respond intelligently: from the Quran's contradictory references to Jesus to the question of abrogated verses that shift the text's meaning over time, from Jihads in Islam's expansion to the call for biblical spiritual warfare, from Sharia law that merges religion and state to the new covenant's emphasis on free moral agency under grace.

Encouragement to the Reader

As you journey through the pages that follow, you will find recurring themes of biblical reliability, the unity of the Hebrew and Greek Scriptures, the mismatch between the Quran's narrative and biblical prophecy, and the abiding Christian calling to share Jesus' message with gentleness and respect. This book does not aim to incite hostility but to equip believers with reasoned arguments firmly anchored in Scripture. Our desire is that you come away with renewed confidence in the biblical worldview, seeing yet again the "unchangeable purpose of God" (Hebrews 6:17), a purpose culminating in Christ rather than in additional revelations centuries later.

Some readers may be new to Christian apologetics or to the specifics of Islam's teachings. Others might have experience discussing matters of faith with Muslim friends. Regardless of your background, you will find in these chapters a structured approach that starts by analyzing the Quran's own claims (Chapters 1–4) and then broadens out to discuss key theological issues such as Jihad, Sharia, worldview, eschatology, and historical authenticity (Chapters 5–11). The concluding chapter addresses the practical side of gospel witness: how do we speak about our hope without giving needless offense, yet still proclaim the fullness of biblical truth?

Pray for guidance as you read, asking that God provide clarity of mind. If you are reading from a Muslim viewpoint, we invite you to consider carefully the biblical evidence for Jesus' unique role as Messiah and Mediator. Explore the vast manuscript tradition that secures the Bible's content across millennia. Reflect on the difference between a purely rhetorical sign and a scriptural record replete with prophecy and divine confirmations. For Christians, the call is to handle God's Word accurately (2 Timothy 2:15), ready to engage Muslims with Christ's love and the unwavering teaching of Scripture.

As you proceed, may you be reminded that the Bible stands alone as the abiding Word of God, tested by prophecy, historical integrity, moral power, and the resurrection of Christ as the ultimate sign. While the Quran occupies an important place in world religious discourse and has shaped entire civilizations, it does not meet the criteria or unify with the biblical message—particularly regarding Jesus' identity and God's redemptive plan. Hence, we approach these pages with reverence for God's truth, recognizing the weight of the question: Is the Quran truly God's Word, or is it a human text that restates partial biblical narratives while diverging from Scripture's culminating gospel? This question compels each of us to examine carefully which path we will follow.

In the end, we hope that the chapters presented here, culminating in practical strategies for Christian witness, strengthen your assurance that "the faith that was once for all time delivered to the holy ones" (Jude 3) abides in the Bible's sixty-six books. The new covenant instituted by Christ stands complete and unrepeatable, sealed by his sacrificial blood. None can add or subtract from that covenant without straying from the foundation the apostles laid. May the Holy Spirit guide you to glean from these discussions both a deeper appreciation for the Bible's reliability and an equipped readiness to share the good news with Muslim seekers who yearn for the redeeming power of the Messiah's cross. May God bless your reading, reflection, and conversations, leading hearts to the fullness of truth in Jesus Christ.

Edward D. Andrews

Author of 220+ books and Chief Translator of the Updated American Standard Version (UASV)

INTRODUCTION to Islam

Introductory Thoughts on Islam's Emergence

When we consider Islam from a Christian apologetic perspective, questions naturally arise about the origins, theology, and practices of this major world religion. Islam began in Arabia in the early seventh century C.E., and its historical narrative holds that the prophet Muhammad was chosen to receive revelations from God through the angel Gabriel. From a Christian vantage point, these claims invite thoughtful examination. Why did Islam arise in Arabia at that particular time? How does Islam understand previous divine revelations allegedly given to the ancient Hebrews, as well as to the early Christian congregation? These questions set the stage for exploring Islam's foundational events, comparing the teachings of the Qur'an with the Bible, and reflecting on the differences that shape Christian and Islamic thought.

Before discussing the life of Muhammad and the rise of Islam, it is necessary to acknowledge that Islam presents itself as a continuation and culmination of earlier revelations. Many of its adherents believe that the prophets of the Old Testament, including Noah, Abraham, and Moses, received genuine revelations from God. They also maintain that Jesus was a righteous prophet of God, though not divine. To many Christians, these ideas resonate with the biblical theme of prophetic succession, yet they diverge significantly from certain pivotal biblical tenets. Consequently, we have to weigh the Islamic narrative with the biblical record to decide if the revelations of the Qur'an truly harmonize with what Christians understand as Jehovah's unfolding purpose.

The vast scope of Islam defies simple summaries, but a faithful introduction to its development will help us better appreciate Islamic beliefs. We can begin with the geographic and cultural milieu that molded the Arabian Peninsula, particularly Mecca, around the time that Muhammad was born.

The Arabian Setting at Islam's Advent

Arabia in the sixth and seventh centuries C.E. was a region crisscrossed by trade caravans connecting Byzantium to the north and African kingdoms to the south. It was dotted with tribal societies bound by elaborate codes of honor and loyalty. Although they honored a supreme deity called Allah, they also revered other gods and practiced idolatry. In Mecca, in the present-day region of Saudi Arabia, many worshipped at a building known as the Ka'bah. It housed numerous idols, apparently including a black meteorite that people venerated. The desert environment, commerce, and polytheistic worship contributed to an intermingling of beliefs, setting the stage for the emergence of a faith that insisted on pure monotheism.

IS THE QURAN THE WORD OF GOD?

When Muhammad was born around 570 C.E., the religions of the peninsula combined a traditional worship of multiple deities with traces of Jewish and Christian influence. Some pockets of Arabia followed monotheistic beliefs, likely gleaned from contact with Jewish and Christian communities. Muhammad's tribe, the Quraysh, guarded the sacred shrine in Mecca and gained prosperity from the commerce that flowed into this city of pilgrimage. Against this background, Muhammad's questioning of idolatry and his inclination toward monotheism were unusual but not unprecedented. The unsettled nature of Arabia's spiritual landscape made it ripe for a message of singular devotion to God.

Muhammad's Early Experiences and Revelation Claims

Islamic sources relate that Muhammad lost both parents while he was young, which left him under the care of relatives. As he reached adulthood, he exhibited a sense of moral indignation at the rampant polytheism and moral laxity among his people. Some traditions suggest that he retreated to a cave on the outskirts of Mecca for meditation and prayer. At about 40 years old—around 610 C.E.—he reportedly received his first revelation from an entity identified as the angel Gabriel. According to these accounts, Muhammad was commanded to "Recite," an imperative that would allegedly transform him into a messenger of God.

As the narrative goes, Muhammad, initially anxious and unsure, found solace in the belief that the divine had selected him to guide his people to pure worship of God. The earliest revelations—later compiled into the Qur'an—demanded a return to the worship of one God, free from idolatrous rituals. From a Christian perspective, any claim of new revelation is subject to biblical scrutiny. The Hebrew Scriptures and the Greek New Testament present a narrative of God's dealings that culminate with the arrival of the Messiah and the establishment of Christianity in the first century. For many conservative Christians, the question arises: Is there any biblical foundation for another prophet after Christ's apostles? This leads some to examine the Qur'an's teachings in detail, comparing them with biblical theology to see whether these revelations align with the pattern of biblical prophecy. Nonetheless, the historical fact remains that Muhammad gained a following and shaped a community of believers.

Consolidation of the Qur'an

According to Islamic tradition, Muhammad continued receiving revelations for about 22 or 23 years, until his death in 632 C.E. Since many in that era possessed strong memories, they reportedly committed large sections of these recitations to heart. Historians note that early written fragments of the revelations were penned on pieces of parchment, bone, or palm leaves. After Muhammad's passing, there arose an urgency to preserve these revelations in an authoritative script. Under the first two caliphs (successors) of Muhammad, committees were formed to gather every recorded verse. Eventually, under the third caliph, 'Uthmān, the collected revelations were standardized into what became known as the Qur'an. This text, especially in Arabic, is revered by Muslims as God's very speech, though many scholars and historians observe differences of nuance in various early manuscripts.

From a Christian standpoint, no text outside the Bible is recognized as divinely inspired Scripture. While we might acknowledge the Qur'an's historical significance, we do not view it as an inspired continuation of the biblical canon. Nevertheless, it still offers an important perspective on how Islam interprets biblical history and prophecy. One of the points that interest many Christians is that although the Qur'an contains references to figures like Adam, Noah, Abraham, and Jesus, it does not parallel the Bible's entire narrative. It frequently repeats sections about patriarchs and prophets, while also framing Jesus not as the Son of God but as a respected prophet. In this way, readers see an intricate interaction—albeit from a non-biblical vantage point—between the Qur'an and earlier Hebrew and Christian traditions.

The Migration to Medina and Expansion of Islam

In Mecca, Muhammad's preaching drew resistance from many local inhabitants who wanted to preserve their idol-worship at the Ka'bah. Persecution increased, leading Muhammad and his small band of followers to flee north to the oasis city of Yathrib, later renamed Medina, in 622 C.E. This flight—called the Hijrah—became the starting point for the Islamic calendar (A.H. for Anno Hegirae). In Medina, Muhammad assumed a more pronounced leadership role, both religiously and politically. Over time, conflicts arose between Medina and Mecca, with battles and negotiations shaping the future of the Arabian Peninsula. Eventually, Muhammad and his followers gained control of Mecca. He is reported to have removed the idols from the Ka'bah, thereby reorienting it as the focus of worship for Allah alone.

After Muhammad's death, Islam's expansion continued under the caliphs who succeeded him. By the middle of the eighth century, Islamic rule had spread from North Africa and Spain in the west to parts of Central Asia in the east. This swift expansion was influenced by many factors, including the weakening of the Persian and Byzantine Empires, the zeal of Islamic leadership, and the internal divisions of rival states. For the Christian, one aspect to ponder is how Islam might fit into the biblical view of human governance and religious diversity emerging after the apostolic age. While the Bible does not provide direct commentary on Islam, it outlines the progress of kingdoms and empires that often overshadow God's people. The rapid proliferation of Islam was a monumental event in history, marking the establishment of a new religious power that would interface—often contentiously— with Christian communities for centuries.

Sectarian Splits: Sunnis and Shi'ites

Muhammad did not designate a clear successor before he died in 632 C.E. In the immediate aftermath, many of his followers supported the claim of Abu Bakr as caliph. Yet others insisted that 'Alī, Muhammad's cousin and son-in-law, should be the rightful successor. Those loyal to 'Alī eventually became known as the Shi'ites, and they claim that legitimate leadership for the Muslim community follows the bloodline of the prophet. By contrast, the Sunni majority holds that leadership can be elective and that the first four caliphs, including Abu Bakr and 'Umar, had rightful authority, though 'Alī was included as the fourth caliph.

The leadership dispute grew increasingly bitter. It culminated in violent confrontations, including the murder of 'Alī and the martyrdom, in Shīʿite eyes, of ʿAlīʾs son Ḥusayn. This tragedy is commemorated in Shīʿite communities even today. The historical schism between Sunnis and Shiʿites endures, shaping theological nuances and religious practices that define these two major branches of Islam. For outsiders, this divide may seem like a mere internal political squabble, but to devout Muslims it involves weighty doctrinal questions regarding succession, legitimate religious authority, and devotion to the family of the prophet. A Christian is reminded that even in early Christianity, disputes arose about leadership, though the biblical record provides apostolic writings that helped unify believers under scriptural direction. Islam, on the other hand, continued without a single unifying ecclesiastical structure, leading to the formation of distinct sects. Understanding these differences can clarify why there is such diversity within Islam, much like Christendom's fragmentation over theological and ecclesiastical issues across time.

The Authority of the Qur'an, Hadith, and Shariʿah

Islamic tradition rests on three foundational sources. First and foremost is the Qur'an. Muslims believe it to be the exact speech of God given in Arabic. Thus, many prefer to read it only in Arabic, asserting that any translation loses its purity. Second is the body of narratives called the Hadith, which supposedly preserve the sayings, approvals, and actions of Muhammad and sometimes his closest companions. Third is the Shariʿah, the body of Islamic law that derives from the Qur'an and the Hadith. It regulates almost every aspect of a believer's life, from daily rituals and moral conduct to complex matters of finance and governance.

For most devout Muslims, the Qur'an is unparalleled in authority. Christians, of course, respect the right of adherents of other faiths to hold their texts in high esteem, but they also note that the Bible stands alone as a divinely inspired revelation. In Christian apologetics, the question often posed is: Does the Qur'an's teaching uphold or alter biblical truths? Many Christians find that the Qur'an diverges from key biblical doctrines about God's nature, Christ's identity, and humanity's path to salvation. They might emphasize that Scripture warns about messages contradictory to the teachings of Christ and his apostles, referencing passages like Galatians 1:8, where Paul cautioned against accepting an altered gospel. Nevertheless, for a thorough grasp of Islam, one must acknowledge that the Qur'an and the Hadith form the bedrock of Islamic practice. The Shari'ah, with its comprehensive moral and legal code, ensures that Islam extends beyond private devotion to encompass social governance.

Islamic Views on God's Name and Divine Oneness

The fundamental tenet of Islam is absolute monotheism—Allah is one. From the vantage point of the Qur'an, there is no plurality in the divine. Muslims affirm a radical monotheism that disavows any concept of God incarnate or God in triune form. Indeed, Islamic teachings repeatedly stress that attributing partners to God is the gravest error. This resonates in certain respects with the strict monotheism taught to the ancient Hebrews: "Listen, O Israel: Jehovah our God is one Jehovah" (Deuteronomy 6:4). Biblical usage of the divine name in the Hebrew Scriptures underscores a personal name, Jehovah, for the God of Israel. Devout Muslims typically use "Allah" to reference the supreme being, though an observant Christian might argue that the personal name Jehovah conveys a more intimate biblical identity than the generic title for "God."

Islamic scholars sometimes point to textual alterations in what they regard as Jewish and Christian Scripture, insisting that Jews and Christians have strayed from pure monotheism. They especially repudiate the notion of the Trinity, asserting that it undermines God's absolute oneness. The Christian faith, however, rests on a distinction between the Father, the Son, and the Holy Spirit, though many conservative Christians differ from traditional dogmatic definitions that equate Jesus with God. Some highlight biblical passages wherein Jesus is depicted as subordinate to the Father (John 14:28) or lacking knowledge reserved for the Father (Mark 13:32). These considerations remind us of important tensions between standard Christian dogma and the Qur'an's statements about Jesus' nature. In sum, Islam staunchly defends a singular view of God, which shapes all of its worship, prayer, and daily life.

Islamic Teaching on Jesus and His Prophetic Role

A crucial point of divergence between Islamic and Christian beliefs lies in the identity of Jesus. Islam esteems Jesus ('Isa in Arabic) as a remarkable prophet and messenger, but never as God's Son or as part of a triune God. The Qur'an also denies that Jesus was actually crucified, describing his death as an illusion or attributing the crucifixion to someone who resembled him. This is a dramatic break from the New Testament account, where the crucifixion is pivotal for redemption. Indeed, the apostle Paul wrote that the resurrection stands at the center of Christian faith (1 Corinthians 15:12-14).

Conversely, Muslims cherish Jesus as an essential prophet who performed miracles, honored his mother Mary, and brought the gospel in a line of preceding revelations. They uphold the moral teachings attributed to him but redefine much of his biblical role. From a conservative Christian standpoint, the denial of Jesus' crucifixion and resurrection unravels the heart of the gospel message that proclaims Jesus as "the Lamb of God," the ransom sacrifice for humanity (John 1:29). Moreover, the scriptural record identifies Jesus as the "Mediator between God and men" (1 Timothy 2:5). Thus, this difference is not a mere technicality but a substantial theological gap between Islam and biblical Christianity.

Man as a Soul and the Afterlife According to Islam

Islam teaches that humans possess a soul that survives physical death and will experience either reward or punishment in an afterlife. The Qur'an depicts scenes of resurrection, the day of judgment, and either entry into gardens of paradise or banishment to a place of fiery torment. Many Muslims hold that the dead have a conscious existence in the Barzakh, a kind of intermediary state before the final resurrection. In contrast, biblical passages such as Ecclesiastes 9:5 and Ezekiel 18:4 can be understood to show that the dead are unconscious in the grave. Many conservative Christians do not believe in a separate immortal soul that departs the body at death. Instead, Genesis 2:7 is understood to mean that man is a "living soul," not that man possesses an immaterial entity. This biblical stance likewise conflicts with notions of a conscious soul surviving bodily death.

Moreover, Islam emphasizes a scorching hell as the destiny of unbelievers, a place of unending torment. Conservative Christians who accept the historical-grammatical reading of Scripture typically see references to "hell" (Sheol, Hades, Gehenna, and Tartarus) as the grave or common pit of humankind. The notion of everlasting torment is not consistent with the believer's perspective that Jehovah God, who is love, would not inflict conscious suffering forever. The Qur'anic depiction of fiery punishment, with sinners receiving perpetually renewed skin to ensure ceaseless torment, is indeed a pointed contrast to the biblical teaching that death is the result of sin (Romans 6:23) and that the dead are not tormented in any perpetually burning underworld. This divide over the afterlife underscores that Christianity and Islam often depart widely in their doctrine of final destiny.

Marriage Practices in Islam

Islamic teaching accommodates multiple marriage types, including monogamy and polygamy. In the time of Muhammad, many widows were left after battles, prompting the Qur'an to allow up to four wives, provided the husband can treat them fairly. Throughout Islamic history, opinions have varied as to whether polygamy was meant as an exception or a normative practice. Men in more traditional Islamic societies may still have multiple wives, though countless Muslims choose monogamy, both for practical reasons and because they view it as more harmonious with modern societal frameworks.

A related practice is known as mut'ah in Shī'ite Islam, sometimes referred to as temporary marriage for a designated time. While the Shī'ites consider it permissible, Sunnis generally denounce it. For Christians, the biblical blueprint commonly references monogamy. Jesus taught that marriage was intended for one man and one woman (Matthew 19:4-6). The Old Testament narratives do describe instances of plural marriages, as with Abraham, Jacob, and David, yet these accounts are descriptive rather than prescriptive, and believers often note the practical complications and family strife that ensued. In any case, the Christian approach typically argues that God's original design was a single spouse union. These distinctions about marriage practices reflect differing moral and social norms across the two faiths.

Daily Life and Pillars of Islamic Practice

Edward D. Andrews

Many are aware that Islam contains practical pillars, sometimes listed as five obligations: public confession of faith (shahādah), daily prayers (ṣalāt), almsgiving (zakāt), fasting (especially during Ramadan), and pilgrimage to Mecca (Ḥajj). Because a devout Muslim's life revolves around these practices, the religion offers a well-defined structure. Although Christians do not observe these specific obligations, they may see parallels in how biblical faith calls for constant prayer (1 Thessalonians 5:17), generosity (2 Corinthians 9:7), and heartfelt devotion to God (Deuteronomy 6:5).

One aspect of Islam that many find impressive is the tradition of communal prayer in the mosque, especially on Fridays. The faithful arrive, remove their footwear, perform ritual washings, and line up shoulder to shoulder in reverent worship. The sermon (khuṭbah) may address doctrinal or moral themes, often laced with quotations from the Qur'an. This communal spirit fosters solidarity among believers. Meanwhile, Christians, though worshipping in churches on varying days of the week, also gather regularly and place great value on fellowship. Still, the forms of worship differ substantially, reflecting the distinctive truths each religion embraces.

Early Encounters and Tension With Christendom

From the seventh to the eighth century C.E., the Islamic empire advanced through the Middle East, across North Africa, and into parts of Europe. Byzantium was weakened, the Persian Empire collapsed, and entire regions embraced the new Islamic faith. These lands included historically Christian territories in Syria, Egypt, and North Africa, and at times local Christians were under pressure to convert or pay special taxes as non-Muslims. Such encounters fueled hostilities. By the eleventh century, Catholic forces launched the Crusades in an effort to reclaim the Holy Land from Islamic governance. History shows that these conflicts brought about centuries of bloodshed and resentment on both sides. Such episodes do not represent true Christian practice based on Jesus' teachings to love enemies (Matthew 5:44), but they do illustrate how religion and politics can merge into violent confrontations that overshadow the message of God's Word.

Other interactions between Islam and Christianity involved scholarship, with significant translations and debates on philosophical,

24

scientific, and religious questions. During periods of relative tolerance, Jewish and Christian communities could coexist with Muslims, contributing to a shared body of knowledge in places like the Iberian Peninsula. Nonetheless, these moments of peace were interspersed with oppression and war, often inflamed by political ambitions disguised as religious zeal. Conservative Christians look beyond these historical episodes of cross-faith conflict, discerning that the kingdom of God is not established through violent conquests or forced conversions. True Christianity has always been a matter of free will and heartfelt conviction (John 18:36).

The Qur'an and Its Use of Biblical Narratives

An intriguing aspect of the Qur'an is how frequently it refers to biblical personages: Adam, Noah, Abraham, Moses, David, Solomon, John the Baptist, and Jesus. Because the Qur'an is not arranged in a strictly chronological sequence, these figures reappear scattered throughout the text. At times, the Qur'an's retellings differ significantly from the biblical accounts, emphasizing or omitting details in accordance with Islamic theology. These variations have fueled centuries of debates among both Muslim and Christian interpreters.

For example, the Qur'an highlights Abraham's monotheism, with an emphasis on his willingness to submit entirely to God. He is portrayed as an exemplary Muslim, meaning "one who submits." While the biblical narrative does present Abraham as faithful, it also shows him waiting for the promise to be fulfilled through Isaac (Genesis 17:19). The Qur'an, however, seems to honor Ishmael to a great degree as an important part of Abraham's legacy, linking Ishmael's line to the ancestry of the prophet Muhammad. The biblical text likewise honors Ishmael as Abraham's son, but the main covenant promise flows through Isaac (Genesis 21:12). This difference in emphasis underscores the distinct identity that Islam forges with patriarchal figures, shaping a narrative that reorients some biblical accounts to point forward to Muhammad's prophetic mission.

Evaluating the Claim That the Bible Was Corrupted

The Qur'an purports to confirm the Torah and the Gospel, yet it also accuses Jews and Christians of altering their sacred texts over time.

In the eyes of many Muslims, this alleged corruption explains why the Bible differs from the Qur'an. Conservative Christians reply that the manuscripts of the Hebrew Scriptures and the Greek New Testament have been preserved with remarkable fidelity, as attested by numerous ancient fragments, manuscripts, and translations that predate Islam by centuries. While certain translation or transcription issues can arise, there is no evidence of the widespread textual tampering that would be needed to align with the Qur'an's claim. From a historical standpoint, the tens of thousands of biblical manuscripts, some dating back to the second century C.E., stand as a formidable testimony to the consistent transmission of Scripture.

Those reading the Bible will note that its content reveals a cohesive narrative that from Genesis onward describes God's interactions with humankind, culminating in Christ's ministry. On the other hand, the Qur'an does not quote extensive passages from the Bible. Instead, it alludes to numerous biblical stories and characters while at times adjusting their details. This approach can raise questions: If the Qur'an genuinely endorses earlier revelation, why are there such marked divergences? For a devout Muslim, the answer lies in the notion of biblical corruption. For a conservative Christian, textual history affirms the Bible's preservation, casting doubt on the idea of large-scale alterations. In apologetic discussions, these contrasts become highly relevant when testing Islam's claim to finalize God's revelation.

Islam's Philosophical and Cultural Contributions

During the medieval period, Islamic civilizations contributed significantly to science, medicine, mathematics, and philosophy. Centers of learning flourished in Baghdad, Cordoba, and other cities under Muslim rule. Classical Greek works were translated into Arabic, later reaching Latin-speaking Europe, thus influencing theological and academic discussion in medieval Christendom. While these developments are notable historically, from a purely biblical perspective, cultural and philosophical achievements do not in themselves validate a religion's theological claims. True worship does not hinge on the ability to make scientific discoveries or produce intellectual discourse, though it can reflect a community's passion for learning. In the Christian view, any genuine faith is measured primarily by adherence to divine revelation, humility, and obedience to the moral imperatives of Scripture (Micah 6:8).

Toward a Christian Apologetic Understanding of Islam

Christians who approach Islam from an apologetic standpoint do so with several convictions. They affirm the reliability of the Bible as the supreme written Word of God. They testify that Jesus' identity as the Messiah and divine Son of God was vindicated by his resurrection, attested in Scripture (1 Corinthians 15:3, 4). They also maintain that there is no additional inspired Scripture beyond the sixty-six canonical books, making the Qur'an extraneous in terms of biblical authority. At the same time, Christians recognize that many Muslims share a reverence for the moral codes found in earlier revelations, believing they all come from the same divine source.

Believers might also note that certain Islamic critiques of Christendom historically refer to the worship of images or saints, or teachings about God's triune nature that can be misunderstood as polytheistic. A conservative Christian relying on Scripture alone could concur that venerating images and saints is not biblical (Exodus 20:4, 5), and that confusing definitions of the Godhead can obscure scriptural truth (John 14:28; 1 Corinthians 15:28). Yet where the Qur'an diverges from the biblical portrait of Christ's redemptive death, the Holy Spirit's role in inspiring Scripture (though not indwelling all believers), and the nature of salvation, Christians must hold firmly to the apostolic record. They do so while calling attention to the historically faithful transmission of the biblical texts and the biblical witness that "there is salvation in no one else" besides Christ (Acts 4:12).

The Quranic Portrayal of Judgment and Responsibility

Another theme prominent in the Qur'an is divine judgment based on works, both good and bad, measured on scales of justice. While the Bible also features the concept of each person being judged, it stresses God's grace extended through Christ and teaches that salvation cannot be earned merely by works (Ephesians 2:8, 9). The Christian scriptures reveal that faith in Christ, coupled with repentance and obedience, is what leads to justification before Jehovah (Romans 3:23-25). Islam, however, frames the path to paradise as rooted in submission to God and fulfillment of the five pillars, with hope that one's sincere devotion can tip the balance in one's favor on judgment day. Moreover, Islamic thought suggests that individuals undergo some suffering after death to atone for any sins not rectified in life, a teaching absent from biblical teaching, which instead points to Christ's sacrifice as all-sufficient (Hebrews 10:10).

Examining Claims of Muhammad's Prophethood

For Islam to be consistent with biblical precedent, Muhammad's claim to prophethood would have to align with biblical prophecy and teaching. Yet the New Testament closes with strong admonitions not to add or subtract from the divinely inspired Word (Revelation 22:18, 19). Furthermore, the biblical test of a prophet includes harmony with existing revelation (Deuteronomy 13:1-3) and one hundred percent accuracy in pronouncements (Deuteronomy 18:20-22). Many Christians believe that some Qur'anic claims conflict with key biblical doctrines. They conclude, therefore, that Muhammad, although a remarkable figure historically, does not stand within the prophetic tradition that the Bible authenticates. From this vantage point, whatever revelations he may have presented are not recognized as an extension of Jehovah's plan. Muslims obviously view these matters differently, revering Muhammad as the final prophet in a line that includes Jesus and culminating in the Qur'an.

Jesus' Promises to His Apostles and the Spirit's Role

Some sects within Islam assert that Muhammad was the fulfillment of Jesus' statements about a coming helper or comforter. However, a careful reading of John chapters 14 to 16 shows that Jesus was addressing his first-century apostles, promising them special guidance through the Spirit that would lead them into truth. Those words, as many conservative Christians emphasize, were not extended to future prophets or religious founders. Christianity sees the Spirit's guidance culminating in the completion of the apostolic writings, forming the canonical New Testament. Therefore, the notion that Muhammad's ministry was directly prophesied by Jesus lacks biblical support. Traditional Christian exegesis holds that John 16:13 points to the Spirit's role in equipping the apostles, not to a seventh-century messenger in Arabia.

Islam's Perspective on Humankind's Need for Guidance

Islamic texts frequently underscore humankind's reliance on divine guidance, echoing the biblical assessment that people are prone to moral and spiritual misdirection. The Qur'an calls for consistent remembrance of God, daily prayers, and living in a way that reflects submission to the Almighty. It also sets forth legal prescriptions for personal conduct, family relations, business dealings, and governance. The Christian worldview shares a belief in humanity's fallen nature, requiring redemption and alignment with God's moral laws. The difference lies in how that redemption is secured. Islam envisions a meticulous set of obligations, sincere repentance, and hope in God's mercy. Biblical Christianity proposes that humans cannot deliver themselves from sin solely by fulfilling laws, for "all have sinned" and need Christ's atoning sacrifice (Romans 3:23-26). While both faiths exhort ethical conduct and worship of the one true God, they diverge on the ultimate means of reconciliation with the Creator.

Modern Global Spread of Islam

Islam stands as one of the largest religions in the world, often cited as the second-largest after forms of professed Christianity. It continues to grow rapidly in Africa and has gained footholds in Europe and North America. Conversion can be attributed to various factors, including demographic growth, immigration patterns, and in some cases, genuine religious conviction. Christians who meet Muslims in workplaces, schools, or neighborhoods can attest that many Muslims uphold a disciplined life of devotion. They pray regularly, avoid certain substances, fast during Ramadan, and strive to conform to the moral standards set out in the Qur'an. This active faith can attract those seeking a structured path of spirituality. Simultaneously, Christians who hold to the historical-grammatical approach to Scripture may engage in dialogues with Muslim neighbors, sharing biblical truths and clarifying misconceptions about Christian beliefs. Such conversations can be fruitful when approached with respect and genuine kindness.

Approaches to Christian Witness Among Muslims

From a conservative perspective, Christian apologetics aims to present the biblical gospel to all peoples, including Muslims, without resorting to political force or cultural imperialism. Faithful Christians might attempt to build on the common ground that both faiths revere Abraham, honor Jesus (albeit differently), and observe the existence of a righteous Creator. Respectful communication avoids caricatures and focuses on scriptural truths. For instance, explaining that biblical Christianity rejects idolatry and venerates no images or saints can remove certain misconceptions. Emphasizing that Jesus never presented himself as equal to the Father can open dialogue about the unique Sonship of Jesus, his role as Messiah, and how Scripture teaches that Jesus is "the way and the truth and the life" (John 14:6).

Since Islam rejects the sacrifice and resurrection of Jesus, presenting the testimony of the Gospels and apostolic letters is key to showing how early disciples staked their lives on that central truth (1 Corinthians 15:14, 15). While Muslims may counter that such events are not accurately recorded in the Bible, demonstrating the textual reliability of Scripture can build confidence. Ultimately, conversion cannot be forced, and while biblical Christians remain certain of their foundation in Christ, they also recognize that faith is a personal, voluntary step.

The Question of Religious Authority and Tradition

Islam's emphasis on the absolute transcendence of God, along with the authority of the Qur'an and the example of Muhammad, creates a firm religious identity for its adherents. Muslim scholars interpret the Qur'an and Hadith to formulate rulings on every aspect of life, from dietary habits to financial dealings. This is quite different from biblical Christianity, in which believers rely on canonical Scripture as the final authority. Although some denominations add traditions, a conservative biblical approach holds that any tradition must align with God's Word. Jesus sharply criticized religious leaders of his day for elevating human traditions above divine commands (Matthew 15:6). By contrast, Islam has consolidated centuries of commentary and legal precedents within religious jurisprudence, leading to a robust but complex set of guidelines. Christians who hold the Bible as all-sufficient may question the development of elaborate religious laws beyond what Scripture describes.

Contrasts in View of Warfare and Jihad

Another notable area of contrast is the Islamic concept of jihad, which at times in history was interpreted to justify expansion through warfare under religious auspices. Although many Muslims today emphasize a spiritual or defensive understanding of jihad, historical records do show conquests that were at least partly inspired by religious motives. Meanwhile, the New Testament portrays Christ's followers as politically neutral, instructed by Jesus that his kingdom is no part of the world (John 18:36). Consequently, the biblical framework does not endorse holy wars. While the Old Testament does describe divinely mandated warfare for Israel under specific circumstances, Christians view those examples as part of an earlier covenant. Through Jesus, a new covenant was established, making such conflicts unnecessary. Because Islam lacks a parallel concept of final revelation in Christ and fosters a religious-political union, many Islamic states historically fused governance and religion, sometimes enforcing their beliefs through political power. The question remains whether that structure can be reconciled with the biblical principle of free, willing submission to God.

The Importance of Understanding Islam Today

Given Islam's widespread influence, it is vital for Christians to be accurately informed about its teachings and history. This awareness fosters effective conversations with Muslim friends or colleagues. It also counters misconceptions on both sides, reducing hostility based on ignorance. Many Christians find that responsible study of Islam deepens their appreciation for the truths they see affirmed in Scripture while also revealing the significance of doctrinal differences. Although both faiths share certain moral and ethical values, such as avoiding immorality and honoring family, they differ over foundational matters of atonement, salvation, and the person of Christ.

Studying the early centuries of Islam, the formation of the Qur'an, and the subsequent development of Islamic law underscores that world religions do not grow in a vacuum. They emerge in historical settings and interact with other faiths. For the believer who stands on the authority of the Bible, the rise and endurance of Islam present a challenge: how to demonstrate biblical truth in a gracious, persuasive manner without compromising the essentials of the faith. In so doing, Christians can recall that scripture calls for respectful engagement, urging believers to speak with mildness and reverence (1 Peter 3:15).

Reconciling God's Sovereignty and Human Freedom

Muslim theologians often stress divine predestination, though schools differ on its precise nature. Some hold that all events occur by the will of God, while others allow for some human freedom within God's overarching plan. Christianity also grapples with foreknowledge and the extent of predestination. Yet many conservative Christians maintain that God's omniscience does not necessitate fixing every human choice in advance. People retain free will, bearing responsibility for their decisions. Islam similarly upholds moral accountability, though the theological frameworks can diverge. Ultimately, each faith sees God as supreme over history. Christians add that Jehovah does not use suffering as a means of refining or testing individuals, in harmony with James 1:13, which says that God does not test anyone with evil. Believers hold that human suffering arises primarily from human disobedience and the flawed independence of humankind, not from a divine plan for shaping character.

The Christian View of Fulfilled Prophecy

One question that arises is whether the biblical pattern of prophecy ended with Christ and his apostles. Scripture presents ample evidence that the coming of Jesus fulfilled numerous messianic prophecies spanning from Genesis to Malachi, culminating in his redemptive sacrifice during the first century C.E. Prophecies about events such as the destruction of Jerusalem in 70 C.E. were also fulfilled within the lifetimes of some apostles. Consequently, conservative Christians see no place for later prophets who would alter or supersede the revelation provided by Christ and his apostolic circle. They point to Jude 3, which says that the faith was "once for all delivered to the holy ones," and interpret that as an indication that the Christian canon and apostolic teaching remain definitive. This position rejects the possibility of a seventh-century Arabian prophet offering a final revelation. The sincerity of Muhammad's claims notwithstanding, biblical theology finds its anchor in Christ, "the way and the truth and the life" (John 14:6), whose teachings are recorded and preserved in the canonical Scriptures.

Assessing Islamic Practices Compared to Biblical Commands

Some Islamic practices, such as daily prayer, fasting during Ramadan, and giving alms, highlight devotion, discipline, and generosity. Although biblical faith also commends prayer and self-control, Christians differ in how these commands are implemented. Jesus instructed his disciples not to make an outward show of fasting or prayer (Matthew 6:5-18). He warned them that righteousness must surpass ritualism and come from heartfelt love of God and neighbor (Matthew 22:37-40). This sense of voluntary devotion under the new covenant contrasts with the more regimented pillars of Islam, which, while beneficial as acts of worship, can become external markers rather than internal transformations. At the same time, devout Muslims may indeed pray and fast out of heartfelt sincerity. Christians are reminded that God alone reads the heart (1 Samuel 16:7), and they should not presume to judge individuals while still upholding biblical truth.

Distinctions in Authority: Caliphate vs. Apostolic Leadership

Whereas early Christianity spread largely by preaching and persuasion, Islam rapidly expanded with a combination of da'wah (invitation to faith) and, in certain instances, military conquests under the early caliphs. Thus, religion and state became intertwined in many Islamic domains. By contrast, the apostles never wielded political or military power, choosing instead to rely on Jehovah's support as they proclaimed the gospel in synagogues, marketplaces, and private homes (Acts 5:42). The Greek New Testament depicts believers as "resident aliens" in the present world, seeking a heavenly government under Christ (1 Peter 2:11). This difference in how religious authority interacts with political structures remains evident in various Islamic theocracies or states with strong Islamic identities. Conservative Christians emphasize that genuine worship must never be enforced by civil edict, for true faith cannot be imposed. This perspective can clarify why Christianity often developed within and sometimes in opposition to existing political orders, whereas Islam frequently shaped government from the top down.

The Crossroads of Dialogue and Evangelism

A Christian apologetic approach to Islam is not about condemning Muslims personally. Many conscientious Muslims adhere to moral standards and show a sincere desire to honor God. The approach instead involves contrasting doctrine and inviting honest analysis of Scripture. Christians affirm that the Messiah's sacrifice is the cornerstone of salvation, something the Qur'an explicitly denies in its narratives about Jesus. Consequently, bridging this gap in belief is no small endeavor. It necessitates a careful presentation of the biblical record, highlighting that Christ's death and resurrection were well-attested facts for first-century believers (1 Corinthians 15:3-8). Dialogues that revolve around the theme of atonement may allow Muslims to glimpse a dimension of God's love and justice as portrayed in the Bible.

While the pursuit of truth remains paramount, the conversation must also reflect Christian qualities such as kindness, patience, and respect (2 Timothy 2:24, 25). Merely amassing historical and textual arguments without displaying Christlike love can hinder genuine understanding. Christians who sincerely desire to share biblical truths must do so under the conviction that the Bible is God's Word, while recognizing the deeply rooted devotion Muslims feel for the Qur'an. The objective is never to belittle but to open a pathway for examining whether the gospel reveals a greater clarity about humanity's plight and Jehovah's plan for salvation.

Christian Hope in Contrast With Islamic Eschatology

The Christian hope centers on the resurrection, coupled with a new heavens and a new earth where righteousness dwells (2 Peter 3:13). It does not hinge on an unending cycle of punishments for those who fall short. Rather, Scripture describes a resurrection for both the righteous and the unrighteous (John 5:28, 29), offering the possibility of reconciliation with God. While Islam also envisions a resurrection day, it accentuates the fearsome torment awaiting unbelievers in hellfire. This portrayal misaligns with the biblical understanding that those perishing simply remain in death, "the common grave of mankind," until God's future judgment (Romans 6:23). For Christians convinced by Scripture, the final destruction of the wicked is not an everlasting burning torment but a complete removal of life (2 Thessalonians 1:9). This difference highlights the contrasting views of divine justice, with the Islamic understanding focusing more intensely on ongoing punitive measures, whereas biblical teaching often emphasizes the wages of sin being death, not perpetual agony.

Reflecting on Islam's Global Significance

Although conservative Christians do not accept the Qur'an as inspired, they acknowledge that Islam wields a powerful influence on cultures and societies worldwide. Millions are drawn to Islam's clear moral codes and emphasis on divine sovereignty. Yet for Christians, the aim is to recognize these features while maintaining that the ultimate revelation of God's purpose culminated in Jesus. The New Testament describes him as "the exact representation of God's very being" (Hebrews 1:3). Since Christians hold that Scripture alone is the authority, they remain steadfast in proclaiming the biblical gospel as the way to reconciliation with Jehovah. In that sense, Islam's prevalence calls believers to carry on proclaiming Christ in a spirit of love, gentleness, and unwavering conviction.

Concluding Thoughts

For conservative Christians, Islam is a faith that shares a belief in one creator but ultimately diverges from biblical teaching on vital questions of Christ's nature, atonement, and the reliability of the canon of Scripture. Its historical rise in Arabia, the consolidation of the Qur'an, the early conflicts over succession, and the later global spread all highlight a religion with deep roots and strong claims to truth. Christians who evaluate these claims through Scripture see no basis to regard Muhammad as a genuine prophet or the Qur'an as a complementary revelation. Yet they also acknowledge that many Muslims manifest commendable devotion and sincerity in their quest to please God.

A robust Christian apologetic response engages these matters with a commitment to what the Bible teaches, accompanied by honest respect for Muslims as fellow humans made in God's image. Christians endeavor to bear witness to the teachings of Jesus and the apostles, trusting that the Word of God can appeal to honest hearts. While Islam proclaims submission to God, the Bible depicts Jesus as the pivotal agent of reconciliation and the ultimate expression of divine grace. The hope in Christ—rooted in his resurrection—remains central to Christian faith, in stark contrast to the portrayal of Jesus in Islamic texts. Ultimately, each person must decide how to weigh the Qur'an and the Bible, guided by the conviction that Scripture was reliably transmitted and that Christ's message has never been supplanted by subsequent revelations.

CHAPTER 1 Is the Quran a Literary Miracle?

A recurring claim in Islamic apologetics is that the Quran stands as a literary miracle. This assertion holds that the beauty, coherence, and stylistic elegance of its Arabic text cannot be matched by human effort, thus proving it to be divinely inspired. Many adherents of Islam regard the language of the Quran, in its original Arabic, as a sign of its supernatural origin. Because of that, they see no need for a miraculous authentication like those performed by biblical prophets. From a Christian standpoint, especially one rooted in a historical-grammatical interpretation of Scripture, a careful investigation of these arguments is vital. Questions arise concerning the standard for divine inspiration, the role of verifiable miracles in authenticating prophecy, and whether literary mastery alone suffices to prove a text's divine origin.

The subject bears significance for conservative Christian apologetics. The Bible demonstrates God's direct intervention in authenticating prophets, including Moses in 1513 B.C.E. at Sinai (Exodus 19:16-18), and Jesus in the first century C.E., whose miracles confirmed him as Jehovah's appointed Messiah (Matthew 11:5; John 10:37, 38). By contrast, Muhammad's claim to prophethood, made in early seventh-century Arabia, is not accompanied by comparable signs of miraculous power. Instead, Islamic tradition often presents the Quran itself as the proof, contending that no human, especially one deemed illiterate, could produce such a text. Yet historical and textual analysis can illuminate whether the Quran's composition alone is adequate to demonstrate divine authorship.

This chapter examines key arguments for and against the proposition that the Quran is a literary miracle. It also compares the Quran's internal claims of uniqueness with the biblical standard for testing inspired writings. In the process, we take into account the fundamental question of how the Bible has set forth the need for authenticating miracles when a new prophet or message arises.

Exploring these issues provides a basis for evaluating both the Quran's literary dimension and the broader question of whether it fulfills the role of inspired Scripture.

Historical Background of the Quran

The Quran emerged in the early seventh century C.E., a time when the Arabian Peninsula was populated by various tribes adhering to forms of polytheism interspersed with some monotheistic influences. Muhammad, born in Mecca around 570 C.E., began proclaiming a message that there is no god but Allah and that he, Muhammad, was the messenger of God. Islamic sources hold that around 610 C.E., Muhammad received his first revelation through an entity said to be the angel Gabriel while meditating in a cave near Mecca. These revelations continued over a period of about twenty-three years, until Muhammad's death in 632 C.E.

The Quran, meaning "Recitation" in Arabic, is believed by devout Muslims to be a direct transmission from God through Gabriel to Muhammad. Since Muhammad is described in Islamic tradition as illiterate, the text was dictated and preserved initially by memorization and by writing on assorted materials, including parchment and palm leaves. Within two decades of Muhammad's death, efforts began to produce an official version, ultimately leading to the standard text recognized by the majority of Muslims. The Quran is divided into 114 suras, or chapters, of varying lengths and topics, arranged mostly from longer to shorter rather than chronologically.

The Quran's self-testimony repeatedly upholds its divine origin, asserting that its Arabic style is peerless and beyond human capacity to replicate. Passages like Sura 2:23, 24 invite skeptics to produce a sura comparable in quality if they doubt the revelation's authenticity. Islamic tradition regards this literary challenge as a standing miracle, an eternal proof that the Quran is from God. Since the text does not record Muhammad performing supernatural wonders on the scale of Moses or Jesus, defenders of Islam frequently refer to the Quran's eloquence as the chief sign of his prophethood.

The Significance of Literary Style in Islamic Apologetics

Literary style matters greatly to Islamic apologetics because the Quran is said to have emerged in a culture highly attuned to oral poetry. Arabian tribes prized poetic skill, and many forms of expression involved structured rhyme and prose. According to tradition, the Arabic of the Quran displayed a magnificent eloquence that exceeded anything previously known. Scholars of Islamic history note that, at least by the time the Quran was compiled, Arabic had developed poetic forms that were widely admired. The idea that an "illiterate" merchant could produce a text of such sophistication has often been treated as evidence of divine intervention.

The argument rests on two principal assertions. The first is that the Arabic text of the Quran is inimitable, meaning that no human has ever produced a work of equal literary excellence in that language. The second is that Muhammad's personal inability to read or write further elevates the miracle, proving that he could not have borrowed from existing sources or refined his style through literary study. Proponents hold that if the text is impossible to duplicate, then its origin must be supernatural.

Yet Christian apologetics typically calls for a more expansive measure of inspiration. Throughout the Scriptures, the test of divine revelation involves prophetic accuracy, historical reliability, and, at times, miraculous signs. Moses led Israel out of Egypt around 1446 B.C.E. with dramatic events that showed God's power (Exodus 7 through 15). Jesus of Nazareth was authenticated by healings, resurrections, and his own resurrection on the third day (Matthew 11:5; 1 Corinthians 15:3, 4). The biblical pattern reveals that God did not rely solely on literary beauty to validate a new prophet or covenant. The authors of the Gospels mention Christ's miracles as an incontrovertible proof that he was sent by Jehovah (John 10:37, 38). This broader perspective raises the question of whether literary excellence alone suffices to establish a text as divinely inspired.

The Place of Miracles in Authenticating Scripture

Biblical precedent shows that genuine prophets came bearing confirmatory signs that left no doubt about their commission from God. In Exodus 4:1-9, Jehovah equipped Moses with the ability to perform wonders to ensure that Israel would know he was truly sent.

When Jesus began his ministry, his healing of the blind, deaf, and lame in fulfillment of messianic prophecies served as undisputable authentication (Matthew 11:2-6). The early Christian congregation also displayed signs (Acts 2:1-11; 1 Corinthians 14:22), with many eyewitnesses attesting to the miracles that accompanied the apostles' preaching.

Muhammad did not present such miraculous signs to his listeners. Hadith literature contains isolated suggestions of wonders, but the Quran itself consistently points to the recited revelations as Muhammad's validation. Islamic tradition explains that previous prophets came with supernatural signs but were met with unbelief, so God withheld miraculous signs in Muhammad's era as a kind of test of genuine faith. This shift in approach is not supported by biblical models, which emphasize that the true God desires clear evidence for his servants, especially when establishing new covenants or major turning points in salvation history.

In Sura 17:59, the Quran indicates that signs were withheld because unbelievers in previous generations had rejected them. However, in the biblical record, unbelief never dissuaded Jehovah from providing miraculous proofs of a prophet's authenticity. Israel's frequent lack of faith did not stop Moses, Elijah, Elisha, or other prophets from performing miracles. Jesus did not deny his wonder-working power merely because some refused to believe. This discrepancy underscores that the biblical and Quranic patterns for authenticating a prophet diverge profoundly, which then brings the Quran's literary claim into sharper focus: is an internally proclaimed "literary miracle" truly sufficient as a sign from God?

Comparing the Quran With Biblical Literature

The Hebrew and Christian Scriptures collectively span millennia, with diverse literary genres: historical narrative, prophecy, poetry, gospel accounts, epistles, and proverbs. Many biblical passages exhibit literary excellence: the Psalms convey profound prayer and praise, Isaiah's oracles display majestic expression, and the Sermon on the Mount (Matthew chapters 5 to 7) stands as a timeless discourse on morality. The story of Joseph in Genesis reveals a compelling narrative filled with intricate detail, while the book of Job presents philosophical discussions on suffering and divine justice with elevated language. The parables of Jesus are masterpieces of brevity and insight.

Translators of the Bible have repeatedly remarked on its literary power in many languages, noting that key themes are preserved even when Hebrew or Greek poetic devices cannot be fully transferred. The biblical texts invite readers of all backgrounds to consider the God behind its words. Many Christians observe that if one singled out only literary quality, the Bible could well claim remarkable beauty in passages like Psalm 23: "Jehovah is my shepherd; I will not lack anything." Yet the Bible does not rely solely on rhetorical appeal to prove divine authorship. It includes fulfilled prophecies such as the foretelling of Babylon's downfall (Isaiah 13:19-22) and Cyrus' decree (Isaiah 44:28; 45:1), events unfolding well after Isaiah's era (late eighth century B.C.E.). That sort of predictive prophecy testifies to something beyond eloquence.

The Quran, by contrast, frequently repeats certain narratives of biblical figures (Adam, Noah, Abraham, Moses, Jesus) but without the same chronological or thematic flow. Its arrangement often seems topical or based on length of suras rather than narrative development. Some of its retellings differ from the biblical accounts in important details, making them less cohesive from a biblical perspective. The Christian exegete may ask: if the Quran recasts biblical material, does it surpass the original in theological depth or literary impact when examined carefully? Historically, many have concluded that the literary merit of the Quran, though containing eloquent passages in Arabic, is not the decisive test for divine inspiration.

The Role of Repetition and Coherence

An aspect that has drawn scholarly attention is the Quran's noticeable repetition. The same accounts, like that of Moses, are recounted in multiple suras, often with similar language and purpose: to underscore the call to faith and warn against disbelief. Sura 55 continually repeats the refrain, "Then which of your Lord's favors will you deny?" a phrase that appears dozens of times, signifying rhetorical emphasis. While repetition can be a powerful device in oratory, repeated content can also indicate a developing text that responded to changing circumstances in Muhammad's ministry.

Moreover, many suras lack a clear chronological order. Longer chapters like Sura 2 incorporate numerous themes: from directives on prayer and fasting to references to the "Cow" incident, interspersed with mentions of prophets and of final judgment. Passages from the Meccan period are sometimes said to be embedded in Medinan suras, or vice versa. Scholars of Quranic studies often note that discerning the original context for each verse requires reconstructing which portion belongs to which historical phase of Muhammad's life. The result is that the unity of the sura is not always self-evident.

Some devout Muslims view this arrangement as part of the Quran's divine structure, while others see editorial or pragmatic reasons for how it was compiled under the Caliphs. Conservative Christian readers, who approach Scripture with an emphasis on historical background and coherent narrative, may find the Quran's structure less orderly than biblical books. This assessment does not deny the presence of elevated passages but challenges the claim that the entire text is organized with a literary perfection beyond human capability.

The Prophet's Illiteracy in Islamic Tradition

Islamic tradition holds that Muhammad was unlettered, reinforcing the idea that he could not have crafted the Quran from personal study. The Arabic text of the Quran itself sometimes alludes to him as the "unlettered prophet" (Sura 7:157). Many Muslims interpret this literally, concluding that Muhammad could neither read nor write. They cite his early life as a merchant and the region's general lack of written materials for the plausibility of this claim. In this view, producing a text with refined literary structure was far beyond his capacity.

Yet the historical record shows that Mecca had robust commercial activities, and oratory was a prized skill. An individual who was not literate in the technical sense might still be a talented communicator. Illiteracy need not imply ignorance or a lack of oratorical flair. The text of the Quran was formed over more than two decades, during which time numerous scribes wrote down revelations that Muhammad recited. The composition did not occur in one sitting, and there was a constant interchange with existing religious traditions, including discussions with Jewish and Christian residents. The question arises: does illiteracy truly guarantee an absence of exposure to, or assimilation of, stories, motifs, and rhetorical methods?

A conservative Christian perspective stresses that the Holy Scriptures themselves, although penned by men "unlettered and ordinary" (Acts 4:13 in paraphrase), still reflect God's inspiration because of verifiable prophecy, thematic unity, and historical accuracy, not because of literary style alone. Luke, for example, was well-educated and wrote a polished Greek. Peter and John, fishermen by trade, wrote more simply. Both sources are recognized as part of inspired Scripture, but not for rhetorical magnificence. Therefore, whether Muhammad was literate or not does not in itself settle the question of divine inspiration.

The Absence of Miracles by Muhammad

Another critical consideration is that if the Quran's style is the only miracle of Islam, the claim contrasts sharply with the biblical record of prophets who performed visible signs. Moses turned water into blood and parted the Red Sea around 1446 B.C.E. (Exodus 7:14-21; 14:21, 22). Elijah called fire down from heaven (1 Kings 18:36-38). Elisha, his successor, multiplied oil for a widow, resurrected a child, and even cured Naaman of leprosy (2 Kings 4:1-7; 4:32-37; 5:1-14). Jesus demonstrated an unprecedented series of miracles, culminating in his own resurrection after three days in the tomb (Matthew 28:1-10). When challenged, Jesus could say: "If I do not do the works of my Father, do not believe me. But if I do them, though you do not believe me, believe the works" (John 10:37, 38). The early Christian congregation also performed wonders through divine power, and thousands in Jerusalem believed (Acts 2:41-43; 3:1-10).

By contrast, the Quran acknowledges that skeptics demanded signs from Muhammad yet states that God withheld them for fear that people would reject them as earlier generations did. From a Christian standpoint, this is not consistent with the biblical model, which shows that God repeatedly confirmed his messengers with supernatural signs regardless of the unbelief of some observers. The willingness of God in Scripture to confirm his prophets powerfully is evident in many historical accounts (Judges 6:36-40; 1 Samuel 12:16-18). The question for a conservative Christian is why a God who consistently provided visible miracles in earlier generations would rely solely on a literary claim for a messenger proposing a universal revelation.

The Challenge Verses in the Quran

Certain verses in the Quran issue a challenge to produce something comparable to its suras. Sura 2:23, 24 states: "If you are in doubt of what We have revealed to Our servant, produce a sura like it." Sura 17:88 claims that all humanity and spirits together could not match the Quran. Muslim commentators sometimes propose that the best Arab poets, even at the height of their craft, were unable to replicate the style or clarity of the Quran. This is generally taken as a spiritual sign of the text's origin.

Yet rhetorical challenges can appear in many works, with authors inviting others to outdo them. The success of the challenge depends partly on subjective literary standards. The question is whether the style and content are genuinely impossible to replicate or whether the text has become so revered in the Islamic cultural framework that no alternative can be acknowledged as equal. Historically, there have been attempts by individuals to compose works mimicking the Quran's style. Such efforts have not been well-received by devout Muslims, and are typically dismissed as inferior.

Christians note that the Bible never makes a purely aesthetic challenge. Instead, biblical texts emphasize faith grounded in historical acts of God and verifiable prophecies. The Gospels proclaim that a person could believe in Jesus partly because of eyewitness testimony to his miracles and resurrection (John 20:30, 31). As for writing style, Scripture does not insist that no one could ever produce equally poetic passages. Rather, it focuses on the authenticity of prophecy and historical events as proof of God's involvement.

The Need for External Validation

In biblical revelation, external validation stands as a hallmark of true prophets. Elijah did not merely say, "My oracles are written so beautifully that you should believe them." He confronted false prophets and demonstrated Jehovah's power. Moses' staff became a serpent, water turned to blood, and even the Egyptian magicians attested to a power beyond mere human skill (Exodus 7:20-22; 8:18, 19). Jesus, confronted by those questioning his authority, referred to miracles as decisive proofs.

If one contends that the Quran's rhetorical brilliance itself is a sign, the question arises: how does one objectively measure rhetorical brilliance across languages and cultures? The fact that the Quran is deeply revered within Islamic tradition might generate a cultural consensus about its unmatched style, but that does not necessarily constitute an external or universal verification. Many readers from outside the Arabic-speaking world do not find the translations of the Quran to be an astonishing literary masterpiece. Translations naturally fail to capture aspects of the original Arabic, but the Bible has likewise been translated countless times while preserving powerful content recognized worldwide. Consequently, a purely stylistic claim is difficult to validate across languages and historical contexts.

Additionally, the intricacies of the Arabic language at the time of Muhammad, and the poetic competitions that flourished then, could have shaped the expectation for a certain grand style. The rhetorical traditions in seventh-century Arabia prized certain forms of structure and recitation, and the Quran undeniably reflected and advanced those forms. However, a parallel might be drawn with Shakespeare's transformative impact on Elizabethan English. One might argue that no one has matched Shakespeare's mastery, yet that is not considered a miracle. The Christian perspective would likewise say that literary beauty, however splendid, is not the biblical test for divine scripture.

The Bible's Perspective on True Prophecy

Deuteronomy 13:1-3 sets a test for individuals claiming to speak in Jehovah's name. If a prophet, or a dreamer of dreams, arises with a sign or portent but then leads people away from worshipping the true God, they are not to be heeded. Deuteronomy 18:20-22 adds that a prophet whose predictions do not come true has not spoken from God. The emphasis is on doctrinal fidelity, predictive accuracy, and consistent worship of Jehovah.

The New Testament likewise insists that believers "test the spirits to see whether they are from God" (1 John 4:1). The Christian congregation recognized apostolic authority because Jesus himself selected the apostles, and they were confirmed by miracles such as speaking foreign languages without prior knowledge (Acts 2:1-11). True prophecy in the Bible involves external events fulfilling predictions or divine acts confirming the messenger.

While the Quran does speak reverently of the prophets mentioned in the Hebrew Scriptures, it does not rely on or present verifiable prophecies of future events that confirm its own authenticity. It also largely omits details about the covenant through Moses that date to about 1513 B.C.E. and that formed the backbone of Israel's worship. Instead, the Quran's logic is that it confirms earlier revelations but corrects the supposed corruptions introduced by Jews and Christians. This position draws attention away from verifying new prophecies and redirects the focus to how well the text's style and moral exhortations surpass prior scriptures. A historical-grammatical reading of the Bible, though, sees an unbroken lineage of revelation culminating in Christ, with no scriptural basis for a subsequent revelation that supplants the apostles' testimony. The Bible's stance that Jesus is the final spokesman (Hebrews 1:2) leaves no room for a seventh-century revelation that claims to override the new covenant.

The Quran's Reliance on Biblical Figures

Many suras draw upon biblical figures such as Adam, Noah, Abraham, Moses, David, Solomon, and Jesus. Yet the narratives presented often diverge in details from the biblical accounts. For instance, the Quran recounts aspects of Moses' confrontation with Pharaoh but does not align precisely with the Exodus narrative that places this event around 1446 B.C.E. The story of Jesus is also recast, denying his crucifixion and thus negating the resurrection as taught in the Gospels. Despite referencing these key biblical characters, the Quran does not bolster the claim of literary miracle by presenting expanded historical contexts or new, objectively verifiable events.

In the Bible, the genealogies and historical markers place these characters in a coherent timeline. The historical setting of Moses, including the mention of Egyptian oppression, the plagues, and the crossing of the Red Sea, can be studied with reference to Egyptian and Near Eastern archaeology. The Gospels place Jesus in a definite first-century Jewish context under Roman rule, with references to specific historical figures (Pontius Pilate, Herod, Caesar). By contrast, the Quran's narratives of these figures appear more episodic, focusing on moral or doctrinal lessons that align with Islamic belief. This shift in focus does not imply an elevated or miraculous literary form; it simply shows that the Quran reuses biblical figures with a different theological framing.

Coherence and Chronological Disarray

Another issue arises from the arrangement of the Quran. The text is not organized chronologically. The typical ordering of suras from longest to shortest sometimes confuses the historical flow. Material said to date to Muhammad's early preaching in Mecca is interspersed with passages from his later time in Medina. Because no transitional statements indicate the shift, readers can encounter abrupt changes of topic or references to events that are not explained until later suras or were introduced previously without warning.

A devout Muslim might argue that the Quran's arrangement transcends ordinary literary norms and should be accepted as part of its miraculous structure. A Christian, however, compares such an approach with the clarity and progression found in many books of the Bible. The Pentateuch, for instance, describes Israel's journey from bondage in Egypt to the edge of the Promised Land in relatively coherent segments (Exodus through Deuteronomy). The Gospels give enough narrative continuity to trace Jesus' ministry from Galilee to Judea, culminating in his death and resurrection in Jerusalem. The epistles in the New Testament, while not ordered strictly by date, carry thematic or author-based coherence and situate themselves in real congregational contexts (Romans, Corinthians, Ephesians, etc.). This clarity contrasts with the editorial complexity observed in the Quran's final form.

Testimony of Historians on the Quran's Style

Several historians and literary critics have commented on the Quran's style. Thomas Carlyle, an admirer of Muhammad's leadership in some respects, found the Quran's text difficult and jumbled. Edward Gibbon, an eighteenth-century historian known for his work on the

Roman Empire, noted that the Quran weaves together fables, precepts, and declamations in a way that can grow wearisome. This does not dismiss the profound religious and cultural effect the Quran has had over centuries, but from a literary standpoint, scholars often highlight the discontinuities and repetitions within the text. These assessments, voiced by individuals not hostile to the fundamental premise of monotheism, cast doubt on the notion that the Quran is self-evidently miraculous in its literary form.

Conversely, devout Muslim interpreters rebut that Arabic must be experienced in its original purity, and that non-Arabic-speaking critics fail to appreciate the true sublimity of the Quran's eloquence. While it is certainly possible that some of the text's aesthetic qualities can be lost in translation, the question remains whether literary impressiveness alone validates a text as divinely authored. Christians historically have recognized Scripture's power in all languages, consistent with the gospel's universal mission (Matthew 24:14). The biblical message does not require mastery of Hebrew or Greek for its beauty or power to shine through, nor does it rely solely on rhetorical form to claim inspiration.

An additional consideration is that devout communities often treat their sacred texts with reverence, attributing extraordinary qualities to them. Over time, religious enthusiasm can magnify perceived qualities, with believers testifying to the uniqueness of their text in a devotional context. Yet for those outside that community, the text may or may not strike them as miraculous. When tested by external literary standards, the Quran exhibits strengths and weaknesses akin to any text that underwent a complex process of composition, oral transmission, and final editing.

Conclusion

Literary excellence alone is not the biblical standard for identifying divine inspiration. The entire scope of Scripture shows that God provides compelling signs—fulfilled prophecy, miracles, historical confirmations of key events—to validate his revelations. Moses' leadership in the mid-1400s B.C.E. was attested by stupendous acts that demonstrated Jehovah's direct intervention. Jesus' messiahship was confirmed by healings and his resurrection in the first century C.E.

IS THE QURAN THE WORD OF GOD?

The apostles manifested miraculous gifts that showcased divine power in the fledgling Christian congregation. The Bible's cohesive narrative, extending from Genesis to Revelation, underscores verifiable acts of God in real historical settings.

Islamic tradition asserts that the Quran is incomparable in its Arabic eloquence. However, critics, including some sympathetic to Muhammad's cause, have noted repetitions, an uneven structure, and difficulties with coherence. While many devout Muslims remain profoundly moved by its recitative style, the claim that it constitutes an exclusive literary miracle does not align with the biblical pattern of how God authenticates his prophets. In the Christian view, even the most eloquent text must be tested against the biblical criteria of prophetic veracity, doctrinal faithfulness to Jehovah's revealed nature, and confirmation through undeniable divine acts.

A purely literary claim does not suffice for Christianity, which recognizes that beautiful language, though valuable, is not a conclusive seal of God's authorship. The test of a true prophet involves both the moral and doctrinal fidelity of the message and the external confirmation of God's power. Since the Quran does not align with that pattern and contradicts core biblical doctrines about Christ's crucifixion and resurrection, conservative Christians do not accept it as a final or superior revelation from God. They affirm the standard set forth in the Bible: "If I am not doing the works of my Father, do not believe me. But if I am doing them, . . . believe the works" (John 10:37, 38). The Quran's reliance on literary quality to authenticate Muhammad's mission stands apart from this biblical model. For that reason, the belief that the Quran is a literary miracle is not a sufficient basis—by the biblical definition—for deeming it divinely inspired.

Edward D. Andrews

CHAPTER 2 Is There Evidence That the Quran Is the Third Installment of the Inspired, Inerrant Word of God?

Among those who value sacred writings, questions arise concerning the authority, inspiration, and harmony of various texts that claim divine origin. The two central collections held by Christians are the Hebrew Scriptures and the Greek New Testament, recognized by many believers as inspired and coherent works spanning centuries. These books form what is commonly referred to as the Bible, a library of writings unified in purpose and harmony (John 5:39; 2 Timothy 3:16). By contrast, Muslims hold the Quran to be the final and perfect revelation from God, superseding all that came before. The Quran references biblical figures such as Adam, Noah, Moses, and Jesus, yet it also presents teachings that appear to diverge from, or even contradict, the biblical message.

It is important to examine whether the Quran truly confirms previous revelation or whether it diverges from the patterns long established by the Hebrew and Greek Scriptures. Some hold that the Quran is the "third installment" of revealed writings, meant to correct supposed errors in the Bible and bring final guidance to humanity. Others maintain that the Hebrew and Greek Scriptures remain complete in themselves, lacking any internal indication that an additional volume of revelation would supersede them. Since God is a God of order and not confusion (1 Corinthians 14:33), any further revelation should align with what He has already given. The question becomes whether the Quran fulfills that expectation or departs in key doctrines and historical claims.

50

Christians who base their faith on the objective historical-grammatical interpretation of Scripture consult passages that affirm God's consistent dealings with His servants across centuries. The Hebrew prophets, culminating in the Messiah, unveil a plan of redemption that hinges on the atoning work of Christ, the promised seed of the woman (Genesis 3:15) and descendant of Abraham (Genesis 22:15-18). The Greek New Testament declares the fulfillment of these promises in Jesus of Nazareth, whose sacrificial death and resurrection remove the curse of sin (Galatians 3:13). The Quran, compiled around the middle of the seventh century C.E., arrives six centuries after Christ's ministry. Muslims believe that Muhammad stands in the line of prophets, offering a final word that both confirms and transcends the Bible. Does the Quran bear marks of genuine inspiration or demonstrate inerrancy consistent with earlier Scriptures? This chapter explores that question at length, drawing on Scripture references and key elements of Islamic teaching.

The Quran's Claim to Confirm Previous Revelation

The Quran makes strong assertions that it corroborates earlier divine revelations, such as the Torah and the Gospel. In Sura 5:50-52 (Rodwell), the text asserts that God granted Jesus the Evangel "with its guidance and light, confirmatory of the preceding Law," and that the Quran likewise confirms the truth of what came before. In theory, if the Quran is to be viewed as a final chapter of inspired writing, it should demonstrate continuity with the Hebrew Scriptures and the Greek New Testament. Since Jehovah is not a God of contradiction, any genuine revelation must harmonize with what He has already revealed.

Throughout the Hebrew Scriptures, there is a consistent emphasis on the name of God, rendered in English as Jehovah. This name occurs thousands of times in ancient Hebrew manuscripts (Exodus 6:3; Psalm 83:18). The Greek New Testament, while often transmitted in manuscripts that replaced the divine name with generic titles, retains references to the importance of upholding God's name (John 17:6). Early Christian writers were aware of the Tetragrammaton, and many Greek translations of the Hebrew Scriptures used that name in quotations. Authentic revelation that seeks to confirm prior Scripture should at least display consistency with the divine name's significance. Yet, in the Quran, references to the name Jehovah are entirely absent, replaced by the more general "Allah." Some manuscripts of the Quran do not preserve or highlight the distinct personal name that the Hebrew Scriptures proclaim. This absence is one initial indication that the Quran, if it were truly the direct successor to biblical revelation, might be expected to retain or honor the unique name of the God of Abraham, Isaac, and Jacob (Exodus 3:15). Instead, it introduces a different emphasis, focusing on Allah as an unnamed divine figure. This difference stands out as a crucial point for discerning whether the Quran truly confirms the heritage of the Hebrew and Greek Scriptures.

Discrepancies Over the State of the Dead

The Bible teaches that sin results in death, and that death is an unconscious state (Genesis 3:19; Ecclesiastes 9:5, 10). Paul's inspired statement that "the wages sin pays is death" (Romans 6:23) further underscores that humans do not suffer forever in a blazing inferno at the moment of death. The Hebrew prophets and the apostles maintained a consistent view: the dead are not conscious and thus do not feel torment. Various symbolic passages, such as the parable of the rich man and Lazarus (Luke 16:19-31) or segments of Revelation, are understood as figurative or illustrative, not literal descriptions of a fiery afterlife.

By contrast, the Quran frequently references a literal, tormenting hellfire as a punishment for unbelievers (Sura 4:56; 25:13, 14, Ali). The text describes repeated skin-roasting or anguish without end, asserting that the wicked will plead for annihilation but never receive it. This portrayal conflicts with the biblical teaching that death itself is the penalty for sin, not everlasting conscious torment. Jesus and the apostles never taught that the majority of humankind would writhe in literal flames for eternity. Instead, the Bible proclaims hope of resurrection and reconciliation through Christ (1 Corinthians 15:20-22), or final destruction for the willfully unrepentant (2 Thessalonians 1:9).

A text claiming to be the next installment of revealed Scripture would be expected to maintain continuity on such a fundamental matter as the nature of the soul and the final destiny of the wicked.

While some Christian groups over the centuries borrowed from pagan notions of torment, the earlier Hebrew and apostolic writings do not contain such a teaching in their literal sense. The Quran's repeated emphasis on an unending, torturous hell underscores a difference in theology that cannot be reconciled easily with the earlier books. Rather than confirming the consistent biblical stance on death as unconsciousness, the Quran presents a different doctrine, indicating it is not fulfilling a confirmatory function.

The Father-Son Relationship of God and Christ

Biblical writings affirm that Jehovah has "sons" in a spiritual sense, including angels (Job 38:7; Psalm 82:6, 7) and humans like Adam (Luke 3:38). Among those sons, the Messiah holds a foremost position, being uniquely begotten as the promised seed (Psalm 2:7; Isaiah 9:6). The Greek New Testament clarifies that Jesus is the Son of God who willingly took on flesh, died, and was resurrected for humankind's salvation (Matthew 3:17; John 1:14; Hebrews 1:5). The entire biblical narrative from Genesis forward builds toward the coming of this special Son, who would redeem Adam's descendants from the penalty of sin. The fatherhood of God in these passages is never portrayed as involving a literal spouse or physical union; instead, it expresses a divine act of creation and the imparting of life.

In contrast, the Quran repeatedly insists that God does not beget offspring (Sura 6:101; 19:36, 91-93). It argues that if God had a son, He would require a consort or sexual partner, a notion the text repudiates. That stance reflects a literal interpretation of "sonship" that fails to capture the biblical nuance, where God's fatherhood is spiritual and not dependent on physical processes. The biblical idea that Jesus is God's Son does not imply that Jehovah engaged in marital relations, an accusation that is foreign to Scripture. The Quran's emphatic rejection of the concept of God's offspring thus departs from the biblical explanation that the Messiah is a begotten Son in a spiritual sense (John 10:34-36). Far from confirming the biblical teaching, the Quran replaces it with an outright denial that God has any son at all, whether figurative or otherwise. This major divergence in Christology indicates that the Quran is not a natural continuation of earlier revelation, which revolves around the Father-Son relationship as pivotal for human redemption (John 3:16).

The Denial of Jesus' Crucifixion

A critical tenet of the Greek New Testament is that Jesus died on a Roman instrument of execution and was resurrected on the third day (Matthew 27:35; 1 Corinthians 15:3, 4). This event is central to the gospel message. The Hebrew prophets, such as Isaiah, spoke of a coming servant of Jehovah who would bear the sins of the people (Isaiah 53:4-12). The Christian Scriptures consistently identify Jesus' death as the fulfillment of these messianic prophecies, presenting his blood as the means by which sins are forgiven (Romans 5:8-11). The apostle Paul expressed that if Christ was not truly crucified and resurrected, the Christian faith would be futile (1 Corinthians 15:14).

The Quran rejects this central historical and theological claim, stating: "They said (in boast), 'We killed Christ Jesus… but they killed him not, nor crucified him'" (Sura 4:157, Ali). It suggests instead that the Jews only thought they crucified Jesus, whereas in reality he was neither killed nor crucified. This stance directly contradicts biblical testimony and Christian belief that Jesus was truly put to death under Roman authority. By negating Jesus' atoning death, the Quran also denies the doctrine of substitutionary sacrifice, which appears consistently in the Hebrew sacrificial system and is explained in the Greek New Testament as the reality that Jesus' death is a ransom for many (Matthew 20:28; John 1:29).

A text that proclaims itself the next revealed word from God should confirm key redemptive acts already set forth in prior revelation, including the sacrifice central to God's plan. The denial of Jesus' crucifixion undermines the entire biblical structure of atonement, which begins in Genesis 3:15 and culminates in the Gospels' accounts of Jesus as the Lamb of God (John 1:36). Thus, instead of bearing witness to the fulfillment of messianic prophecies, the Quran deviates entirely on a point that the biblical writings affirm as foundational. This gap in doctrine further underlines that the Quran is not simply adding a final volume to a consistent canon.

The Question of Textual Corruption

In light of these discrepancies, some Muslim apologists argue that the Bible was corrupted prior to Muhammad's era, so that the Quran cannot be expected to align with a corrupted text. If the original Torah and Gospel had vanished or been substantially altered, the argument goes, then the Quran is simply restoring truths that were lost. However, a careful reading of the Quran itself shows that it never plainly states that the Scriptures were textually corrupted. Rather, it accuses Jews and Christians of misquoting or concealing portions of the text (Sura 2:70-73; 3:63-64), implying that the Scriptures remained intact but were mishandled by some religious leaders. The text mentions "torturing" or twisting Scripture with the tongue, not that the manuscripts themselves were thoroughly falsified.

History provides extensive evidence that the Hebrew and Greek Scriptures circulated widely in various lands and languages well before the seventh century C.E. By Muhammad's time, numerous manuscript families and translations (such as the Syriac or Latin versions) were already in existence, making a universal corruption impossible to carry out. The discovery of ancient scrolls, including those at Qumran (the Dead Sea Scrolls), demonstrates remarkable stability in the text of the Hebrew Scriptures across centuries. In the case of the New Testament, thousands of manuscripts predating the Quran by centuries show a high degree of textual integrity, allowing scholars to confirm that the text is substantially the same as in ancient times.

Thus, if the Quran claims to confirm earlier Scripture, it cannot argue that the original revelations disappeared entirely. The texts of the Law and the Gospel were well known in various communities, and even the Quranic charges imply that copies of the prior books existed. In Sura 10:94, the reader is told that if there is doubt regarding the revelations, one should consult those who read the former Scripture. This verse presupposes that the biblical text was still present and reliable enough to be consulted for confirmation. Accusations of widespread textual corruption cannot be sustained by either the historical data or the Quran's own statements.

Harmonization or Contradiction?

A hallmark of genuine revelation is consistency across the span of centuries and among different writers. The Hebrew Scriptures, penned by more than thirty individuals over a millennium, show doctrinal and thematic unity. The Greek New Testament, written within the first century C.E., affirms the Hebrew writings, referencing them as "the Scriptures" given by God (2 Timothy 3:15). When Jesus rebuked religious leaders, he often quoted or alluded to the Law, the Psalms, and the Prophets, underscoring that their testimony pointed forward to him (John 5:39; Luke 24:44). The apostles commended those who carefully compared their teachings against the Hebrew Scriptures, as with the Beroeans (Acts 17:11).

If the Quran were truly a third installment meant to complete the biblical narrative, it would be expected to display such coherence with the Law and the Gospels. Instead, the evidence shows theological departures. Jesus' identity as the Son of God, the atonement, the nature of man's soul after death, and even fundamental historical facts like the fate of Noah's family (Sura 11:36-47) differ from biblical accounts (Genesis 7:13; 10:1; 2 Peter 2:5). The repeated disclaimers that God does not have a son, the omission of Jehovah's name, and the portrayal of unending torment in the afterlife all conflict with earlier teachings. Such contradictions cannot be explained away by appealing to textual corruption of the Bible without undermining the Quran's claim to confirm that same Bible.

Contrasts in the Doctrine of Atonement

One of the most striking divergences is the doctrine of atonement. From the earliest chapters of the Hebrew Scriptures, the principle that "the soul that sinneth, it shall die" (Ezekiel 18:4) runs through the entire biblical history. Sin brings death, and only a sacrifice can provide a covering for transgression (Leviticus 17:11). The Levitical system of sacrifices emphasized that blood had to be spilled for forgiveness to take place, pointing prophetically to Christ's ultimate sacrifice. The Greek New Testament explains that Jesus, as the greater High Priest, entered the Most Holy on behalf of humankind and "offered one sacrifice for sins perpetually" (Hebrews 10:12). Paul summarizes this when he says, "Christ died for our sins according to the Scriptures" (1 Corinthians 15:3), referencing the body of Hebrew prophecy that announced the Messiah's redemptive work.

The Quran, however, rejects the necessity of blood atonement. It sees no need for a sacrifice to remove sin's penalty. Since it denies that Jesus was even crucified, it also denies the doctrine of substitutionary death. Islamic theology instead proposes that salvation rests on God's mercy and on the faithful practice of religious duties, including the Five Pillars. Though some might see parallels in the emphasis on divine mercy, the overall biblical concept that a blood sacrifice is indispensable to cover sin is absent from the Quranic narrative. This gap calls into question whether the Quran can be viewed as the next stage of revelation, because it does not confirm the extensive biblical teaching on atonement woven into the Law, the Prophets, and the apostolic writings.

Discrepancies Over Historical Details

Another test of genuine inspiration is historical accuracy. The Bible situates its narratives in concrete settings, naming kingdoms, rulers, and genealogies that can often be checked against external historical and archaeological sources. The Hebrew Scriptures trace lineages from Adam down to the tribes of Israel, while the Greek New Testament includes the genealogies of Jesus (Matthew 1:1-17; Luke 3:23-38), connecting him to Abraham and David. Such detail helps readers place the biblical narratives in their broader ancient Near Eastern context.

The Quran references many biblical figures but alters certain details. One example involves Noah's family during the Flood. The Bible explains clearly that Noah, his wife, their three sons, and those sons' wives were preserved through the waters (Genesis 7:13; 10:1). The Greek New Testament reaffirms that eight persons in total survived (2 Peter 2:5). The Quran, however, suggests that one of Noah's sons refused to believe and perished (Sura 11:36-47). This difference in detail signals a contradiction rather than a confirmation of the Bible. If the Quran were simply clarifying an ambiguous point, that might be defensible, but Genesis is explicit in naming the three sons who survived. The presence of such discrepancies suggests that the Quran is not simply an extension of the biblical record; it may incorporate variants of earlier traditions that do not align with the Hebrew text.

Edward D. Andrews

Assessment of Transmission and Manuscript Evidence

Muslims sometimes assert that the original Torah and Gospel have been lost or significantly altered, leaving the Quran to provide the final truth. The documentary history of the Bible, however, reveals that copies and translations proliferated across diverse communities. By the first century C.E., synagogues had scrolls of the Hebrew Scriptures, and early Christian congregations began circulating letters from the apostles alongside the Septuagint translation of the Hebrew texts. The discovery of ancient manuscripts and fragments, such as the Dead Sea Scroll of Isaiah, has consistently demonstrated that the text remained remarkably intact over centuries. Greek New Testament papyri, dated within a few generations of the apostles, confirm that the content of the Gospels and epistles has not undergone the supposed radical corruptions that some allege. Scholars examining these texts note that minor variants exist, but they do not alter the core doctrines or the historical framework.

Sir Frederic Kenyon, an English biblical scholar, once observed that the interval between original composition and earliest extant evidence is small enough to be "negligible." This means there is no realistic scenario in which the foundational events of the Messiah's life, death, and resurrection could have been overturned by copying errors or conspiratorial editing. Archaeologists and textual critics likewise affirm that no major portion of Scripture is absent from the ancient manuscripts. If the Quran were genuinely from God, one would expect it to attest to this textual preservation rather than dismiss it with vague allusions to corruption.

The Biblical Model of Progressive Revelation

The Scriptures show a pattern of progressive revelation, from the earliest hints of the coming Messiah (Genesis 3:15) to the more detailed prophecies delivered by Isaiah, Daniel, and other prophets, culminating in the arrival of Jesus in the first century C.E. Once Christ came, the apostolic writings declared that in him God had spoken conclusively (Hebrews 1:2). The entire structure of redemption is declared complete in Christ, who is described as "the way and the truth and the life" (John 14:6). The prophecies focus on his death and resurrection, establishing the means by which humankind can be

58

reconciled to God. The apostle John concluded the canon with the book of Revelation, which envisions the ultimate victory of God's kingdom and contains a warning against adding to or taking from the words of inspired prophecy (Revelation 22:18, 19).

A new revelation that arises six centuries later, claiming to supersede or correct the gospel of Christ, disrupts the internal logic of the biblical canon. Early Christians recognized the Hebrew Scriptures as God's word, and the Greek New Testament as the fulfillment of those prophecies. There was no anticipation of a further prophet who would rewrite the narrative of Jesus' crucifixion or deny his role as the unique Son of God. The question, then, is whether the Quran can be part of that biblical progression or whether it stands in conflict with the established revelation. Since the Quran denies cardinal truths about the Messiah and proposes doctrines foreign to the biblical record, it does not fit naturally into the sequence of revelation that runs from Genesis to Revelation.

The Role of Miracles in Validating Revelation

Another element often overlooked is the role of miracles in authenticating God's messengers. Moses performed powerful signs that compelled Pharaoh to release the Israelites (Exodus 7 through 12). Elijah and Elisha demonstrated divine backing through miraculous acts (1 Kings 17:1; 2 Kings 5:1-14). Jesus offered signs such as healing the blind, casting out demons, and even resurrecting the dead (Matthew 11:5; John 11:43, 44). The apostles, though not superhuman in themselves, performed miracles and spoke in foreign tongues as manifestations of divine endorsement (Acts 2:1-11; 2 Corinthians 12:12). These supernatural events served to confirm that the message and messenger were from God.

The Quran, by contrast, provides no record of Muhammad performing tangible miracles akin to those of the biblical prophets. Instead, it declares that the Quran itself is a literary miracle, unmatched in style and content. That claim, however, is subjective and largely dependent on the Arabic language's capacity for rhetorical beauty. The biblical model for confirming a prophet's authenticity consistently involves observable signs. Since the Quran does not present such signs, it does not align with the established pattern by which God validated new revelation in the past. Although some extra-Quranic traditions in Islam attribute miracles to Muhammad, these do not appear in the Quran itself, where the emphasis remains on the text's style as proof of divine origin.

Examining the Quran's Engagement With Biblical Figures

The Quran refers to numerous biblical characters, including Abraham, Joseph, Moses, and Jesus, often recasting their stories in brief suras. Where the Hebrew Scriptures provide thorough narratives, genealogical data, and an extensive historical context, the Quran typically supplies partial retellings that accent moral or doctrinal lessons. For instance, the account of Joseph in the Bible spans many chapters and includes intricate details of dreams, betrayals, and ultimate reconciliation (Genesis 37–50). The Quran's version (Sura 12) is much shorter, highlighting particular scenes without the same historical depth.

If the Quran were a true continuation of the biblical story, one might expect it to expand or clarify ambiguous areas. Instead, it either summarizes or alters established details. Recasting biblical events with divergent outcomes suggests that the Quran is working with traditions that were circulating in Arabia rather than confirming the canonical texts recognized by Jewish and Christian communities. Although there can be value in new perspectives, a text aiming to be the inspired sequel would logically align with the recognized canonical accounts and maintain fidelity to key details. The presence of clear contradictions—such as the fate of Noah's son—indicates a departure from the earlier narratives rather than a helpful expansion or clarification of them.

The Central Focus on Christ's Role in Scripture

The Hebrew and Greek Scriptures revolve around the promise and fulfillment of God's solution for sin and death. From the moment sin entered the world, the narrative steadily advances toward a coming deliverer (Romans 5:12-19). Abraham is promised that through his seed all nations would bless themselves (Genesis 22:18). The prophets point to a future Messiah who would rule in righteousness and bear the sins of many (Isaiah 9:6; 53:5, 6). The Greek New Testament proclaims that Jesus is that promised Messiah, who suffered willingly and conquered death on the third day (Luke 24:46). The Gospels, Acts, and letters of Paul stress repeatedly that redemption comes solely through Jesus (Acts 4:12; Ephesians 1:7).

The Quran, however, diminishes this role by denying both the crucifixion and the Sonship of Christ. It does affirm Jesus as a great prophet born miraculously of a virgin but stops short of allowing that he is the unique Son of God or that his death has any significance for sin's removal. For believers who see the entire biblical record as culminating in the cross, this shift is irreconcilable with Scripture's message. It suggests that the Quran is not simply the next stage in revelation but a separate religious text with teachings that stand apart from the Bible's central focus on Jesus' redemptive sacrifice.

The Nature of God's Name and Personality

From the earliest chapters of the Hebrew Scriptures, God reveals Himself as Jehovah, declaring this to Moses as His memorial name "to generation after generation" (Exodus 3:15). The personal name appears almost seven thousand times in ancient Hebrew manuscripts, underscoring its central importance. Biblical writers invoke that name in appeals for deliverance, praise, and worship (Psalm 83:18; 2 Samuel 7:23). Jesus, in his ministry, made known his Father's name, teaching disciples to pray that it be sanctified (John 17:6; Matthew 6:9). Early Christians, inheriting the Hebrew Scriptures, understood that name's significance, even if later copyists replaced it with titles in some manuscripts.

The Quran does not carry forward this singular name. Instead, it employs the term "Allah," a generic Arabic word for "God" used by Arabian tribes, including pagans and monotheists. Although some argue that "Allah" represents the same being as Jehovah in a different linguistic form, there is a marked difference between upholding a revealed personal name and adopting a commonly used title. If the Quran were truly the culminating revelation, one might expect it to build upon the name that God repeatedly stressed in earlier covenants. Its silence on Jehovah's personal name stands out as a major departure. Rather than confirming the continuity of divine revelation, it seems to establish a new framework in which the identity of God is not anchored in the personal name revealed to Israel.

Edward D. Andrews

Why Coherence Matters for Inspired Writings

God's truth, as presented in Scripture, does not present mixed messages or contradictions. The Hebrew Scriptures and the Greek New Testament, though diverse in authorship and era, unite around key themes: God's holiness, man's fall into sin, the unfolding purpose of redemption, and the promise of a Messianic kingdom. Jesus embodies these threads by fulfilling the Law and the Prophets (Matthew 5:17). Cohesion remains a badge of authenticity, reflecting God's stable character (James 1:17).

If the Quran significantly diverges on central doctrines about God, Christ, the atonement, and the afterlife, it calls into question whether it originates from the same divine source. The principle "God cannot lie" (Titus 1:2) implies that any subsequent revelation would restate and further illuminate truths already established, not subvert them. The claim that the Quran "safeguards" the previous revelation while contradicting it on vital points is logically inconsistent.

Considering the Apostolic Testimony

The apostles, who were eyewitnesses to Jesus' ministry, wrote under inspiration to record the life, death, and resurrection of Christ (John 19:35; 21:24). Paul's letters, circulated within years of Jesus' resurrection, reference well-known facts about Jesus' crucifixion and appearances after his rising from the dead (1 Corinthians 15:1-8). If the Quranic assertion is correct that Jesus was not crucified, the apostles and early believers would have perpetuated an enormous falsehood. Yet many of them endured persecution and death for proclaiming what they had personally witnessed (Acts 7:59, 60; 12:2; 2 Timothy 4:6).

A hallmark of the Christian faith is the eyewitness foundation of Christ's resurrection (Luke 1:1-4; 2 Peter 1:16). That event, more than any other, confirmed to the disciples that Jesus was indeed the appointed Messiah. The Quran, which emerged six centuries after these testimonies, offers no verifiable historical basis for overturning the eyewitness accounts recorded by early Christians. If the Quran were simply clarifying a misunderstanding, there would need to be substantial evidence that all those early believers had been mistaken or deceived. No such evidence appears, beyond the Quran's bare statement of denial. Hence, the apostolic testimony further corroborates that the biblical account stands firm.

Doctrinal Foundation or Cultural Shift?

Scholars have noted that the Quran often interacts with traditions circulating in the Arabian Peninsula, where monotheistic and polytheistic beliefs intermingled. Jewish and Christian communities existed there, but so did various pagan tribes venerating idols around the Ka'bah in Mecca. Muhammad's proclamation of one God resonated with biblical monotheism, yet it also introduced fresh elements that shaped a distinct religious identity. The absence of references to the name Jehovah, the shift away from atonement through Christ's sacrifice, and the denial of Jesus' Sonship all contributed to a new theological system that diverged from biblical precedent.

Muslims hold that this divergence arises from the Quran's role in correcting biblical corruption or misunderstandings introduced by religious authorities. However, as shown by the presence of ancient manuscripts, the biblical text was stable and widely disseminated in multiple languages by the seventh century C.E. The fundamental claims of Jesus' crucifixion, resurrection, and atoning role are well attested by numerous sources long before Muhammad's birth. This suggests that the Quran did not correct an error but rather presented an alternative account reflecting local traditions and beliefs. Claiming that a text which overturns a foundational biblical event is "confirmatory" requires a redefinition of the term confirmatory. Instead of confirming, it rewrites.

Unity of Hebrew and Greek Scriptures vs. Quranic Distance

The Hebrew Scriptures and the Greek New Testament exhibit remarkable continuity: genealogies connect the Messiah to earlier covenants, prophecies find fulfillment, and themes of redemption carry through. When the gospel writers quote Old Testament passages, they do so consistently, demonstrating unity of thought regarding God's purpose. The entire Bible tells one story, from creation to the promise of a future reign of righteousness under the Messiah. Although penned by many individuals over centuries, these books maintain a consistent portrayal of God's character and salvation plan, focusing on Christ as the culmination.

The Quran, arriving much later, does not simply omit minor genealogical details or omit obscure references. It denies the crucifixion, the very apex of the gospel narrative. It introduces an eternal torment in a manner foreign to biblical teaching, it sets aside the central atonement doctrine, and it insists that God has no son. Each of these elements is in tension with the earlier scriptural witness. Rather than bridging the Old and New Testaments, the Quran erects a new framework that cannot be integrated without dismissing large portions of biblical doctrine. For conservative interpreters of Scripture who rely on the Bible's internal consistency, the Quran's claim to be the "third installment" does not withstand scrutiny.

The Uniqueness of Christ's Mediatorship

From Genesis to Revelation, the Bible presents an ongoing pattern of mediation between God and humankind. Patriarchs like Abraham offered sacrifices, Moses served as a mediator of the old covenant (Exodus 24:7, 8), and the Levitical priesthood performed ritual sacrifices to atone for sins temporarily. All these pointed forward to the true Mediator, Christ Jesus, who accomplished a once-for-all sacrifice (Hebrews 9:24-28). The scriptures emphasize that there is "one mediator between God and men, a man, Christ Jesus" (1 Timothy 2:5).

The Quran, however, posits Muhammad as the final messenger, implying a shift in mediatorship away from Christ's unique role. Some interpretations hold that each prophet served in a line culminating in Muhammad, but the biblical view of Christ's priesthood, anchored in the order of Melchizedek, is singular and untransferable (Hebrews 7:23-25). If the Quran were truly continuing the biblical storyline, it would reaffirm Christ's permanent mediatorship rather than superseding it. Yet by dismissing the crucifixion and downplaying Jesus' Sonship, the Quran logically negates his continuing role as an enthroned mediator.

Addressing the Charge of Bias

Some might argue that criticizing the Quran's claim to confirm previous Scripture arises from Christian bias. Yet from a purely textual and historical standpoint, contradictions in theology, historical details, and interpretive frameworks are visible. The question is not whether Islam and Christianity can coexist in a broader social sense. Rather, it is whether the Quran fits the model of a final God-breathed revelation that completes or confirms the Bible. The evidence demonstrates consistent departures from the cohesive biblical narrative, not the anticipated continuity.

Examining the Quran's text reveals that it does not preserve the central teachings of the Hebrew prophets and the apostles of Christ in a manner that aligns with biblical teaching. Instead, it introduces new emphases and denies core elements of Christian faith, such as the need for a sacrificial death to atone for sin. The fact that these divergences exist on major doctrinal points, rather than peripheral matters, is significant. An addendum or continuation would require harmony on such central truths, or else it would disqualify itself from the claim of being the next link in God's progressive revelation.

Concluding Reflections

Does the Quran stand as the third installment of inspired and inerrant Scripture, seamlessly confirming the Hebrew Scriptures and the Greek New Testament? Evidence weighs against that claim. Numerous points of divergence—whether in the denial of Jesus' crucifixion, the rejection of God's unique Son, the assertion of perpetual torment, or the omission of Jehovah's personal name—signal a new set of beliefs rather than a faithful continuation. Biblical revelation presents a coherent message culminating in Christ's atoning sacrifice, which the Quran disavows. The notion that the biblical text was corrupted lacks credible historical or manuscript support. The Quran's own acknowledgment of the prior Scriptures and its references to them do not specify a complete loss of their integrity; rather, it suggests some religious leaders misquoted or concealed them.

The passages in the Quran that insist it confirms the Law and the Gospel stand in tension with the actual doctrinal content found within. While one can respect the dedication of devout Muslims to the Quran, from a conservative Christian perspective rooted in Scripture, the

Quran does not fulfill the role of a final revelation that completes the biblical canon. It is better understood as a separate religious text that incorporates some biblical themes while substantially modifying or contradicting core teachings.

Believers who uphold the Hebrew and Greek Scriptures as the complete written revelation see no further canonical writings that override or supplant the gospel. The biblical account closes with the resurrection and ascension of Christ, the outpouring of the Spirit in the first century upon the apostolic community, and the prophetic visions recorded in the book of Revelation. Those wishing to align with the historical-grammatical interpretation of Scripture conclude that the Quran, despite its reverence for some biblical figures, does not confirm the earlier canon but rather departs from it on vital doctrines. In that sense, no compelling evidence suggests that the Quran is the third installment of the inspired, inerrant Word of God.

CHAPTER 3 Is the Quran Harmonious and Consistent?

The Quran claims to be a revelation sent down by the same God who gave the Pentateuch to the Israelites and the Gospel to early Christians. Devout Muslims hold it in the highest regard, viewing it as the final and purest expression of God's will, free from the corruption they attribute to older Scriptures. Some present the Quran as a literary miracle, while others say its message contains incontrovertible truths that mere humans could not produce. From a conservative biblical viewpoint that upholds Scripture as God's inerrant revelation, these claims warrant close scrutiny. A primary test for any text that claims divine authorship is whether it is logically consistent and self-harmonious (James 1:17). Since God is not a God of confusion (1 Corinthians 14:33), His Word should not reflect contradiction or need abrogation. This chapter addresses whether the Quran meets the standard of internal harmony and consistency.

The examination begins by noting that the Quran itself acknowledges the possibility of contradiction. Sura 4:82 suggests that if the book contained any inconsistencies, that would prove it was not from God. Yet many passages and interpretative difficulties have prompted even Muslim commentators to propose that certain verses are "abrogated" by later ones. The Arabic term for abrogation, naskh, appears in disclaimers that God can substitute or forget earlier revelations (Sura 2:106; 16:101). Why would an all-knowing, all-powerful God provide messages that He later cancels or modifies? This challenge runs parallel to biblical teaching, where no prophet had to correct or annul the revelations of an earlier time. Moses never reversed the miracles granted at the Exodus, nor did the apostles of Jesus disclaim Christ's teachings. Consistency has always been a hallmark of God's communication across the centuries.

Far from focusing solely on the question of abrogation, this chapter reviews other apparent inconsistencies, such as the Quran's conflicting guidance about compulsion in religion, its stance on predestination versus free will, contradictions regarding the direction (kebla) of prayer, and statements about who can attain salvation. These differences are not trivial matters; they involve instructions on worship, war, moral conduct, and the fundamental nature of God's sovereignty. The question is whether an inspired and cohesive revelation from God could exhibit such tensions. Muslims seeking to reconcile these passages have devised complex commentaries, often resorting to the device that later suras override earlier ones. The material below explores these issues in light of biblical principles and the Quran's own claims, aiming to determine if the Quran genuinely stands as a self-consistent, divinely authored text.

The Quran's Claim to Consistency

Sura 4:82 (Ali) states: "Do they not consider the Qur-an (with care)? Had it been from other than God, they would surely have found therein much discrepancy." This verse addresses the standard by which to test divine inspiration in the Quran's own terms. If serious contradictions appear, the text arguably invalidates itself. A fundamental question is therefore whether such discrepancies exist. While Muslims believe the Quran was revealed to Muhammad piece by piece over about twenty-three years, the presence of contradictory instructions or teachings would contradict the notion of unchanging divine knowledge.

In defense of possible changes, Sura 2:106 and 16:101 mention that God can substitute or abrogate previous revelations. To many Christians who rely on the historical-grammatical reading of Scripture, the concept of God retracting or canceling instructions in the same era for the same covenant people is foreign. The Bible does reveal that certain instructions changed when covenants changed (for instance, the Mosaic Law was superseded by the new covenant in Christ). Yet the text of the Scriptures does not show repeated reversals of fundamental moral or spiritual decrees. In the Quran's case, the question is whether these expansions or reversals concern essential doctrine and practice or whether they are akin to the biblical concept of progressive revelation leading from the Law to Christ. Many critics observe that abrogation in the Quran often resolves contradictory statements rather than continuing a progressive plan spanning centuries. This contradiction abatement is distinct from the biblical narrative of covenants that run across large historical epochs.

Abrogation: A Tacit Admission of Contradiction?

One does not find biblical prophets stating that their earlier prophecies should be "forgotten" or "substituted." Indeed, Moses, David, Isaiah, Jeremiah, Jesus, and the apostles delivered messages that remain valid for their designated audience, with the overarching plan culminating in Christ (Romans 10:4). The Bible's storyline is unified: the Hebrew Scriptures point to the Messiah, and the Greek New Testament announces his arrival and saving work (Galatians 3:23-25). No biblical writer introduces contradictory requirements and then proclaims them canceled while the same covenant stands. That pattern is absent.

By contrast, the Quran's statements about abrogation have raised many inquiries. The text specifically says that God can abrogate or cause to be forgotten earlier verses, substituting better ones (Sura 2:106). Rodwell's commentary notes that classical Muslim scholars accept more than two hundred such abrogations. Modern Muslims debate these numbers, but the principle remains. Why would an eternal, perfect text delivered from God require active cancellations within a short span of about two decades? Did God revise His stance on major issues? The matter of compulsion in religion is one of the most cited examples, as discussed below.

Contradictions Over Compulsion in Religion

From a biblical vantage point, true worship of Jehovah is voluntary (Deuteronomy 30:19; Joshua 24:15). Jesus invited listeners to come to him and find rest (Matthew 11:28) but never forced conversion. The Quran, however, has suras that prohibit compulsion in religion and present Muhammad as only a warner. Sura 2:256 says, "Let there be no compulsion in religion." Sura 10:99, 100 poses: "What! wilt thou compel men to become believers? No soul can believe but by the permission of God." These verses align with an earlier, peaceful approach in Mecca when Muhammad lacked temporal power. The text emphasizes kindly persuasion: "Summon thou to the way of thy Lord with wisdom and with kindly warning: dispute with them in the kindest manner" (Sura 16:126).

In tension with that stance, the Quran also includes bellicose directives. Sura 2:186-190 (Rodwell) and Sura 9:5 famously instruct believers to "fight those that join other gods with God" and to "kill them wherever ye find them." Another verse states, "I will cast a dread into the hearts of the infidels. Strike off their heads then, and strike off from them every finger-tip" (Sura 8:12). Sura 9:124 urges believers to wage war against neighbors who are infidels. Such commands contradict the notion that "there is no compulsion in religion." If an unbeliever is threatened with violence or death unless he converts, that is a far cry from a free choice to worship God. Commentators have attempted to harmonize these statements by contending that the militant verses apply only to self-defense in a historical context. Yet many Muslim theologians historically accepted that Sura 9:5, revealed late in Muhammad's career, abrogated the earlier peaceful injunctions. Others propose specific circumstances in which violence is permitted, but the direct language about forcing conversions or punishing idolaters remains in the text.

By biblical standards, Jesus never taught his followers to kill those who reject the gospel (Luke 9:54-56). The earliest Christians spread their faith through preaching, not violence (Acts 2:14-41). If the same God had revealed the Gospel and the Quran, one would expect a consistent stance on using coercion or lethal force to gain converts. The differences in the suras themselves—some advocating nonviolence in religion, others commanding aggression—lead to confusion. Many reason that a perfect revelation from God would not require abrogation to shift from non-compulsion to open warfare and forced submission. Even if the historical context in Arabia changed from Mecca to Medina, God's moral principles do not shift so drastically within a single prophet's lifetime.

Predestination Versus Human Choice

Another area of apparent contradiction lies in the Quran's statements on predestination and free will. On the one hand, Sura 2:256 and 18:28 speak as though humans are able to choose belief or disbelief: "Let him who will, believe; and let him who will, be an

70

infidel." Sura 40:44 references a call to salvation, implying that individuals can heed or ignore the warning. These passages paint a picture of personal responsibility and accountability similar to biblical calls to repentance (Ezekiel 33:11).

On the other hand, many suras depict God as the One who controls who believes or disbelieves, making any choice irrelevant. Sura 76:29-31 (Rodwell) says: "Whoso willeth, taketh the way to his Lord: but will it ye shall not, unless God will it, for God is knowing, wise. He causeth whom He will to enter into his mercy." Sura 11:120 likewise suggests God has decreed some to err. These verses mirror a rigid form of predestination: God predetermines who is guided and who is misled, and individuals have no real power to alter their fate. The text even extends this to daily events. Sura 3:139 and 57:22 speak of events, including warfare, as locked into a "Book" that predates creation.

Similar tensions exist in some Christian circles regarding divine foreknowledge and human freedom, yet Scripture regularly affirms human accountability. The biblical message consistently insists that individuals are responsible for responding to God's offer of salvation, even if God in His foreknowledge discerns outcomes (Deuteronomy 30:19; Joshua 24:15). By contrast, the Quran sometimes suggests that blame for disbelief cannot be pinned on the individual at all if God had predestined that person to be misled. The presence of these two streams of teaching in the Quran—one emphasizing free choice, the other declaring a thoroughgoing predestinarian viewpoint—has historically led to sectarian strife within Islam. Each group finds textual support for its stance, illustrating an internal inconsistency that remains unresolved.

Some try to maintain that the earlier verses about free will were abrogated by later statements, or else they confine the free-will passages to a specific moment in Muhammad's mission. Others argue that only certain kinds of decisions are predestined. However, this requires imposing distinctions that the text itself does not always clarify. The net effect is confusion: can the unbeliever truly be blamed if God made him an unbeliever? Or is the unbeliever personally accountable? The biblical approach tries to hold divine sovreignty and human responsibility in balance without self-contradiction, but the Quran's mixed messages can appear contradictory to outside observers, leaving Muslims themselves debating the correct interpretation.

The Kebla: Conflicting Statements on Prayer Direction

Muslims face the Ka'bah in Mecca during formal prayers, an act known as turning to the kebla. Yet the Quran has verses that seem to downplay the importance of any particular direction. Sura 2:109 (Rodwell) reads, "The East and the West is God's: therefore whichever way ye turn, there is the face of God." Sura 2:172 says, "There is no piety in turning your faces toward the east or the west." One could interpret these verses to mean that direction is irrelevant, since God is omnipresent. No single direction can confine His presence. By analogy, in the Bible, Solomon prayed at the dedication of the temple, acknowledging that God cannot be contained in any earthly structure (1 Kings 8:27). The prophets taught that worship depends on sincerity rather than facing a physical location (John 4:21, 24).

Another series of Quranic passages, however, instruct believers to direct themselves toward the Sacred Mosque in Mecca. Sura 2:139, 144, and 145 (Rodwell) indicate: "We will have thee turn to a kebla that will please thee. Turn then thy face towards the sacred Mosque." This shift apparently arose during Muhammad's time in Medina, where the early Muslim community is said to have initially prayed toward Jerusalem. Then a new command changed the direction of prayer. Whether it was an abrogation or a divine test remains disputed. Yet the final outcome in Islamic practice is unequivocal: facing Mecca is mandatory for canonical prayers.

One might reconcile these verses by claiming that the principle "East and West belong to God" remains theologically true, yet the practical requirement to face Mecca is a specific command. However, for a text that describes itself as fully consistent, the argument from the verses that direction of prayer does not matter stands in tension with the explicit instructions that it does matter. Sura 2:172 undermines the notion of a single correct orientation, while the later suras in the same chapter stress that orientation. The Bible never gave contradictory rules about facing east or west in prayer. Although the

Temple in Jerusalem became a central place of sacrifice, biblical worshipers recognized God's presence worldwide. The discrepancy in the Quran about direction, including the abrupt shift from "any direction is fine" to "face the Sacred Mosque," can reflect an evolving context of Muhammad's leadership. But from a perspective that expects unchanging divine counsel, the question arises: why the contradiction?

Muslims Before Muhammad?

The Quran uses the term "Muslim" to mean one who submits to God. Sura 3:60, 5:48, and 111, among others, suggest that Abraham and Jesus' apostles were "those who surrender themselves" to God, effectively labeling them Muslims. Sura 5:111 says that the disciples of Jesus declared themselves Muslims. Yet Sura 39:14 has Muhammad stating: "I am bidden to be the first of those who surrender themselves to him." One could argue that the earlier patriarchs and apostles displayed the spirit of submission, so they were "Muslims" in a general sense, while Muhammad was the first Muslim in the new formal sense. Nevertheless, the text does not always clarify the distinction. Some suras appear to indicate that the identity "Muslim" predates Muhammad, while another implies that he was the first to adopt that identity. This contradiction, though subtle, points to at least an ambiguity that requires elaborate commentary to resolve.

Biblically, the faithful who lived before Christ (like Abraham, Moses, and David) are not described as "Christians," a term that arose in the first century C.E. among Jesus' disciples (Acts 11:26). While in principle they foreshadowed the faith later embodied in Christ, the Scripture never calls them by that later name. If the Quran had consistently said "Abraham was a sincere worshiper of God, distinct from the idolatry around him," many Christians would concur. Yet the claim that he was literally a "Muslim" raises confusion about historical continuity. Did Abraham follow the pillars of Islam or pray the salat five times daily toward Mecca? The narrative in Genesis, written many centuries earlier, does not suggest that. The difference might appear minor, but it underscores the broader question of how the Quran rewrites earlier biblical narratives to fit a new religious framework.

Salvation for Non-Muslims or Not?

Another inconsistency involves whether salvation is open to "people of the Book" who are not formally Muslims. Sura 2:59 (Rodwell) says, "Verily, they who believe (Muslims) and they who follow the Jewish religion, and the Christians, and the Sabeites,—whoever of these believeth in God and the last day, and doeth that which is right, shall have their reward with their Lord." This indicates that anyone from those groups can be rewarded if they believe in God and the last day. The statement aligns somewhat with biblical teaching that God is not partial (Acts 10:34, 35), accepting worshipers from every nation who fear Him and work righteousness.

Yet suras such as 3:79 and 5:76-77 say that only those who follow Islam are accepted, and that those believing Jesus is the Son of God or claiming God is "the third of three" (a reference to the Trinity) are infidels bound for fire. Sura 9:29 charges Muslims to fight "those who do not believe in God nor in the last day, nor forbid what God and his Prophet have forbidden," including certain people of the Book, until they pay tribute. The second stance is that no religion but Islam is valid. The first stance is that Jews, Christians, or others can be saved if they hold to belief in God and righteousness. Again, the attempts at harmonization have included appeals to abrogation, with some scholars claiming the inclusive verses were replaced by the later, more exclusive verses. Others limit the inclusive verses to righteous Jews and Christians living before Muhammad's time. The text alone, without interpretive traditions, is not always consistent.

By contrast, the Bible remains consistent that those who seek God in line with His revealed will can receive mercy, yet ultimate acceptance rests on faith in Christ as the promised Messiah (John 3:16; Acts 4:12). The new covenant after Christ is not ambiguous: "No one comes to the Father except through me" (John 14:6). The Quran's contradictory signals about the status of other monotheists illustrate the tension among Islamic interpreters. Some adopt inclusive perspectives and see Sura 2:59 as definitive, whereas others emphasize the later suras that brand non-Muslims as doomed unless they formally accept Islam.

Intra-Sura Discrepancies

Another factor is that some suras contain contradictions even within the same chapter. Sura 2:285 (Rodwell) says, "We make no distinction between any of His Apostles," implying that all prophets share equal rank before God. But verse 254 in the same sura says, "Some of the Apostles have we endowed more highly than others." Reconciling these statements can be done by claiming a difference between general respect for all prophets and special honors for some. Yet taken at face value, the statements appear contradictory.

Sura 56 likewise changes its description of how many among the earlier and later generations enter paradise. In the first part of the sura, it emphasizes that only a few from the later generations will attain that blessing, while in a subsequent portion it states that a crowd from the later generations will gain it. Beyond a figurative reading, it seems that the text changes the numeric proportion. If the Quran was perfectly coherent, the same sura would not appear to switch its ratio of saved persons midstream. One might propose that these passages refer to different classes of righteous individuals, but the plain reading suggests a discrepancy.

The Case of Jesus' Death or Non-Death

A well-known issue in Islam is the question of whether Jesus physically died. Sura 4:157 denies that he was crucified, asserting that the Jews thought they killed him but did not. Instead, God raised him up. However, Sura 3:55 can be read to say God caused Jesus to die and then took him up. Classic translations such as Sale's reflect the Arabic phrase that typically means "I will cause thee to die." Yet others, like Ali, paraphrase the phrase as "I will take thee." The result is disagreement among Muslim scholars themselves, some believing Jesus experienced a brief death, others saying he never died at all. This is no small matter, as it intersects with the Christian teaching that Jesus was truly killed and resurrected (1 Corinthians 15:3, 4).

The textual confusion on whether Jesus died or not is significant. If the Quran cannot be definitive on a core question about a major prophet's fate, it suggests internal inconsistency or at least interpretive ambiguity. The biblical Gospels present no ambiguity: Jesus was executed under Pontius Pilate, physically died, was buried, and rose on the third day (Luke 23:46-49; 24:1-7). The Quran, in disclaiming the crucifixion, reworks the narrative. However, even from an Islamic standpoint, the question of whether Jesus died at some later point or was taken to heaven alive remains unsettled, fueling a range of interpretive traditions.

The Historical Explanation for Contradictions

Some historians note that in the early, Meccan suras, Muhammad had little political power. The revelations from that period present a mostly peaceful stance, focusing on persuasion and patience. When he migrated to Medina and gained authority, suras began endorsing military action to secure Islam's ascendancy. The historical explanation is that Muhammad's strategies evolved as his circumstances changed. Yet if the entire text is from God, one wonders why the Creator would instruct peace early on and then command aggressive warfare later, culminating in calls for the subjugation of unbelievers. The notion of abrogation was presumably introduced to manage these shifts. This stands in contrast to the biblical record, where God's overall moral principles remain consistent, even though He deals with Israel as a nation in a unique covenant for a time (Exodus 19:5, 6; Jeremiah 31:31-34).

If one defends the Quran purely on the basis of progressive revelation, it must be explained why the same community under the same prophet needed numerous reversals within only two decades. The biblical transition from the Law of Moses to the new covenant in Christ spanned fifteen centuries, culminating in a once-for-all shift (Hebrews 8:7-13). By contrast, the abrogation principle in Islam allowed older verses to be canceled by later ones, sometimes within a short timeframe. That difference in approach contributes to the sense that the Quran is not a single coherent body of instructions, but a compendium of shifting directives tied to political or social developments. For a text claiming to be perfect and unchanging from eternity, these abrupt changes remain difficult to justify.

Muslim Responses to Apparent Contradictions

Islamic scholars are keenly aware of the issues outlined above. Over the centuries, they have developed various interpretive tools:

1. Abrogation (naskh): The later revelations in Medina override the earlier Meccan ones. This is the most common approach.

2. Contextual re-interpretation: Some claim the militant verses applied only when Muslims were attacked or in unique circumstances.

3. Multiple meanings: Words can be extended to metaphorical senses, allowing contradictory statements to be read as harmoniously addressing distinct contexts.

4. A general acceptance of paradox, with the note that God's ways are beyond human logic.

None of these methods completely erase the sense of internal tension. Indeed, abrogation admits that contradictions exist but are resolved by discarding older instructions. The second approach sometimes contradicts the plain reading of texts that explicitly call for offensive action. The third can stretch the text beyond its immediate sense, while the fourth leaves contradictions unexplained except by appealing to mystery. The net result is that even devout Muslim commentators concede perplexities. Writers such as Imam Râzî acknowledged puzzling passages, sometimes concluding that only God knows their true meaning.

From a conservative biblical approach, any revelation from God should be stable and reflect His unchanging nature (Malachi 3:6). The Scripture indicates that while God can progressively reveal more about His plan, He does not actively negate earlier moral truths. For instance, although some Mosaic ordinances were temporary shadows of Christ (Colossians 2:16, 17), they pointed forward rather than contradicted what would follow. The concept of repeatedly substituting moral or doctrinal teachings within a single generation is foreign to the scriptural pattern. As James 1:17 reminds us, from God "there is no variation or shifting shadow."

Implications for the Quran's Claim of Divine Origin

Because Sura 4:82 uses the absence of contradiction as proof that the Quran is from God, the presence of these contradictions weakens that claim. The argument that the Quran is a literary miracle falls short if one acknowledges that many passages conflict or require abrogation. The biblical yardstick for divine revelation is coherence with God's character and prior revelation, as well as internal consistency. In the

Bible, Jesus never had to revise or negate the teachings of the prophets. Instead, he fulfilled them (Matthew 5:17). The apostles did not discard the Gospels in favor of contradictory letters. Rather, they expanded on Christ's teaching in harmony with the gospel accounts (1 Timothy 6:3, 4).

Some defenders of the Quran say the abrogation principle itself is a sign of divine wisdom, showing that God adapts commands to changed circumstances. Yet the question arises why an omniscient God would give instructions that quickly become outdated. The argument that certain commands served immediate needs in seventh-century Arabia while still claiming eternal validity for the entire Quran is contradictory. The Bible, while set in ancient cultural contexts, does not revolve around instructions that are later canceled within the text itself. When the new covenant replaced the Mosaic Law, the transformation was not contradictory but rather the culmination of what was foreshadowed (Galatians 3:24-25).

These points suggest that the Quran's claim to stand as a perfect, final revelation must be weighed against its own textual record of abrogations, reversals, and inconsistencies. From a Christian apologetic standpoint, one can respect the sincerity of Muslim devotion while recognizing that the Quranic text does not measure up to the standard of inerrant divine inspiration. Instead, it appears shaped by the evolving context of Muhammad's leadership and changing priorities from Mecca to Medina.

The Biblical Model of Consistency

In the Bible, unity pervades the writings of multiple authors living centuries apart. Genesis, written in the second millennium B.C.E., foreshadows themes that Revelation, composed in the late first century C.E., brings to a conclusion (Revelation 22:1-5). Although progressive revelation clarifies details over time, fundamental truths, including the identity of God, the moral law, and the promise of redemption, do not contradict one another. The biblical text does not require disclaimers that earlier revelations might be abrogated. Instead, Jesus said, "Heaven and earth will pass away, but my words will never pass away" (Matthew 24:35), indicating permanence and reliability.

Paul insisted that even if an angel from heaven preached a gospel contrary to what the apostles taught, such a messenger should be rejected (Galatians 1:8). If a subsequent revelation truly came from the same God, it would confirm what was already revealed, not alter it. While Islam claims the Quran confirms the Law and the Gospel, the textual evidence in prior chapters has shown that it frequently conflicts with them or modifies core teachings (for example, denying the crucifixion). The question of internal consistency in the Quran itself thus compounds the problem. If the text repeatedly changes directions on compulsion, salvation, or the role of previous prophets, how can it confirm the consistent biblical narrative?

Observations From Muslim Commentators

Classical Muslim commentators such as Imam Râzî recognized that numerous verses conflict on the surface. The typical solutions revolve around classifying suras or particular passages as Meccan or Medinan, then establishing an abrogation hierarchy. For instance, militant verses in Sura 9 abrogate earlier peaceful verses from Meccan suras. But the details of which verse abrogates which can vary among scholars, leaving no unanimous blueprint for resolving all tensions. Ali's footnotes also sometimes mention that multiple interpretations exist, with no consensus. The frequent use of statements like "the Lord only knows best" or "these are the various explanations" shows that even within the tradition, reconciling these internal discrepancies is a difficult, unresolved challenge.

By comparison, the biblical text is studied through historical context, but believers typically do not rely on a principle of abrogation for contradictory passages. Genuine difficulties in the Bible are addressed through context, grammar, cultural background, or parallel references that illuminate the text. Yet the core doctrinal stances remain consistent—God's nature, sin's penalty, the redemptive purpose in Christ, and the moral commands do not vanish in the blink of an eye. No portion of the New Testament claims to abrogate earlier apostolic writings. Paul corrects misunderstandings in some congregations but never proclaims that prior epistles or gospels are null and void. James' emphasis on works complements Paul's emphasis on faith, but neither abrogates the other (James 2:14-26; Romans 5:1-

2). That difference in approach underscores how the biblical model fosters coherence, whereas the Quran's abrogation principle acknowledges the presence of real contradictions.

Consequences for Apologetic Discourse

Christians engaging in conversations with Muslims should be aware of these internal difficulties. The aim is not to disparage individuals who cherish their faith. Instead, it is to evaluate whether the Quran can stand as a final revelation surpassing the Hebrew and Greek Scriptures, especially on the question of consistency. If one sees the hand of an all-knowing God in Scripture, that same God would not produce a text requiring multiple cancellations and contradictory teachings within a short timeframe. The biblical God reveals moral truths that remain stable across generations. Even the shift from the Mosaic Law to the law of Christ is portrayed as a fulfillment, not a contradictory retraction (Hebrews 10:1-18).

When raising these questions, it is helpful to show empathy for the reverence Muslims hold toward their holy book. Yet believers in the Bible have strong reasons to doubt that the Quran is an equal or superior revelation, partly because of these internal contradictions. The differences regarding forced conversion, predestination, the direction of prayer, or who can be saved—alongside how abrogation is deployed—illustrate that the Quran does not function as a purely consistent message from eternity. If these contradictions were minor editorial details, they might be more easily overlooked, but many involve crucial matters of faith and conduct.

Comparing New Testament and Quranic Revelation Timelines

The timeline for the revelation of the Quran is also noteworthy. Unlike the Old Testament or the Gospels, which span centuries of prophecy, the Quran was compiled within a few decades after Muhammad's death (632 C.E.). It claims finality and completeness yet was shaped by immediate historical conditions, from persecution in Mecca to ascendancy in Medina. If biblical texts had introduced contradictory instructions in such a short period, those instructions would undermine claims of divine inspiration. Instead, across the entire biblical era of more than 1,500 years from Moses to Christ, the central message remained that Jehovah is sovereign, sin leads to death, and God provides redemption through the Messiah. There is no record of earlier prophets canceling the revelations of prior prophets. Rather, they build on a consistent foundation.

The Quran's internal changes, advanced as abrogation, stand at odds with the biblical standard that "the gifts and the calling of God are without repentance" (Romans 11:29). God's purpose is not undone or reversed within a few years. Once again, if the shift from no compulsion in religion to open warfare and forced conversions was truly God-ordained, it would contravene the biblical pattern of stable moral teaching. Instead, one sees evidence that these changes reflect the conditions in Arabia at the time, suggesting a text shaped by the historical circumstances of its prophet, rather than a suprahistorical, perfect revelation from an unchanging God.

The Wider Contrast With the Bible's Message

Christians who affirm the reliability of Scripture do so partly because the Bible tells a cohesive narrative from creation to final restoration, with minimal confusion about God's character or demands. The Law of Moses pointed forward to Christ's sacrifice (Galatians 3:24), and the new covenant replaced the old in an orderly, prophesied manner (Jeremiah 31:31-34; Hebrews 8). The apostles never launched violent campaigns to coerce believers into the church, nor did they proclaim that "some epistles are now abrogated." Instead, they taught that the Holy Writings "are able to make you wise for salvation" (2 Timothy 3:15). By contrast, the Quranic principle of abrogation and the contradictory rulings on vital matters create an environment of interpretive confusion.

Furthermore, the question of whether the earliest revelations from the Meccan period or the later revelations from Medina hold ultimate authority remains contested among Muslims. This fosters complexities in Islamic law, theology, and geopolitics. Many look to the later suras to justify certain strict or militant stances, while others cite the earlier suras to advocate tolerance and peace. The biblical counsel is that God is "the Father of lights, with whom there is no variation or shifting shadow" (James 1:17). This theological premise is difficult to square with the Quran's vacillation on pivotal issues.

Final Reflections on Harmony and Consistency

Given the evidence, the Quran demonstrates significant internal contradictions, particularly in core matters such as religious compulsion, free will versus predestination, the status of earlier revelations, the direction of prayer, and the possibility of salvation for non-Muslims. The text's own mention of abrogation suggests an awareness that newer verses conflict with older ones. If it were truly from the unchanging God of the Bible, one would expect a steadier continuity of teaching, free from repeated reversals in a short timespan.

Muslim commentators have offered various rationales: abrogation is divinely ordained, the historical context changed from Mecca to Medina, or different suras address different situations. Nonetheless, these explanations do not fully dispel the reality of contradiction. Contrastingly, biblical revelation, though progressive, remains internally consistent in its portrayal of God's nature, the moral law, and the Messiah's role in redemption. While the Bible acknowledges separate covenants, the shift from the old covenant to the new does not revolve around contradictory commands that are simply canceled. It is a planned development culminating in Christ's sacrifice.

Consequently, from a conservative Christian perspective that rests on the objective historical-grammatical method and the integrity of Scripture, the Quran's claim to be a perfect, divine revelation is not supported by its internal evidence. Its abrogation principle and conflicting instructions point to a text shaped by temporal circumstances rather than a single, unchanging divine voice. As believers in the Bible's God who does not lie (Titus 1:2), and whose Word endures (Psalm 119:160), one can respectfully conclude that the Quran does not exhibit the harmony or consistency required to establish itself as another inspired testament in line with the earlier Scriptures. The net result is that the biblical test—"Had it been from other than God, they would surely have found therein much discrepancy" (Sura 4:82)—applies here, revealing that the Quran, by its own standard, falls short of complete self-consistency.

CHAPTER 4 Is the Quran from God or Man?

When believers who rely on the Bible as God's revelation examine the Quran, questions inevitably arise about the Quran's origin, authority, and message. Countless Muslims throughout the world hold that the Quran is coeternal with God, existing on a celestial tablet before being transmitted to the prophet Muhammad by an angel. According to orthodox Islam, this holy book was not created at any point in time but has always existed alongside God. Additionally, many believe that the Quran not only supersedes earlier Scriptures, such as the Pentateuch and the Gospel, but that it stands as the highest revelation free of any flaw or corruption.

From a conservative biblical stance, claims about the Quran's origin, especially the view that it is eternal, raise searching questions. Does the Quran offer evidence of genuine divine authorship, as the Hebrew Scriptures and the Greek New Testament do? Does it reflect the character and consistency of the God who spoke through Moses, the prophets, and Christ Jesus? Or does it exhibit features that point to human sources, local influences, and changing needs in early seventh-century Arabia? The biblical test for divine inspiration involves not only miracles of confirmation and internal consistency but also harmony with previous revelation (Deuteronomy 13:1-4). A message from Jehovah should not contradict or reverse the fundamental truths He already delivered through the prophets and Christ. In addition, if a writing is truly from God, one would expect it to exhibit a consistency free from self-contradiction and from reliance on the circumstances of one man's life.

Earlier chapters reviewed the absence of accompanying signs or miracles to confirm the Quran's revelation, the lack of alignment with the Bible's core doctrines, and the presence of contradictions that lead to the practice of abrogation within the Quran. This chapter builds on that background to address the central question: Does the Quran originate from God, or does it reflect human composition influenced by local traditions and possibly other spiritual sources that deviate from Jehovah's message in the Scriptures? Addressing this question requires an in-depth look at how the Quran portrays itself, how it treats Scripture, what it teaches about God, and how the historical circumstances surrounding Muhammad shaped its suras and religious customs. Those who seek truth must consider the weight of evidence to determine whether the Quran demonstrates divine hallmarks or whether it more readily aligns with the imprint of human authorship.

Orthodox Muslim Views on the Quran's Eternity

Orthodox Islam has long held that the Quran is uncreated and eternally present in the heavenly realm. According to this understanding, Muhammad merely served as the conduit through whom the text was conveyed. The standard tradition states that the angel Gabriel delivered the Quran to Muhammad in separate revelations over about twenty-three years, culminating in 632 C.E. Some devout Muslims have even contended that the text is coequal with God in the sense that the Quran, as God's Word, shares divine attributes. Opponents of that view have pointed out the paradox of suggesting that a coeternal being can be a written text. Historically, heated debates arose over whether the Quran was created in time or uncreated and eternal, leading to theological controversies in the Islamic world.

For believers acquainted with the Bible, the notion of an eternal book existing on a heavenly tablet conflicts with how God revealed truth through Scripture. While the Bible does teach that Jehovah's Word is everlasting in the sense that His purposes endure (Isaiah 40:8), it does not depict the Hebrew Scriptures or the Greek New Testament as coeternal with God. Rather, it shows that God progressively revealed His will over the centuries through human prophets and apostles, culminating in Christ (Hebrews 1:1, 2). The idea of a text literally existing in heaven from eternity before being communicated to humankind is foreign to biblical presentation. The Christian Greek Scriptures do acknowledge that Jesus is the Word of God in a personal sense (John 1:1), but that is distinct from ascribing eternity to a book of suras.

If one holds that the Quran is literally coeternal with God, then it raises the immediate question of how it could be written on a physical tablet in heaven, and by whom. The notion of an eternal tablet that presumably was composed or inscribed contravenes the logic of "eternal and uncreated." Such philosophical difficulties hint that the claim might have arisen from reverent exaltation of the Quran rather than from rational or biblical reflection. Beyond these philosophical points, an informed Christian approach scrutinizes whether the text's content measures up to the standard of God's Word. If it fails on that level, then insisting that it is an eternal text coequal with God is simply untenable.

Absence of Miracles Authenticating Muhammad's Role

When Jehovah introduced major covenants, He provided authenticating signs. The Law covenant mediated by Moses was accompanied by dramatic miracles, including plagues on Egypt and the parting of the Red Sea around 1446 B.C.E. (Exodus 7-14). The Christian Greek Scriptures indicate that Jesus healed lepers, restored sight to the blind, and raised the dead, culminating in his own resurrection, thus confirming his messiahship (Matthew 11:5; John 5:36; 1 Corinthians 15:3-8). The absence of such confirming miracles in Muhammad's life stands as a marked difference. While Islamic tradition sometimes attributes miraculous events to Muhammad in the hadith, the Quran itself repeatedly points to the text of the Quran as the main sign.

The idea that "the Quran is the miracle" has been addressed in earlier chapters, specifically its claim of being a literary miracle. That claim rests on the assumption that no one could replicate the Arabic eloquence or style. The preceding chapters have weighed that assumption against the presence of repetitious passages, contradictory instructions (resulting in abrogation), and a structure that relies heavily on local Arabian customs. Meanwhile, the biblical standard of a miracle always involves something publicly verifiable, such as healing diseases or controlling the forces of nature, to confirm the messenger (John 10:37, 38; Acts 2:22). Basing a prophet's credentials solely on an assertion that no one can produce a similar text is at odds with the biblical pattern of God's dealing with His servants.

Additionally, Scripture nowhere indicates that a final prophetic figure would appear six centuries after Christ, lacking miracles, to announce a revelation reversing or modifying established doctrine. If God intended to introduce a new and final covenant, it would presumably bear the same level of miraculous attestation found in earlier pivotal events. Instead, the Quran offers no record of external signs. The suras occasionally refer to demands for a sign and repeatedly respond that God chose not to send one. Sura 17:59 says that earlier peoples did not believe miracles, so God withheld further signs. Yet biblical revelation never uses people's unbelief as a reason to stop giving miraculous confirmations. Even if many in Israel disbelieved, God still performed miracles through Moses, Elijah, and other prophets. The consistent pattern across Scripture does not align with the Quran's explanation.

Does the Quran Confirm Previous Scripture?

The Quran insists that it confirms earlier revelation, particularly the Law and the Gospel. Yet upon close inspection, as previous chapters have shown, it often diverges from biblical teaching or explicitly contradicts it. For instance, it denies that Jesus was crucified (Sura 4:157), a fundamental event in the New Testament. It dismisses the notion that God has a unique Son, whereas the Greek Scriptures affirm Christ's sonship (John 3:16). It reworks narratives about Abraham, Moses, and other biblical figures in ways that differ markedly from the Hebrew text. These discrepancies undercut the Quran's claim to "confirm" prior revelation. The biblical measure for a valid prophet is that he does not direct people away from Jehovah's message (Deuteronomy 13:1-3). The New Testament likewise insists that no new gospel can supersede the one preached by the apostles (Galatians 1:8). Because the Quran diverges from that biblical witness, it cannot stand as a confirmation of earlier revelation.

One might question whether the biblical texts were corrupted, thereby forcing the Quran to restore their original meaning. Yet historical manuscript evidence testifies to the stability of both the Hebrew Scriptures and the Greek New Testament over many centuries, well before Muhammad's time. The Dead Sea Scrolls, dating as far back as the second century B.C.E., confirm the general reliability of the Hebrew text. New Testament papyri from the second and third centuries C.E. show that its text has not been radically altered. Indeed, the Quran itself does not consistently claim that the older Scriptures vanished or were thoroughly corrupted. It accuses Jews and Christians of misquoting or hiding parts of their texts, implying the texts were intact but misused. Attempts to resolve conflicts by alleging large-scale biblical corruption lack historical and textual support.

If the Quran truly confirmed Moses and Jesus, it would align with their central teachings: the atonement, the identity of the Messiah, and the message of salvation by faith. Instead, it rejects the cross, the blood sacrifice for sins, and the divine Sonship of Christ. That negation stands in direct conflict with the heart of biblical revelation. Since the God of the Bible does not contradict Himself (Isaiah 46:9-11), there is no basis for a new "revelation" that dismantles core biblical truths. Such an approach leads to the conclusion that the Quran's claim of confirmation is not founded in Scripture.

Internal Discrepancies and Abrogation

A prominent reason for doubting the Quran's divine origin is the existence of internal contradictions, which have led Islamic scholars to adopt the doctrine of abrogation (naskh). The Quran itself indicates that God can replace or annul previous revelations (Sura 2:106, 16:101). This principle has been used to explain why certain suras that counsel peace and tolerance can be overridden by later suras that command violence toward unbelievers until they submit (Sura 9:5). The effect is that older instructions get canceled while the final stance, presumably from the Medina period, holds greater authority. If the entire Quran truly existed from eternity, the notion that God is substituting or forgetting prior verses in real-time context raises questions about divine consistency.

The Bible also describes progressive revelation. The Mosaic Law was superseded by the new covenant in Christ (Romans 10:4; Hebrews 8:13). However, that was a single shift that the Scriptures had foretold in Jeremiah 31:31-34, culminating in the sacrificial death of Christ. The question of abrogating moral or doctrinal instructions within the same covenant over a short period of time, and then leaving contradictory verses still embedded in the text, does not arise in the Bible. In

Scripture, God might refine or clarify commands, but He does not repeatedly cancel them. The presence of these contradictory statements in the Quran, some urging no compulsion in religion, others advocating violence, illustrate a form of inconsistency that stands at odds with the biblical pattern of a stable, unchanging message. Malachi 3:6 says that Jehovah does not change. Repeated abrogation of prior divine instructions suggests a text shaped more by circumstance than by a timeless divine will.

Revisiting Prophecies About Muhammad in the Bible?

Another frequent claim is that the Bible foretold Muhammad's ministry, thus authenticating the Quran. Muslim scribes often point to Deuteronomy 18:18, where God promises Moses He would raise up a prophet like him from among the people's brothers, placing His words in that prophet's mouth. They also reference Jesus' words about a coming helper or comforter in John chapters 14 to 16. Yet neither text supports an Arabian prophet appearing six centuries after Christ.

Deuteronomy 18:15-19 refers to a prophet among the Israelites, a prophecy Peter applies to Christ in Acts 3:22, 23. Jesus, a Jew from the tribe of Judah, indeed spoke in Jehovah's name, performed miracles like Moses, and perfectly revealed the Father. The text does not point to a descendant of Ishmael living in seventh-century Arabia who never spoke in the name Jehovah. Moreover, the comforter or "helper" in John 14:16, 16:7 is explicitly said to be the Holy Spirit poured out at Pentecost (Acts 2:1-4). Jesus told his apostles that they would receive this helper not many days after his ascension, which happened in 33 C.E. They were not told to await a prophet centuries later. The book of Acts records the immediate outpouring of the Spirit, leading to powerful preaching and dramatic growth of the Christian congregation (Acts 2:41). This clearly does not describe or point to Muhammad in 610 C.E.

References to an alleged final prophet in Song of Solomon or other Old Testament passages sometimes appear in certain Islamic apologetic works, but these claims rest on ambiguous wordplay, not any direct textual evidence. Evaluating these claims in the light of scriptural context shows they do not foretell a new religion overshadowing Christ's fulfillment. Biblically, Jesus is presented as the final spokesman, the culmination of God's revelation (Hebrews 1:1, 2). The apostolic writings repeatedly stress that no further mediator or prophet of new laws is anticipated. Hence, claims that the Bible predicts Muhammad fail under a straightforward reading of Scripture.

The Quran's Prophetic Element

Genuine prophecy is a hallmark of divine inspiration. The Bible's accuracy in foretelling events underscores its divine origin (Isaiah 42:8, 9). Critics or believers can test predictions about future events to see if they come to pass. Moses prophesied plagues upon Egypt, Isaiah named Cyrus two centuries before his rise, Jeremiah gave a seventy-year timeframe for Judah's exile, Daniel outlined successive world empires, and Jesus prophesied Jerusalem's destruction (Luke 19:43, 44). These fulfillments abound in Scripture, strengthening faith in its inspiration.

What about the Quran? Does it offer prophecies that confirm its divine source? A cited example is Sura 30:1-3, which references the defeat of the Roman Empire followed by a reversal within a few years. Defenders of the Quran argue that this prophecy was fulfilled when the Byzantine (Eastern Roman) forces later gained victory over the Persians. Yet critics note that any astute observer might have guessed that the massive Roman Empire could rally. Additionally, textual ambiguity arises because the original lacked vowel points, so some translations read that the Romans would be defeated further. Even if one granted the correct reading, it would not match the specific, detailed predictive nature of biblical prophecies that name individuals or specify exact timelines. The prophecy about Cyrus in Isaiah is far more explicit, demonstrating that real divine foreknowledge includes identifying the deliverer by name (Isaiah 44:28; 45:1).

Another alleged Quranic prophecy is that Islam would triumph over every other religion (Sura 9:33). Historically, Islam never did conquer the entire world. Today, it remains a significant faith, but not dominant in all regions. About 30 percent of the world's population identifies with various forms of professed Christianity, while Muslims number around 1.9 billion, which is roughly 24 percent, though demographics vary. Despite centuries of expansion, Islam did not surpass or eradicate all other religions. Consequently, the prophecy remains unfulfilled if taken literally. Meanwhile, the Bible's prophecies about the global preaching of the gospel and the moral and societal conditions of the last days have been widely observed, even though many reject biblical faith. In short, the Quran's so-called prophecies do not match the specificity or success found in biblical prophecy. That deficiency undermines the argument that the Quran is divinely inspired on prophetic grounds.

Local Arabian Influences on the Quran

A major factor suggesting that the Quran is of human origin is the extensive incorporation of local beliefs, customs, and controversies in seventh-century Arabia. Historians note that many pre-Islamic tribes worshipped around the Ka'bah in Mecca, revering a black stone, engaging in pilgrimages, and respecting certain months as sacred. Far from discarding these rituals, the Quran embraces them, turning the Ka'bah into the focal point of worship for Muslims worldwide (Sura 2:139-145). If a new revelation were truly universal, without dependence on local pagan customs, one might expect God to guide worshippers away from venerating a stone building or continuing the pagan practice of circling it. The Hebrew Scriptures, for instance, vigorously condemned idolatrous shrines (Exodus 20:3, 4; Deuteronomy 12:2-4). Yet the Quran transformed the Meccan pilgrimage, or hajj, into a central pillar of Islam, despite its roots in pre-Islamic worship.

Polygamy as practiced in the desert environment likewise becomes codified into the Quran, which allows a man up to four wives (Sura 4:3). In biblical times, polygamy existed but was never explicitly instituted by God as the standard for all worshippers, and the Christian arrangement encourages monogamy (Matthew 19:4-6; 1 Timothy 3:2). The Quran's stance that a faithful man can have multiple wives does not reflect the pattern taught by Christ, though it does reflect the norms of seventh-century Arabia. The religion of Islam in the Quran also borrowed certain elements from local monotheistic movements known as the Hanifs, who already proclaimed the unity of God and criticized idolatrous practices.

Additionally, the strong fatalism in the Quran resonates with pre-Islamic Arabic beliefs that a person's destiny is inescapable. In the biblical record, Jehovah's sovereignty coexists with meaningful human choices, but the Quran sometimes portrays a more rigid predestination, with individuals forced to the path of belief or disbelief (Sura 76:29-31). That emphasis is reminiscent of local Arabian culture's sense that fate (time) is inexorable. Rather than transcending the region's worldview, the Quran frequently merges with it. This synergy between the text and local beliefs suggests adaptation rather than pure divine revelation.

Use of Jewish, Apocryphal, and Folklore Traditions

The Quran draws on stories from Jewish tradition, apocryphal gospels, and even Zoroastrian ideas. It references Mary's miraculous speaking infant (Sura 19:27-34), a concept parallel to the apocryphal "Gospel of the Infant." It recounts Jesus forming birds from clay and bringing them to life, found in the "Gospel of Thomas." These are not narratives from canonical Scripture but rather from later, spurious writings. Similarly, the Quran's denial of the crucifixion of Jesus echoes the Manichaean notion that someone else was substituted in Jesus' place, an idea that circulated among certain heretical sects in late antiquity. The biblical Gospels are unanimous about Jesus' crucifixion. The presence of such apocryphal or folkloric elements in the Quran indicates reliance on non-biblical traditions circulating in or near Arabia at the time.

Jewish Talmudic influence may appear in the Quran's references to angels, demonology, and the idea of balances on Judgment Day. The Talmudic tradition included discussions about spirit creatures and elaborate afterlife concepts. The Avesta, from Zoroastrian Persia, also described a final judgment with a bridge and weigh scales for souls. The Quran depicts a narrow bridge or a place like Al-Araf for those not fully righteous or wicked. These parallels strongly suggest that Muhammad had contact with individuals from diverse religious backgrounds—Jews, Christians, Zoroastrians, and local Hanifs—and synthesized aspects of their beliefs into the suras. Instead of representing a pristine revelation from God, the result appears as a blend shaped by multiple influences. If the Quran were truly an eternal text from the same God who inspired Moses and Jesus, it would not rely so heavily on non-canonical Jewish and Christian folklore.

Accommodations to Muhammad's Personal Circumstances

Another telling feature of the Quran is how frequently it addresses personal incidents in Muhammad's life by providing revelations that resolve his immediate problems. For instance, after an unpleasant rumor circulated about his wife Aisha and a young warrior, Sura 24 came forth to exonerate her and condemn the rumor. When Muhammad wished to marry the divorced wife of his adopted son Zaid, Sura 33 excused this union even though local custom considered an adopted son's ex-wife out of bounds. Later, Sura 66 spoke to an incident in which Muhammad had relations with a Coptic concubine in the home of one of his wives, leading to a household dispute. The sura permitted him to continue his relationship with the concubine while rebuking his wives for objecting.

Had these revelations come from God, an observer might ask why God would inscribe such personal episodes on an eternal heavenly tablet. The biblical prophets sometimes recounted personal struggles, but they seldom invoked direct revelations that solved domestic quarrels or authorized specific marriages. Indeed, the Scriptures usually hold God's prophets to a high moral standard, sometimes rebuking them for personal errors (2 Samuel 12:7-14; Galatians 2:11-14). The repeated pattern of suras aligned with Muhammad's immediate desires or controversies indicates a text shaped by local and personal considerations rather than an unchanging, eternal message. This phenomenon has led some critics to conclude that the Quran was partly shaped by personal convenience, as opposed to emanating from an impartial and timeless divine source.

Contrasts with the Biblical Progression of Covenants

One might ask why God, who revealed the far superior new covenant through Christ (Hebrews 8:6), would revert seven centuries later to a system emphasizing ritual washings, dietary rules, and other practices reminiscent of, or even more restrictive than, the Mosaic Law. The Book of Hebrews contrasts the shadows of the old covenant with the reality found in Christ (Hebrews 10:1). The new covenant moves beyond a rigid code to an inward transformation through faith in Jesus' sacrifice. The Quran, however, reintroduces elaborate external rites, including ritual prayer in a precise direction five times a day, proscribed fasts, strict dietary regulations, and veneration of a physical shrine. This is not an advancement beyond the gospel but a regression, from the vantage point of the biblical narrative. Jeremiah 31:31-34 promised a better covenant, inscribed in hearts, fulfilled in Christ.

If the Quran truly came from the same God who orchestrated salvation history culminating in Jesus, it would not instruct believers to adopt ceremonies foreign to the gospel or revert to polygamy and ritual obligations reminiscent of older systems. Jesus spoke of worship in spirit and truth, not tied to sacred mountains or temples (John 4:21-24). The Christian congregation recognized freedom from the Mosaic code, focusing on moral law and the Spirit's guidance. The Quran's reemphasis on external forms strongly suggests it is not a continuation of biblical covenants but a separate religious tradition shaped by the environment of seventh-century Arabia. This stands in tension with any claim that the Quran supersedes the teachings of Christ.

Evaluating the Alleged Perfection of the Quranic Text

Muslims often uphold the Quran as impeccably preserved and free from human corruption. They compare this presumed textual purity with what they consider a corrupted Bible. However, historical records of the early Islamic community indicate that variant recitations existed, prompting the third caliph, Uthman, to produce an official version, discarding other manuscripts. If the text had been meticulously dictated by God in an unaltered form, one wonders why these divergences required a unification process. Meanwhile, the Bible, with thousands of manuscripts in multiple languages, displays remarkable consistency. Variants exist, but the essential message remains intact.

Beyond the textual transmission, the content itself reveals contradictory instructions that led to abrogation. If the Quran was authored by God from eternity, it would not need to revise earlier suras. Indeed, the final text preserves the older suras side by side with the abrogating ones. This scenario suggests that the text's formation was an unfolding historical process rather than a deposit from a timeless heavenly tablet. Some might retort that the same argument could be leveled at the Bible. Yet the Bible's internal progression from the Law to the gospel is consistent with prophecy and does not rely on repeated short-term reversals. The official canon of Scripture formed over centuries, but the biblical community did not discard older manuscripts as invalid. The differences in approach are substantial, pointing to the biblical text's stable continuity across many centuries as opposed to the Quran's more immediate editorial standardization.

Could the Quran Have Unseen Spiritual Influence?

A possibility arises that the Quran might have an otherworldly source, not from God but from spirit beings opposed to Jehovah's purposes. The Scriptures acknowledge that Satan can appear as an angel of light (2 Corinthians 11:14). Satan is described as the god of this system of things who blinds minds, preventing them from seeing the light of the gospel of Christ (2 Corinthians 4:4). If one rejects the idea that the Quran is from the true God, the question remains whether it is purely human or if malevolent spirit forces contributed to its composition. Muhammad initially experienced fear, suspecting that an evil entity might be contacting him, until his wife encouraged him that it was a good spirit.

Biblically, deceiving spirits can produce counterfeit revelations. Paul warned about teachings that turn people away from the truth in Christ (1 Timothy 4:1). The Quran leads billions to deny Jesus' crucifixion and Sonship, central to Christian salvation doctrine. It also calls for aggression against those who do not accept Muhammad's prophethood. This pattern might reflect a spiritual strategy to obscure the redemptive work accomplished on the cross. Some might regard that as too strong an allegation. Still, it is consistent with the biblical narrative that evil spirits sow confusion and false gospels to deter individuals from Christ's saving message (Galatians 1.6-9).

Whether one believes the Quran is purely a product of Muhammad's reflection on local beliefs or influenced by wicked spirits, it is clear that the text does not align with the redeemed life and atoning sacrifice taught in the Greek Scriptures. If it were truly from Jehovah, it would not steer people away from the cross and the resurrection. The negative portrayal of Jesus' death suggests that the fundamental biblical teaching on ransom for sin has been deliberately removed, which fits the apostle John's warning that many deceivers have gone forth, refusing to acknowledge the Christ who came in the flesh (2 John 7).

Comparing the Quran's Moral Framework to Christian Liberty

Some might argue that the Quran's moral code improved the pagan environment of Arabia, discouraging female infanticide, regulating polygamy, outlawing certain idolatries, and teaching the unity of God. The question is not whether Islam improved local conditions but whether it truly came from the same God who had already revealed His ultimate plan through Christ. The apostle Paul wrote that the new covenant freed believers from Mosaic burdens (Galatians 5:1). The Quran, though beneficial in some aspects for that culture, reintroduces many ceremonial practices and leaves out the atoning sacrifice of Jesus. That difference is essential. While one can acknowledge that Islam stands above raw paganism, it need not be from God. Many religious or philosophical systems have introduced partial improvements without aligning fully with biblical revelation.

Consider that the Bible's moral teachings, culminating in Jesus' command to love even one's enemies (Matthew 5:44), surpass a system that endorses holy war to subjugate unbelievers. The Quran's approach allows forced conversions and ongoing hostility, as reflected in certain suras. By contrast, the New Testament advocates preaching and peaceful persuasion. If the Quran were the final revelation, one might expect an even higher moral standard than the gospel. Instead, the moral trajectory suggests a partial step forward from Arab paganism but a retreat from the radical love ethic taught by Christ. That disparity underscores the argument that the Quran is not from the God who perfected revelation in Jesus.

Reflecting on the Quran's Focus on Arabic Culture

The repeated emphasis in the Quran on its Arabic language and appeal to Arabs reveals a context-bound revelation. The text itself often states it is an Arabic recitation for people who understand Arabic (Sura 12:2; 13:37; 16:105). If the Quran was truly for all nations as a final revelation, one might anticipate broader outreach or a statement encouraging translation for every people. The Christian Greek

Scriptures not only were written in Koine Greek, a lingua franca of the time, but their content quickly spread to many cultures without the claim that the gospel is only "pure" in Greek. Indeed, Scripture encourages the translation of the message so that everyone can hear (Matthew 28:19, 20; Acts 2:6-11). The repeated insistence in the Quran on its Arabic form as a sign of divine favor suggests an approach shaped by local concerns rather than a universal perspective.

Furthermore, the biblical narrative extends from creation in Genesis to the new heavens and new earth in Revelation, engaging multiple cultures over centuries. The Quran begins in seventh-century Arabia, referencing local disputes, religious practices, and battles. Little of universal history or prophecy emerges. The text includes mention of earlier biblical figures but often in ways that revolve around persuading the immediate audience in Mecca or Medina. This narrow cultural scope does not negate all moral teachings, but it stands in contrast to the broad sweep of biblical revelation that has shaped countless cultures. The Quran's repeated mention of local events, like friction with certain tribes, suggests a historically contingent text rather than a timeless communication.

The Question of a Return to Mosaic-Like Rituals

Another major puzzle is the Quran's emphasis on dietary laws, ritual ablutions, prescribed fasts (especially Ramadan), and abstinence from specific foods such as pork. These rules mirror or extend aspects of Old Testament law and sometimes reflect local Arabian taboos. By the time of Christ, the biblical record points to a shift away from external ceremonialism toward inward moral purity (Mark 7:18, 19). The apostolic council in Acts 15 did not require Gentile believers to follow the entire Mosaic code, focusing only on a few prohibitions related to idolatry and blood. If a final revelation were coming six centuries later, one might expect it to reflect the new covenant's emphasis on freedom in Christ, not restore a system of dietary and ceremonial prescriptions.

The reintroduction of a highly regulated code with obligations reminiscent of Mosaic worship—albeit with an Arabian slant—does not match the trajectory established by Jesus and the apostles. Instead, it demonstrates a departure from the biblical narrative of redemption and transformation. Observers might note that the Mosaic law had a divine purpose for a specific time (Galatians 3:19), pointing to Christ. Once Christ completed his sacrifice, the old covenant was done away with (Hebrews 8:13). The Quran's reimplementation of external constraints is more plausibly explained as an effort to shape a distinct communal identity in a new Arab monotheism than as a revival from the same God who had previously set aside those ceremonial requirements. That discrepancy speaks to a human or possibly demonic impetus, rather than a message from Jehovah.

Considering Muhammad's Initial Fears of Evil Spirits

Biographies of Muhammad recount that when he first started receiving what he believed to be revelations, he experienced terror and doubts, suspecting demonic influence. He initially confided in his wife, who reassured him that no evil spirit would approach a man of his piety. Over time, he embraced the conviction that an angel was guiding him. Nonetheless, from a biblical vantage point, the devil and his angels can appear benign, disguising themselves as helpers (2 Corinthians 11:14). One does not have to conclude dogmatically that a demon personally dictated the entire Quran. Yet the presence of unbiblical teachings, denial of crucial aspects of Christ's identity, and calls for compulsion in religion raise serious concerns about where the message truly originated.

The apostle John declared that many false prophets would go into the world, acknowledging that deceiving spirits can lead people away from the gospel (1 John 4:1-3). He stated that the spirit from God would confess that Jesus came in the flesh, a reference to the incarnate Son fulfilling redemption. The Quran, by contrast, denies Jesus' crucifixion, effectively denying the fullness of his work in the flesh (1 Corinthians 1:23; 1 John 2:22). If one weighs these elements, it becomes plausible that a spirit opposed to Christ might exploit partial truths and religious fervor to produce a system that obstructs the gospel.

The Impact of the Ka'bah Veneration

An additional consideration involves the Ka'bah in Mecca. Muslims believe this structure was originally built by Abraham and Ishmael as a house for God, though the Bible never references

97

Abraham traveling to Mecca or erecting a cubic shrine. Historical sources suggest that the Ka'bah was a local pagan center containing numerous idols, each tribe worshiping its own deity. Muhammad eventually cleansed the shrine of idols, preserving only the black stone, which remains an object of reverent kissing and circumnavigation during the hajj. If the Quran is from God, why maintain a stone building as the holiest site, with rituals that strongly echo the region's pre-Islamic idol worship? The biblical pattern is that once the revelation of Christ came, the physical temple in Jerusalem itself lost its exclusive sanctity (Matthew 24:2; John 4:21). The Christian congregation worships God everywhere in spirit and truth, no longer tied to a single shrine (Acts 17:24, 25).

The ongoing reverence for a black stone reveals that the new religion inherited the very object-centered veneration that biblical revelation rejects. Isaiah 44:13-20 condemns worship involving physical objects as meaningless. Jesus did not call his followers to gather around an ancient stone but to gather in his name, reflecting a spiritual fellowship (Matthew 18:20). The presence of these inherited practices supports the conclusion that the Quran emerges from local Arabian religion rather than from the God who led Israel out of idol-based worship.

Summation of the Evidence

In sum, the Quran does not pass the biblical tests for a God-given revelation. It lacks accompanying miracles that would attest to Muhammad as a true prophet. It claims to confirm Scripture yet contradicts essential biblical doctrines. It exhibits internal inconsistencies that require abrogation. Its alleged biblical prophecies of Muhammad do not stand up to straightforward exegesis, and its own prophecies fail to match biblical standards. It draws heavily on local Arabian customs, pre-Islamic rituals, Jewish folklore, and apocryphal writings. Revelations conveniently appear to resolve domestic matters for Muhammad. The text endorses reversion to external ceremonies at odds with the new covenant's spiritual freedom. The revered Ka'bah with its black stone remains a remnant of pagan practice. All of these factors align more with a humanly generated text, possibly with darker spiritual influences, than with an authentic Word from Jehovah.

Hence, from a conservative Bible-based viewpoint, the Quran originates from man, not from God. A sincere quest for truth must note that the biblical canon already provided the fullness of God's plan of salvation in Christ. The New Testament warns that after the apostles' time, false teachers and rival messages would appear, seeking to distort or displace the gospel (Acts 20:29, 30). The Quran fits that pattern by redefining Christ's mission and discrediting his crucifixion. Jesus himself cautioned that "many false prophets will arise and mislead many" (Matthew 24:11). While one can acknowledge the historical importance of Islam and the moral reforms it introduced in certain cultures, those factors alone do not verify it as divine. The fundamental divergences from Scripture are decisive.

Lessons for Christian Readers

Christians should therefore stand firm in the faith once delivered to the saints (Jude 3), remembering that the gospel of Jesus Christ is final and complete. Attempts to add a new revelation must align with God's prior message, but the Quran undermines central biblical truths. Believers can approach Muslim acquaintances with respect and kindness but remain aware that the Quran's origins are not from Jehovah. Scripture upholds that Christ's sacrifice is the only path to forgiveness and that no additional prophet after the apostolic era was ordained to create a new covenant. The biblical record surpasses the Quran in historical reliability, fulfilled prophecy, and doctrinal coherence.

Furthermore, in areas where the Quran champions monotheism against idol worship, Christians might highlight that the biblical call to worship only Jehovah is indeed essential (Exodus 20:3). Yet the greater revelation of God's purpose in Christ goes beyond strict monotheism to the redeeming love displayed on the cross, something the Quran denies. The spiritual consequence is that individuals who follow the Quran's denial of the cross remain in darkness about the single greatest act of divine love. The apostle Paul wrote that the cross is the power of God to those being saved (1 Corinthians 1:18). This stands diametrically opposed to the Quran's teaching. A text that strips the cross of its meaning cannot come from the God who orchestrated redemption through Jesus' atoning death.

Concluding Thoughts

Those who examine the Quran in the light of Scripture, history, and reason find compelling evidence that it stems from human or even sinister sources rather than from Jehovah. Indeed, if it had been simply the product of human endeavor without claims to final revelation, it might still have improved certain social norms in Arabia. But once it sets itself as the definitive revelation superseding Christ, it must be measured by biblical criteria. Without miraculous confirmation, with contradictory teachings requiring abrogation, with borrowed traditions from apocryphal texts, and with a consistent departure from the core of the gospel, the Quran fails the test of divine authorship.

No reason remains for a believer in the Bible to accept that the Quran was authored by the God of Abraham, Moses, and Christ. It stands as an alternate religious tradition, created or shaped in an environment that combined local pagan customs, Jewish folklore, and an incomplete understanding of Christian doctrine. A final note is that Muhammad's personal sincerity in certain early efforts does not transform the Quran into a revelation from Jehovah. Sincerity cannot replace alignment with truth. Even those convinced of their revelations can be mistaken or misled by unseen forces. The test is whether the message accords with God's enduring revelation in Scripture (1 John 4:1). By that measure, the Quran does not pass.

Christians are advised to remain anchored in the knowledge of Christ, as the final messenger through whom God has spoken (Hebrews 1:1, 2). The entire biblical canon bears the unmistakable hallmark of God's unfolding plan, culminating in the crucifixion and resurrection of Jesus. Accepting the Quran's claim means forfeiting the central truths about Christ's ransom and exaltation, which no genuine revelation from God would negate. In evaluating whether the Quran is from God or man, the evidence consistently points to the latter. No mention of any subsequent scriptural canon arises in biblical prophecy, and the Quran itself does not withstand scrutiny as a continuation of the biblical faith. Hence, the conclusion stands that the Quran is of human origin, influenced by local traditions and possibly spiritual deception, but not a revelation from the God of Scripture.

CHAPTER 5 Is Islamic Teaching Rooted in Genuine Divine Revelation or Merely Human Tradition?

Islam stands as one of the significant world religions, claiming adherence by an enormous portion of humanity. At its center lies the Quran, believed by devout Muslims to be the very words of God as revealed to the prophet Muhammad in the early seventh century C.E. The name "Islam" itself points to an ideal of entire submission or resignation to the will of God, a profound commitment reflected in Islamic worship and practice. Historically, Muhammad's rise and the subsequent spread of Islam reconfigured much of the political and religious landscape from Arabia to parts of Europe and Asia.

From the viewpoint of conservative Christian scholarship, questions arise concerning these Islamic teachings. Are they consistent with what Scripture teaches about God, Christ, the path to salvation, and the nature of genuine revelation? Could a system introduced centuries after Christ, with no accompanying miracles, truly be the crowning disclosure of divine truth? Are the calls for holy war found in the Quran a reflection of God's will, or do they represent a significant departure from the spiritual warfare championed by Christ and his apostles? Because Christianity and Islam both profess belief in a single Creator, these questions become even more pressing.

This chapter investigates Islamic teachings in light of what Scripture shows about God's dealings with humankind. It revisits matters such as the absence of validating miracles for Muhammad, the abrogation principle in the Quran, the call for religious warfare, and the contradictions within Islamic practice regarding compulsion in religion. It also explores the historical setting in which Islam arose, the claims the Quran makes for itself, and how those claims intersect or

101

conflict with core biblical doctrines. Individuals who affirm the finality and sufficiency of the Scriptures must grapple with Islam's assertions, including the Quran's insistence on being the supreme revelation from God. Although Christians hold firmly that Jesus is the ultimate messenger and that the Bible provides the complete counsel of God, understanding the essence of Islamic teaching is essential for defending biblical truth.

Overview of Islam's Founding and Core Claims

Islam's early development began in Mecca, a commercial city in Arabia that housed the Ka'bah, a shrine revered by local tribes. Traditions hold that Muhammad—born around 570 C.E. into a family associated with the powerful Quraysh tribe—began to receive revelations about 610 C.E. These recitations were compiled posthumously into the Quran, which now comprises 114 suras of varying length. Islamic tradition also gave rise to extensive collections of hadith, or traditions, that allegedly supplement the Quran with examples of Muhammad's actions, teachings, and rulings.

From the start, Muhammad's success drew on several factors. He insisted there was but one true God—referred to as "Allah"—at a time when Arabia featured polytheistic practices. His message also confronted local immorality and critiqued injustices such as female infanticide. However, as he gained followers, tensions with fellow Meccans rose. Eventually he migrated to Medina, where he assumed a growing political and military leadership role. After consolidating power, he cleansed the Ka'bah of its idols and established it as the center of Islamic worship. This new religion spread with remarkable speed after Muhammad's death in 632 C.E., often through conquest.

Muslims revere the Quran as the uncreated word of God, existing on a celestial tablet and transmitted through Gabriel. That stands in stark contrast to the biblical depiction of revelation, where God progressively communicated through multiple prophets and finally spoke through Christ (Hebrews 1:1, 2). The question posed from a conservative biblical vantage point is whether the Quran's message conforms to the central truths taught by God's servants over the centuries, culminating in the New Testament. If it deviates from that testimony, how should devout Christians weigh its claims to being a final revelation?

The Absence of Accompanying Miracles

When Jehovah raised Moses as a prophet to the descendants of Abraham, Isaac, and Jacob in 1513 B.C.E., He provided miracles that left no doubt about Moses' divine commission (Exodus 4:1-9). Similar wonders attended the ministries of Elijah and Elisha. In the case of Christ Jesus, the Gospels are replete with references to signs of his authority, including healing the blind and lepers, resurrecting the dead, and ultimately rising from the grave himself (John 5:36; Acts 2:22). Such divine endorsements confirmed that these prophets truly spoke in God's name.

Muhammad, however, acknowledged in the Quran that no miracles accompanied his message. He repeatedly taught that his mission was merely to proclaim, not to produce signs. Sura 6:109 (Ali) shows that his contemporaries challenged him to bring wonders as earlier prophets allegedly had done. He responded that God withheld such signs. Sura 2:118 similarly references people demanding evidence that he was from God. Had these demands been answered with actual miracles, the Quran would undoubtedly record them. Instead, it proffers the text itself as the proof, claiming that no human could produce the like of one sura.

Despite this lack of biblical-style miracles, later Muslim traditions or hadith writings began attributing spectacular feats to Muhammad, such as splitting the moon, making water flow from his fingers, or commanding a tree to testify to his prophethood. These narratives emerged in the second or third centuries of the Islamic era. Their late development and the Quran's silence on them strongly suggest these legends arose among the faithful seeking to exalt Muhammad by providing him with miracle stories analogous to Moses and Jesus.

One example is Sura 54:1, which mentions the moon's being cleft asunder. Some interpret that passage as alluding to a miraculous splitting of the moon, but the text does not explicitly credit Muhammad with performing this act. Many authoritative Muslim commentators either treat it figuratively or as a future event. No historical evidence points to a literal splitting of the moon. Further, the Quran's own statements, such as Sura 17:59, reaffirm that signs were withheld in Muhammad's era. This is all the more remarkable when measuring it against the standard set by Moses and Christ. Both performed extraordinary wonders to authenticate their roles as channels of revelation.

From a biblical perspective, if a new covenant prophet were to arise, one might expect to see some confirmation that matched or surpassed what accompanied prior pivotal revelations. The absence of such miracles undercuts the claim that Islam is a new, final message from God. The immediate reason for its success, historically, appears more grounded in social, political, and military developments in Arabia rather than in visible divine acts reminiscent of the plagues in Egypt or the healings in the Gospels.

Abrogation and Contradictions in the Quran

Another noteworthy feature of Islamic teachings is the principle of abrogation, which allows later suras to cancel or supersede earlier ones. The Quran acknowledges contradictions. In response to critics pointing out inconsistencies, it provides the explanation that God can abrogate certain revelations and replace them with better ones (Sura 2:106; 16:101). This concept stands at odds with how Scripture depicts divine communication. Scripture may show progressive revelation from the patriarchs to Moses, and from Moses to Christ, but it never portrays God repeatedly discarding or nullifying laws He gave only a few years earlier within the same covenant community.

The existence of contradictory instructions in the Quran is illustrated most starkly in the matter of religious compulsion. Some verses say, "Let there be no compulsion in religion" (Sura 2:256). Yet others command believers to "kill those that join other gods to God wherever ye find them" (Sura 9:5, Rodwell) and to fight until the worship of God alone remains. Muslims throughout history have recognized that these verses conflict. The typical solution is to say that later verses from Muhammad's period of political power override earlier verses from his time as a persecuted prophet in Mecca. This abrogation principle leads to confusion about which instruction is binding.

From a biblical vantage point, any revelation from Jehovah remains consistent in moral standards, although certain ceremonial laws changed when Jesus fulfilled the Mosaic covenant. That shift was prophesied centuries beforehand (Jeremiah 31:31-34; Hebrews 8:8-13). The repeated retraction of previous statements in the Quran lacks the clarity and continuity that mark the biblical revelation. While some modern Muslims deny that the Quran abrogates itself, many classical interpreters, including recognized commentators, do affirm that numerous verses have been canceled. Since the text seldom identifies which suras are canceled, readers are left uncertain, with the result that contradictory verses remain side by side. By contrast, Scripture does not rely on short-term abrogations but features an overarching plan of God culminating in Christ. This discrepancy suggests that the Quran's content was shaped by evolving circumstances rather than a single, coherent eternal decree from God.

Freedom of Religion or Coerced Conversion?

An especially troubling contradiction within Islamic teachings revolves around religious freedom versus compulsion in matters of faith. Early suras from the Meccan era appear to advocate tolerance or at least forbearance. Sura 2:256 famously says, "Let there be no compulsion in religion," reflecting a stance that one's duty is solely to preach, leaving acceptance to the hearer's conscience. Sura 10:99, 100 implies that belief is only valid by God's permission, hinting that forced conversion is meaningless. This approach, in principle, aligns better with the biblical pattern that calls for voluntary faith (Deuteronomy 30:19; Luke 9:55, 56), though in the Christian arrangement there is no place for warfare at all.

However, the Medinan suras—revealed after Muhammad gained political and military power—contain repeated calls to fight unbelievers until they submit to Islam. Sura 9:5 instructs, "Kill those that join other gods to God wherever ye find them... but if they shall convert, and observe prayer, and pay the obligatory alms, then let them go their way." This text fosters the notion that non-Muslims may be killed or subdued unless they accept Islam or pay tribute (Sura 9:29). Many of the conflicts in Muhammad's later career align with these verses. He led raids against caravans, besieged Jewish tribes, and upon conquering Mecca, demanded submission.

The difference between these two stances—one forbidding compulsion, another commanding violence—cannot be dismissed as mere misinterpretation. Classical Islamic jurisprudence acknowledges that the suras advocating war hold priority for expanding Muslim rule. This outlook shaped centuries of conquests under the caliphs, culminating in the spread of Islam into Africa, Asia, and parts of Europe. While some modern Muslims argue that these verses applied only to self-defense or to unique historical contexts, the plain reading of passages like Sura 9:5 or Sura 8:12 indicates more than defensive warfare. The historical record of Islamic expansion, including repeated invasions and calls to impose Islamic rule, confirms that these texts were understood literally for much of Islamic history.

From the standpoint of the biblical message, Christ never commanded violent expansion. Instead, he instructed his followers to lay down the sword (Matthew 26:52) and rely on preaching to spread the gospel (Matthew 28:19, 20; Acts 1:8). Genuine conversion in Scripture is always a matter of personal conviction. This divergence is profound. While Old Testament Israel did engage in wars, those conflicts were divinely ordered for a limited period and territory, fulfilling specific covenant promises (Deuteronomy 7:1, 2). The new covenant under Christ ended those physical wars for his followers and announced a spiritual warfare fought with the Word of God, not swords or siege. The Quran's repeated endorsement of violent jihad as a means of advancing the faith stands in stark contrast to Jesus' instructions and the practices of the apostolic congregation.

Comparing Islamic Warfare With Israel's Ancient Conflicts

Defenders of Islamic jihad sometimes point to Israel's warfare under Moses or Joshua, arguing that the Bible likewise authorized conquering enemies by force. However, the two situations differ significantly in context and theological purpose. In Israel's case, God appointed the nation as an instrument of judgment against the Canaanites because of their long-standing wickedness (Deuteronomy 9:4, 5). The conquest was limited to a defined land area promised to Abraham's descendants. Israel was not permitted to expand indefinitely. David extended those borders to their God-ordained limits but did not surpass them simply to subjugate other religions or forcibly convert foreign peoples. Moreover, repeated miracles accompanied Israel's conquests, showing that it was God's direct intervention (Joshua 10:11; Judges 4:15). Scripture also clarifies that if Israel itself became wicked, it would face a comparable judgment at the hands of foreign powers, which indeed happened (2 Kings 17:7-23).

By contrast, Islam's wars historically stretched across multiple continents, from Spain to India, without acknowledging a fixed limit. The impetus was the spread of Islamic rule, bolstered by texts commanding believers to wage war against non-Muslims until they submitted to the new faith. While it might be argued that Islam improved the moral climate of some lands by curbing certain forms of idolatry, the biblical pattern reveals no continuing program of forced conversions. The Christian congregation inherited Jesus' command to demonstrate love even toward enemies (Matthew 5:44), an ethic that bars holy wars to expand the faith.

The Contrast With Christ's Example and Apostolic Practice

Christ Jesus emphatically refrained from any form of political or military campaign, stating, "My kingdom is no part of this world" (John 18:36). He refused to let his disciples fight on his behalf, even when the Roman authorities came to arrest him. Instead, he accepted suffering and martyrdom, trusting the Father's will (Matthew 26:50-54). The post-resurrection church likewise never engaged in carnal warfare to secure conversions. The book of Acts shows that believers preached boldly, prayed for boldness, and at times fled persecution, but never took up the sword (Acts 8:1-4; 12:1-5). They recognized that forcibly subduing outsiders would deny the free choice central to the Christian faith (Romans 14:5).

The Quranic teaching that calls for the subjugation or killing of idolaters unless they repent seems irreconcilable with the ethic taught by Jesus and the apostles. Some attempt to reconcile it by noting that these commands appear in suras from a period of intense hostility, implying that the biblical God likewise authorized force under the old covenant. Yet the new covenant stands on a different plane. The synergy between the Old and New Testaments consistently points forward to a spiritual approach in the age of the Messiah (Romans 10:4). Once Christ came, the former system of physical warfare ended. Scripture's prophecy never envisioned a latter-day prophet reinstating religious battles to expand the knowledge of God by compulsion.

Self-Described Gaps in the Quran's Internal Consistency

Unlike the Bible, which presents a unified story culminating in Christ, the Quran shows wide variations in tone and instruction from sura to sura. Scholars classify suras as Meccan or Medinan, with different theological emphases. Muhammad's critics in his day pointed out these shifts, accusing him of inconsistency. The Quran's response was to claim that God can cancel or forget earlier verses at will (Sura 2:106). However, biblical theology sees God as immutable (Malachi 3:6), and though He can issue new covenants, He does not repeatedly negate His own counsel within a short timeframe. Mosaic laws were replaced by Christ's law after fifteen centuries, fulfilling multiple prophetic signs that anticipated this shift (Galatians 3:24, 25). In the Quran's case, abrogation sometimes occurred within a few years to accommodate changing circumstances in Muhammad's leadership. That pattern does not reflect the stable, purposeful revelation one expects from Jehovah.

Additionally, Islamic commentators themselves debate which verses abrogate which. There is no universal agreement, further revealing a system shaped by immediate needs rather than long-term divine foreknowledge. The text was not compiled in chronological order but arranged mostly from longer to shorter suras. This arrangement complicates identifying which verses came first. For instance, suras calling for tolerance might appear after suras advocating violence, although historically the tolerant verses preceded the militant ones. This confusion intensifies the sense that abrogation is a human solution to manage contradictions rather than evidence of cohesive divine authorship.

The Jihad Mandate in Islamic History

Islamic civilization has a complicated history, marked by cultural achievements, scholarship, and a wide range of governance models.

Yet the early centuries of Islam included notable expansions often justified by religious motives. The concept of jihad spurred armies to conquer large areas in the Middle East, North Africa, and parts of Europe. It is a matter of historical record that these expansions went beyond defense. The defeat at Tours by Charles Martel in 732 prevented Islamic rule from overtaking France. Centuries later, Ottoman forces reached the gates of Vienna in 1683, seeking further conquests. These campaigns reflected the dual spiritual-political nature of Islam, which fuses religion and governance in ways foreign to the New Testament. Christians who read the book of Acts see a missionary approach based solely on preaching, not on forming armies to impose the faith. This fundamental difference underscores that Islam does not represent the faith of the new covenant taught by Jesus.

While some might argue that these expansions reflect cultural or imperial ambitions rather than the religion's true essence, the impetus for jihad was frequently supported by suras urging believers to fight unbelievers until they surrender or pay the jizya (tribute). Contrasts with biblical teaching become clearer when comparing the indefinite scope of Islamic conquest to the limited, theocratic arrangement in ancient Israel or the peaceful mission of the apostolic congregation. Instead of overshadowing the old covenant, as the new covenant does in Scripture, Islam reverts to a system reminiscent of worldly powers that merge temporal authority with a legalistic worship code.

Reassessing the Quran's Claims of Authenticity

The Quran's repeated self-affirmation as the ultimate revelation demands scrutiny in light of God's dealings through the prophets and, most decisively, through Christ. If the Quran truly replaced the gospel, it should logically continue the biblical pattern and confirm the central truths taught by Jesus. Instead, it denies the crucifixion (Sura 4:157), disavows Jesus as the Son of God, and offers little parallel to the new covenant's emphasis on atonement (Romans 3:23-25; John 1:29). Its approach to external religious obligations, such as formal prayers at fixed times facing Mecca, repeating traditions drawn from local Arabian practices, and an almost exclusive focus on earthly rulership, differs drastically from the gospel's spiritual orientation. The Christian congregation is a pilgrim community in the midst of the world but not of it, championing free acceptance of the message.

Some Muslims assert that the Bible itself was corrupted, necessitating the Quran's restoration of original truths. However, historical manuscript evidence shows that the text of the Hebrew Scriptures and the Greek New Testament remained stable from centuries before Muhammad. Discoveries such as the Dead Sea Scroll of Isaiah confirm that the text was substantially preserved long before the seventh century C.E. The earliest Greek manuscripts of the Gospels likewise confirm the continuity of the message about Christ's death and resurrection. Hence, the claim that biblical texts were lost or adulterated contradicts objective manuscript data. When the Quran instructs believers in doubt to consult those who read the former Scriptures (Sura 10:94), it presumes the authenticity of those texts in Muhammad's era.

The Significance of the Ka'bah and Pagan Vestiges

A final consideration concerns the Ka'bah itself, now revered as the holiest site in Islam, the direction (kebla) to which Muslims turn in prayer. Pre-Islamic Arabs venerated this cube-like structure containing multiple idols. Muhammad eventually cleansed it of idols, but the black stone remained. The annual pilgrimage or hajj, requiring seven circuits around the Ka'bah and other rites, finds its roots in pre-Islamic tradition. If the Quran were from Jehovah, one might expect it to discard such local vestiges of pagan worship. The Old Testament insisted on tearing down pagan altars (Deuteronomy 12:2, 3). Instead, the Islamic arrangement repurposed the shrine. The biblical pattern would not ordinarily preserve an ancient idol-temple at the center of worship, particularly when the new covenant had already set worship free from the notion of any geographic site (John 4:21-24). That the Quran anchored worship to a pre-Islamic shrine suggests cultural continuity rather than a radical break with pagan tradition. Jesus' message transcended a single location, reflecting a shift from temple-based worship to worship "in spirit and truth."

Does the New Testament Foretell Muhammad's Coming?

Islamic apologists sometimes point to biblical passages they believe reference Muhammad. One example is Deuteronomy 18:18, where God promises to raise up a prophet like Moses from among the Hebrews' brothers. Yet the New Testament itself applies that prophecy to Christ (Acts 3:20-23). Jesus was a Jew from the tribe of Judah, fulfilling the role of a prophet who spoke in God's name. Another frequently cited text is John 14:16, 16:7, where Jesus mentions a helper, the "paraclete" or comforter, that would come to guide the apostles. The immediate context and the events at Pentecost show this was the Holy Spirit poured out upon the apostles (Acts 2:1-4). It was not a reference to a prophet emerging six centuries later. Neither the timing nor the role matches Muhammad's life and mission.

In addition, if God intended to send a major prophet after Christ, one would expect the apostles or Jesus himself to give direct instructions for how that transition would occur. Instead, Jesus affirmed that his words would never pass away (Matthew 24:35). The apostle Paul warned that even if an angel from heaven preached a different gospel, believers should reject it (Galatians 1:8, 9). The scriptural data leaves no room for a revelation that abrogates the cross and denies Jesus' atoning death.

Evaluating Islamic Moral and Social Teachings

Islamic morality, in many respects, condemns vices such as drunkenness, adultery, dishonesty, and oppression of the poor. This condemnation has drawn some to admire Islam's strictness. However, biblical revelation likewise forbids these sins (Galatians 5:19-21; Ephesians 4:28). Mere moral overlap does not prove the Quran's inspiration any more than the presence of moral codes in other religions indicates they are from God. Additionally, the Quran's sanction of polygamy (Sura 4:3) and the acceptance of concubinage reflect a step back from the Christian ethic wherein Jesus emphasized a man being joined to his wife as "one flesh" (Matthew 19:4-6). Muslims often retort that Scripture narrates polygamy among patriarchs. While that is true historically, the new covenant standard for Christian overseers, for instance, is being "a husband of one wife" (1 Timothy 3:2). Polygamy in Scripture is generally portrayed as leading to family strife rather than being a normative practice for all. The

Quran, conversely, institutionalizes polygamy as a permissible aspect of Islamic law.

Another difference is the prohibition of certain foods in the Quran, reminiscent of Old Testament dietary restrictions, which the new covenant sets aside (Mark 7:18, 19; Acts 10:13-15). The emphasis in Christian teaching is on moral and spiritual purity, not ritual uncleanness. By returning to external codes, the Quran goes against the grain of the gospel's freedom from Mosaic-like regulations. This reemergence of ritual law—along with the practice of set prayers repeated in Arabic while facing Mecca—reveals a system that resembles old covenant shadows more than the liberating truths of the new covenant.

The Tension of a Worldly Dominion

The biblical narrative culminates in Jesus, who claims not a present earthly dominion but a future kingdom transcending national boundaries (John 18:36). Christians live under secular governments, obeying them unless those governments demand disobedience to God, but do not form an earthly theocracy (Romans 13:1-7; 1 Peter 2:13, 14). Islam, however, merges religion and state in a single system, historically bringing about caliphates that administered religious and civil laws together. This arrangement is deeply embedded in the Quran, which addresses warfare, tribute, rules for inheritance, punishments for adultery, theft, and apostasy. The biblical congregation deals with moral discipline internally but never claims sovereignty over secular authority. Even ancient Israel's theocracy functioned on the basis of a direct covenant for a defined land, overshadowed by Christ's arrival. The Quran, by contrast, envisions a continuing union of religion and government to enforce compliance with Islamic law.

Hence, the worldly aspect of Islamic governance diverges from the approach taught in the New Testament. The apostolic congregation spread the gospel while living in Roman territory, never seeking to seize political power. The acceptance of the message remained voluntary, guided by conviction rather than compulsion. Meanwhile, the Quran's arrangement fosters a religious state where Sharia law covers both private devotion and public conduct, even applying the penalty of death for certain religious offenses. This difference is not a mere cultural preference; it signifies a fundamentally different concept of how God's people should exist among the nations.

The Issue of Personal Revelations for Muhammad's Domestic Affairs

The Quran includes revelations that settle personal matters for Muhammad, such as controversies surrounding his wives or instructions about specific marital exceptions. For instance, an incident involving slander against his wife Aisha prompted Sura 24 to defend her and threaten accusers. Another episode concerned the marriage to Zainab, the divorced wife of Muhammad's adopted son Zaid, addressed in Sura 33. These passages show revelations that function as immediate solutions to Muhammad's personal or domestic dilemmas. That situational approach stands in contrast to the biblical prophets, whose messages primarily address broad covenant faithfulness and moral direction for entire communities, rarely settling an individual prophet's personal entanglements in a manner that exonerates or benefits him. David, for instance, was reproved by Nathan for wrongdoing (2 Samuel 12:7-14). Jonah was corrected for refusing God's assignment (Jonah 1:1-3; 4:1-11). Scripture does not depict the prophet manipulating revelations for personal advantage.

This pattern in the Quran encourages some to argue that the text is closely tied to local disputes and personal concerns, rather than delivering universal truths from a transcendent vantage point. The biblical prophets confronted their own sinfulness or the sinfulness of the monarchy rather than issuing oracles that justified their private decisions. In Scripture, the impetus remains on revealing God's righteousness, not on ensuring that the prophet's personal interests are protected by new or updated commandments.

Do Islamic Teachings Resolve Mankind's Core Problem?

Christian theology states that humanity's central predicament is alienation from God due to sin, remedied solely by Christ's atoning death (Romans 5:8-11). The new covenant reveals a permanent priesthood in Jesus, the mediator who reconciles believers to the Father (Hebrews 7:24, 25). In Islamic doctrine, the notion of original sin or an inherited fallen condition is rejected. The Quran sees Adam and Eve's wrongdoing as a forgivable lapse rather than an inheritance that burdens subsequent generations, and it places emphasis on personal deeds, hope in God's mercy, and compliance with Islamic law. This shift means that the Quran lacks the biblical concept of a fundamental need for atonement through a Redeemer. Instead, righteous living and God's forgiveness are said to suffice.

By removing the cross from the salvation narrative, Islam offers a moral code but not the transformative deliverance from sin central to the gospel. In place of a Savior, it provides an array of religious observances: fasting during Ramadan, reciting prayers in Arabic five times daily, giving alms, undertaking pilgrimage to Mecca, and professing faith in the oneness of God and Muhammad's role as His prophet. These pillars may instill discipline and devotion, but from a biblical vantage point, they do not solve the irreparable breach caused by sin (Ephesians 2:8, 9). Without Christ's ransom, the condemnation described in Romans 6:23 remains. The apostle Peter stated that there is no salvation in any other name (Acts 4:12). If Islam draws attention away from Jesus' atoning death, it stands in conflict with the heart of the new covenant.

The Quran's Portrayal of Paradise and Judgment

Another revealing angle is the Quranic depiction of paradise as a garden of physical delights, replete with sensual pleasures, food, and drink. Sura 55 and other suras describe a heaven of blissful enjoyment for believers, while the wicked endure fiery punishment. This imagery resonates with certain Jewish and Zoroastrian traditions but contrasts with the biblical emphasis on an eternal kingdom where resurrected believers enjoy communion with God, freed from sin and corruption. While Scripture does describe a future paradise on a new earth for the righteous (Revelation 21:3, 4; Isaiah 65:17-25), it underscores spiritual intimacy with the Creator and the moral perfection of resurrected humanity. The Quran's emphasis on sensual rewards signals a different focus, sometimes described as appealing to the cultural expectations of seventh-century Arabian audiences.

Likewise, the Quran frequently envisions a literal torment for disbelievers, involving hellfire that repeatedly burns their skins and is replaced anew (Sura 4:56). While the Greek Scriptures speak of eternal destruction for the unrepentant, the Bible uses terms like Gehenna symbolically to indicate final judgment (Matthew 10:28). The consistent biblical depiction is that the wages of sin is death, not eternal conscious torment (Romans 6:23). Many Christians see references to a fiery destiny for the wicked as symbolic of total annihilation. The Quran's graphic pictures of repeated torment align more with certain intertestamental Jewish writings or Zoroastrian concepts, again suggesting outside influences that shaped Islamic teaching.

The Challenge of Preserving the Bible's Integrity

Muslims often argue that the Bible's alleged textual corruption necessitated the Quran. Yet the historical record of how the Hebrew and Greek Scriptures were transmitted shows remarkable fidelity. The Dead Sea Scroll of Isaiah, dating to roughly the second or first century B.C.E., matches the Masoretic text in the majority of its content. Early Christian manuscripts of the Gospels and Pauline letters from the second and third centuries C.E. confirm that Christ's death and resurrection were taught from the earliest times, with no sign of a grand textual overhaul. If the biblical message about Jesus were corrupted, one might expect to find older manuscripts lacking the crucifixion narrative. Instead, that event stands as the heart of the earliest Christian texts.

Additionally, the Quran itself does not consistently accuse Jews or Christians of altering their Scriptures. Instead, it sometimes says they hid or misquoted them (Sura 2:75-79), implying the texts remained available. Even after centuries of textual analysis, no evidence supports the idea that the entire biblical narrative about Christ's passion and resurrection was removed or tampered with in a sweeping conspiracy. If God had allowed the complete corruption of Scripture, the question arises why the New Testament authors' extant manuscripts so clearly testify otherwise. Such a position also conflicts with the Quran's instructions that those in doubt should consult "the people who read the book before" them (Sura 10:94), indicating that the earlier revelation was intact.

Summing Up the Scriptural and Historical Evidence

Edward D. Andrews

Combining these various lines of evidence, the Christian scholar sees that Islamic teachings share certain ethical or monotheistic convictions but differ radically from the new covenant's cardinal points, including the nature of Christ, the finality of his sacrificial death, the role of faith, and the separation of the Christian congregation from worldly power. The Quran's acceptance of jihad, abrogation, polygamy, ritual prescriptions reminiscent of old covenant forms, and the fusion of religion and state underscores a stark divergence from the gospel. Whereas the Bible's storyline converges on the cross and resurrection, the Quran denies them, offering no atoning Redeemer. That fundamental disparity cannot be reconciled by mild theological reinterpretations.

Furthermore, Islam's revisionist approach to biblical history—claiming, for instance, that it was Ishmael, not Isaac, who was the child of promise—lacks any documentary basis in older manuscripts. The biblical text is clear about Isaac's role in God's covenant (Genesis 17:19; 21:12). Islam's recasting of these events is more readily explained as an effort to ground Arab identity in the lineage of Abraham by exalting Ishmael. This might be politically or culturally significant but does not align with the consistent witness of the Hebrew Scriptures. Additionally, the biblical genealogies and subsequent references to Abraham's chosen line culminating in Christ remain intact, with no hint that Ishmael carried God's covenant.

Islamic Teachings Versus the Simplicity of the Gospel

The gospel teaches that salvation depends not on a complex system of rites but on faith in Christ's sacrifice and obedience to his teachings (Romans 3:21-26; Ephesians 2:8, 9). The Christian life thereafter flows from the Spirit-inspired Word, shaping moral behavior without an external code of repeated ceremonies (Galatians 5:22, 23). The Quran, however, lays out an extensive framework of external obligations, from daily prayers in Arabic to the mandatory pilgrimage and strict fasting regimes. While such rites may foster discipline, they do not resolve the innate need for redemption from sin. Scripture consistently places the cross at the center of God's solution, which Islam diminishes.

116

Additionally, biblical faith is anchored in the resurrected Christ as proof that his sacrifice was accepted (1 Corinthians 15:12-20). The Quran denies the crucifixion, describing it as a misunderstanding, thereby nullifying the resurrection's importance. Without the cross and resurrection, the message of forgiveness stands on uncertain ground, replaced by the hope of balancing good deeds against bad on scales of judgment. This moral calculus is foreign to the central biblical teaching that no one can earn salvation by works, for "all have sinned" (Romans 3:23). Only Christ's redemptive act grants full reconciliation (John 14:6).

The Core Conflict: Jesus' Identity and Mission

All these contrasts converge on the identity and work of Jesus. Scripture proclaims him as the unique Son of God, who entered the world to redeem sinners, voluntarily offering his life to cover Adam's descendants with a perfect sacrifice. The Quran views Jesus ('Īsa) as a revered prophet, born of a virgin, yet denies his divine sonship and crucifixion. In so doing, it omits the central reason for the incarnation. The apostle John explains that every spirit that does not confess Jesus Christ as having come in the flesh is not from God (1 John 4:2, 3). Denial of the cross is tantamount to denying the heart of Jesus' mission. That denial, according to Christian teaching, cannot come from the same Spirit that inspired the prophets and the apostles.

Therefore, from a conservative biblical perspective, the core teachings of Islam rest on a different foundation than the gospel. The changes introduced by the Quran, including its calls for jihad, abrogation of verses, polygamy, and subjugation of the church-state divide, do not represent a legitimate continuation of biblical revelation. Instead, they deviate from the message of redemption completed by Christ. While acknowledging Islam's moral teachings or monotheistic stance, believers must firmly reject the notion that this is the final revelation from Jehovah.

Concluding Thoughts

Islamic teachings indeed promote certain moral values and unify a broad community around monotheism and structured devotion. Historically, they confronted entrenched paganism in Arabia, eliminating many superstitious practices. Yet from the vantage point of Scripture, Islam's textual claims and doctrinal positions are not reconcilable with the faith taught by Moses, expanded by the prophets, and fulfilled in Jesus. No miracles authenticated Muhammad's prophethood on the scale demonstrated by Moses or Jesus. The repeated abrogations in the Quran reveal contradictory directives. The acceptance of coercive jihad stands in opposition to the free acceptance of the gospel. The overshadowing of the cross means that the essential doctrine of atonement is missing, leaving humanity's core predicament unsolved.

Because Scripture shows that Jehovah does not lead His people back into forms of ceremonial observance that Jesus already supplanted, the new covenant cannot be undone or eclipsed by a seventh-century movement. Christ's sacrifice and resurrection stand at the heart of God's plan (1 Corinthians 1:18). Any religious teaching that diverts attention from that saving act cannot be from God. When the Quran denies the crucifixion and merges religion with state power to impose acceptance, it abandons the new covenant's spiritual thrust and the believer's freedom in Christ.

In sum, a straightforward evaluation shows that Islamic teachings differ profoundly from both the old covenant's transition to the new and the gospel's central message of redemption. Sincere Muslims may exhibit genuine devotion to God as they understand Him, but the system of Islam cannot be equated with the revelation of the Scriptures. Instead, it is a subsequent development drawing on local traditions, Jewish and apocryphal legends, and claims to final authority that stand outside the biblical lineage of faith. The devout Christian must conclude that the Quran's instructions, including the call to fight unbelievers for religious ends, do not arise from the same God who sent Christ to lay down his life and forbade his followers from resorting to the sword.

Christians are thus obligated to weigh and critique Islamic teachings with compassion for those who practice Islam but with unwavering commitment to the biblical revelation. Because Jesus announced that he alone is "the way and the truth and the life" and that "no one comes to the Father except through me" (John 14:6), no subsequent prophet can claim to displace or supersede the gospel's message. The biblical record remains complete, teaching that believers must reject any new gospel, even if it claims angelic origins (Galatians 1:8, 9). This principle leads to the inescapable conclusion that, while Islam might incorporate certain moral truths and a reverence for a single Creator, it does not represent a continuation or fulfillment of biblical faith but rather a distinct religious system, shaped by human tradition and lacking the full power and assurance of divine revelation.

CHAPTER 6 Are Islamic Jihads Truly of Divine Origin or Driven by Human Ambition?

Questions about jihad loom large in discussions of Islam's expansion and religious warfare. Few Islamic concepts have drawn more attention than the call to struggle—often translated from the Arabic as "jihad." Devout Muslims regard this as an important element of faith, one that historically shaped the political and religious strategies of emerging Muslim communities. Outside observers, however, note disparities within the Quran itself: some suras assert that there should be no compulsion in religion, while others urge believers to fight infidels until only worship of Allah remains. For centuries, Muslim theologians and apologists have tried to reconcile these stances, whereas critics have pointed to contradictory verses and the violent expansions in Islamic history to conclude that jihad is far from a merely defensive concept.

From a conservative Christian perspective, evaluating jihad involves measuring Islamic teachings against Scripture. The Old Testament depicts Israel conducting wars by Jehovah's express command, but those conflicts were limited in scope, miraculously validated, and bound to a particular land covenant. The New Testament sees Christ telling his followers to put away the sword, leaving no room for forced conversions. If the Quran indeed supersedes earlier revelation, one might expect continuity with the final message of Jesus. Instead, the calls for offensive campaigns and the concept of abrogating contradictory verses introduce tensions irreconcilable with biblical patterns. This chapter reviews the Quranic depictions of war and compulsion, the historical record of Islamic conquests, and the apparent contradiction between suras advocating freedom of religion and those encouraging religiously motivated aggression. It also examines the frequently raised analogy between Old Testament wars of Israel and modern jihad. Finally, it weighs the question of whether jihad can be squared with any biblical notion of spiritual warfare and how these issues impact the Christian's approach to Islam.

Does the Quran Command Freedom of Religion or Coerced Compliance?

A pivotal tension within the Quran involves statements seemingly affirming religious liberty alongside passages that legitimize violence to impose Islam on unwilling populations. The verse often cited to support tolerance is Sura 2:256: "There is no compulsion in religion." Some suras also present Muhammad as merely a warner, not an enforcer. However, many other suras instruct believers to fight or kill idolaters if they refuse to accept Islam. Sura 9:5, the so-called "verse of the sword," reads: "But when the forbidden months are past, then fight and slay the Pagans wherever ye find them. . . . but if they repent, and establish regular prayers and practice regular charity, then open the way for them." Sura 2:193 similarly exhorts Muslims to "fight therefore until there be no more civil discord, and until the only worship be that of God."

Some Muslim apologists stress that these warlike passages address self-defense or a specific historical context. Yet the plain language in Sura 9:5, Sura 2:191, and others calls for violence until disbelievers convert or yield. Sura 2:193 uses an expression that literally means fighting must continue "until the temptation stops," or until religious opposition ceases. This phrase hardly seems defensive. Sura 8:39 goes further, stating that unbelievers should be combated "until there is no more oppression and all worship is devoted to Allah" (a paraphrase in some translations). Orthodox dictionaries define jihad primarily as "a holy war waged on behalf of Islam as a religious duty." Even if modern interpreters highlight a personal spiritual struggle dimension, historically the dominant meaning has been warfare against unbelievers, as proven by centuries of Islamic expansion and the killing of thousands who refused to convert.

The glaring contradiction between freedom of conscience in Sura 2:256 and the demands in Sura 9:5 has led many Muslim commentators to adopt the principle of abrogation. Later suras, typically from the Medinan period when Muhammad held political power, are said to override the more tolerant verses from his earlier Meccan preaching. This reading places suras like 9:5 at the apex of official policy, meaning that indefinite warfare against idolaters remains a valid approach for devout Muslims. Others prefer reconciling them as purely defensive instructions, but such a stance struggles to align with the text itself and the reality of Islam's expansions, which were not limited to repelling aggressors. Understanding jihad historically confirms that it encompassed far more than defensive action, shaping centuries of conquests into Asia, Africa, and Europe.

Observing Jihad in Islamic History

Historical records show that once Muhammad gained influence in Medina around 622 C.E., Islam grew swiftly, propelled partly by the impetus of warlike suras. After establishing an initial power base, Muhammad oversaw attacks on caravans from rival cities and fought battles such as Badr, Uhud, and the Trench. His later campaigns included the siege of the Jewish tribe Koraiza, where roughly seven hundred men were beheaded in a single day. Historical sources indicate that these prisoners could have been spared by professing Islam, but none accepted, so they were executed and their families sold into slavery. This episode exemplifies forced submission, consistent with suras that promise pardon only upon conversion.

Following Muhammad's death, the first caliphs launched an aggressive expansion known as the Ridda wars, subduing Arab tribes that had sought to break away. The new empire spread across the Middle East, North Africa, and beyond. By 732 C.E., a century after Muhammad, the armies of Islam had conquered parts of Spain and advanced into southern France until halted by Charles Martel. In 1453 C.E., Constantinople fell to the Ottoman Turks, and by 1683 C.E. Islamic forces reached the gates of Vienna—nearly 2,950 miles from Mecca—before suffering defeat. Although some expansions may have integrated local Christians and Jews under a dhimmi system (requiring tribute but allowing limited worship), the impetus for large-scale conquests cannot be credibly labeled "purely defensive."

Comparisons sometimes arise with the crusades launched under medieval Catholic powers, but from a biblical vantage point, those crusades likewise violated Christ's teaching to abstain from carnal warfare for religious ends (Matthew 26:52; John 18:36). Early Christians, as depicted in Acts, never carried out forced conversion, nor did they form armies to conquer neighboring lands. Their growth resulted from preaching, persuasion, and the Holy Spirit's power. By contrast, the impetus behind many Islamic expansions derived from religious texts that mandated subjugation of unbelievers. While it is true that not all Muslims engaged in jihad throughout history, the scriptural basis for it stands clear in the Quranic injunctions.

Are Old Testament Wars a Justification for Jihad?

Muslim apologists often invoke the Old Testament accounts of Israel's conquests to justify Islamic jihad, arguing that the God of the Bible also ordained violence. A more careful analysis reveals deep distinctions. When Jehovah commanded the Israelites to dispossess the wicked Canaanites, He validated those wars with supernatural signs and miracles, such as hailstones, confusion in the enemy's ranks, and other clear manifestations of divine intervention (Joshua 10:11; Judges 5:20). These campaigns carried out God's judicial punishment upon degenerate populations marred by child sacrifice, demonic practices, and extreme moral depravity (Deuteronomy 9:4, 5). Additionally, God set specific geographic limits for Israel, the land promised to Abraham. David's expansions did not exceed those divinely appointed bounds, nor did Israel attempt a global conquest.

Any attempt to draw parallels between Israel's warfare and jihad overlooks the broader context. The law covenant was a unique theocratic arrangement, anticipating the Messiah. When Christ came, he disarmed his followers spiritually, instructing that "all those who take the sword will perish by the sword" (Matthew 26:52). The Christian congregation formed no armies to subdue disbelievers; it spread the gospel by witnessing, not by the sword (Acts 8:4; 2 Corinthians 10:4). Furthermore, biblical revelation indicates that the final judgment of the wicked world is reserved for God and Christ at Armageddon, not for Christians to execute (Revelation 16:14, 16; Romans 12:19; Zephaniah 3:8). Where the old covenant might point forward to divine judgments, no new covenant command instructs believers to forcibly conquer others.

Jihad, in contrast, claims to be an ongoing duty for Muslims to ensure that religious worship is exclusively dedicated to Allah. This differs not only in scope, being presumably indefinite and universal, but also in moral impetus, lacking direct miraculous validation from God. The ancient Israelite wars, embedded within a greater covenant narrative, stand completed with the advent of Christ, who replaced physical conflict with spiritual warfare (Ephesians 6:12-17). Thus, the Old Testament cannot be used as a basis for modern Islamic jihad.

Suras of Abrogation and the Contradiction They Pose

The contradictory nature of jihad verses exemplifies a broader phenomenon in the Quran known as abrogation. Sura 2:106 and 16:101 allow for divine cancellation of earlier instructions. Classic Muslim scholars note that many warlike verses override or abrogate earlier peaceful passages. This principle explains how Surah 2:256 ("there is no compulsion in religion") can be overshadowed by Surah 9:5, which urges believers to kill idolaters unless they convert. Because the final suras typically come from the Medinan period of Muhammad's life, when he assumed leadership roles and engaged in conquest, these militant instructions are viewed as the definitive stance.

Biblical revelation exhibits no such short-term cancelation. While the new covenant supersedes Mosaic law, that transition was foretold by prophets like Jeremiah and spanned many centuries. Furthermore, the Mosaic law was not abruptly undone within the same generation through contradictory edicts. God's progressive revelation upholds consistent moral principles. By contrast, the Quran's statements shift dramatically in a few years, from tolerance in Mecca to forcibly imposed uniformity in Medina. The biblical teaching that "God is not a God of confusion" (1 Corinthians 14:33) underscores a stable, unchanging moral foundation. The repeated disclaimers in the Quran about "some revelations abrogating others" reveal a text shaped by evolving historical pressures rather than timeless divine counsel.

The Arabic Word "Jihad" and Its Historical Weight

While some modern reformers stress that jihad can denote a personal spiritual struggle, historically and linguistically the primary sense has been a holy war against unbelievers. Early Islamic history revolves around expansions explicitly called jihad. The hadith literature abounds with references to the merits of fighting for Islam, with promises of paradise for martyrs. Indeed, Webster's dictionary defines "jihad" foremost as "a holy war waged on behalf of Islam as a religious duty," though it acknowledges the secondary sense of spiritual striving. The prevalence of physically violent jihad throughout 1,400 years of Islamic history attests that these suras are not mere metaphors for personal discipline.

In line with that, the direct context of jihad references in suras 2:191, 193; 9:5, 29; 8:12, 39 is warfare. They speak of killing or capturing nonbelievers, besieging them, or demanding tribute. Surah 9:29 specifically instructs the faithful to fight "the people of the Book" until they pay jizya (a subjugation tax). Over time, the concept of jihad contributed to Islam's identity as a religio-political system, merging spiritual devotions with state governance. The new covenant taught by Christ, however, never merges church and state but calls on believers to remain separate from worldly politics (John 15:19; 17:14, 16; 18:36). The difference cannot be minimized by referencing occasional warfare in the Old Testament or symbolic spiritual conflicts in the Christian era.

The Execution of Critics and the Elimination of Dissenting Voices

The life of Muhammad in Medina demonstrates how early Islam handled dissent. He reportedly ordered the killing of certain poets and opponents who mocked or rejected his prophetic claims. This included the Jewish tribe Koraiza, which faced mass execution. Critics who did not recant or convert were sometimes put to death. Later caliphs extended that policy, often imposing harsh penalties on heretical Muslim sects or on non-Muslims who refused to pay tribute. While Islamic rulers occasionally tolerated Christians and Jews under the dhimmi system, those groups lived under constraints and paid higher taxes.

From a biblical viewpoint, the apostles never advocated eradicating critics. They faced Jewish and Roman opposition but responded with preaching, not violence (Acts 4:18-31; 5:29). Christ endured mockery and crucifixion without calling on angelic legions or instructing disciples to retaliate (Matthew 26:53, 54). Early Christians overcame slander by good conduct and perseverance, not by killing or punishing dissenters (1 Peter 2:12-23). This pattern differs fundamentally from the lethal suppression of opposition seen in early Islam, where suras legitimize removing obstacles to the new religion. The impetus to quell dissent by the sword again reveals a divergence from the gospel's message of peace and trust in divine vindication (Romans 12:19).

Was Islam's Growth Entirely By the Sword?

Muslim scholars sometimes argue that the success of Islam was not solely reliant on warfare, pointing out that trade, cultural achievements, and occasional peaceful missions expanded Muslim influence. In some cases, local populations welcomed the new faith to escape oppressive regimes or to benefit from trade relations. Nevertheless, the role of armed conquest cannot be denied. Large swaths of territory in the Middle East and North Africa were subdued through campaigns waged soon after Muhammad's death. The choice often given to conquered peoples was conversion to Islam, payment of jizya, or warfare. While not everyone was forcibly converted at sword-point, the impetus of these expansions underscores that the overarching environment was shaped by jihad. The religious impetus to unify lands under Islamic rule was part and parcel of the faith's political dimension.

By contrast, the Christian congregation spread widely in the Roman Empire during the early centuries without mustering armies. Persecuted believers gave witness in synagogues, marketplaces, and private homes. Converts in places like Antioch, Ephesus, and Rome embraced the gospel without fear of a conquering Christian army. Indeed, Christian growth preceded any imperial endorsement (Acts 11:19-26). This difference reveals an essential distinction in how each faith advanced. The biblical principle that "the weapons of our warfare are not fleshly" (2 Corinthians 10:4) illuminates the Christian approach. Islamic tradition, especially in its early centuries, testifies to a faith whose spread was intimately linked to military success.

Modern Muslim Apologetics and Denial of Historical Realities

In contemporary times, some Muslim apologists vigorously deny that Islam ever waged aggressive wars or forced conversions. They cite "no compulsion in religion" and interpret jihad in spiritual terms. They depict expansions as purely defensive, repelling external threats to the fledgling Muslim community. But a straightforward reading of Surah 9:5, Surah 8:39, and others cannot be limited to defense alone, especially when examining the historical expansions that occurred far beyond the Arabian Peninsula. The establishment of new caliphates across distant lands, thousands of miles from Mecca or Medina, is not easily construed as defensive.

The advanced push into Europe—reaching France, besieging Vienna, and controlling Spain for centuries—defies classification as purely protective. The large armies that roamed across North Africa and the Middle East did not limit themselves to neutralizing threats but systematically brought entire regions under Islamic rule. The repeated mention in the hadiths of the blessings for mujahideen (those participating in jihad) corroborates that it was not just metaphorical. While the modern climate encourages many Muslims to downplay jihad's militaristic dimension, historical evidence is abundant. The claim of purely defensive jihad stands as revisionist, ignoring countless offensives that shaped the Islamic empire.

Defensive vs. Offensive Warfare in Christian Perspective

Biblical teaching allows for national defense in secular contexts, recognizing that governments can legitimately bear arms to punish wrongdoing (Romans 13:1-4). Believers might serve in the military of their respective lands with a clean conscience, provided they do not engage in wrongdoing or unprovoked aggression. However, the New Testament never condones "holy wars" or crusades to expand the faith. Once Christianity became the official religion of the Roman Empire centuries later, some church leaders endorsed forced conversions or wars against "heretics," but these actions stand contrary to apostolic precedent. They represent the infiltration of worldly methods into a faith that was originally non-coercive.

When the modern world sees examples of so-called Christian armies, these often reflect historical Christendom's failure to adhere to Scripture, paralleling how some modern Muslims critique extremist groups that arise from literal readings of jihad verses. But from a purely biblical perspective, the concept of forcibly converting people does not align with Jesus' command to preach the gospel and let individuals respond freely (Matthew 28:19, 20). By contrast, the notion of jihad as an enduring duty remains embedded in classical Islamic jurisprudence, especially within the schools that rely strictly on the Medinan suras.

The Attempt to Diminish Jihad's Role: A Response to Contemporary Pressures

Some modern Muslim thinkers, faced with global criticism of terrorism and extremist violence, highlight the idea of a "greater jihad," focusing on personal spiritual striving. They emphasize attributes like patience, piety, and moral self-control. This shift might reflect the desire to present Islam in a more peaceful light, distancing themselves from militant movements such as ISIS, Al-Qaeda, or Al-Shabaab. While no one denies that Islam can have a strong ethical dimension, the scriptural context for jihad remains significant. Historically, the "lesser jihad" of armed conflict overshadowed the "greater jihad" in practice. The spread of Islam in many regions was accompanied by or enforced through warfare. Official religious authorities even now debate how best to interpret the principle of jihad amid modern geopolitical realities.

Still, from a conservative biblical viewpoint, the tension persists: the new covenant's approach to spiritual warfare disallows forcibly subjugating unbelievers. The Christian is engaged in a struggle against demonic influences and personal sin but not in mobilizing armies to impose the gospel. Jehovah's arrangement in the Hebrew Scriptures was similarly limited, culminating in Christ who replaced physical conflict with a message of salvation. The Quran's acceptance and codification of holy war signals a departure from that biblical trajectory. Recasting jihad as purely spiritual requires ignoring or reinterpreting the clear language about fighting disbelievers.

Meanwhile, radical groups continue to cite these suras literally to validate their actions.

The Realities of Forced Conversions Under Islamic Rule

Although Islamic rulers historically offered some level of tolerance to "people of the Book" (Jews and Christians), letting them retain their faith by paying a jizya tax, many others—especially "pagans"—did not enjoy such an option. In cases where local populations were not recognized as people of the Book, they faced the stark choice: convert or face violence. Even Jews and Christians under Muslim authority experienced restrictions that made life difficult, encouraging conversions over time. The existence of forced or heavily incentivized conversion across large swaths of territory is well attested by historians.

These forced conversions undermine the notion of free acceptance. Suras like 9:5 align perfectly with the historical impetus to present subjugated peoples with an ultimatum. That practice opposes the free-will emphasis found throughout Scripture, culminating in Jesus' invitation for individuals to "come" willingly (Matthew 11:28). If a prophet truly continued the biblical message, we would expect a consistent approach to conversion—persuasion, not compulsion. Instead, the reliance on arms in many Islamic conquests signals that a very different spirit was at work. This fundamental departure from biblical norms remains a core apologetic critique of jihad.

The Role of Feelings vs. Reason in Confronting Evidence

Believers or sympathizers with Islam sometimes object that focusing on jihad's violent side stokes prejudice, refusing to see the spiritual or moral teachings that also define the faith. A balanced approach can concede that Islam has moral laws, charitable injunctions, and an emphasis on one God. Yet it cannot ignore the frequent commands to subdue or kill unbelievers. If a faith is judged by its sacred texts and historical outworkings, then ignoring jihad's prominence would be intellectually dishonest. As Scripture says, "The heart of the discerning acquires knowledge, for the ears of the wise seek it out" (Proverbs 18:15). Sound reasoning compels an objective look at the weight of evidence, not letting personal feelings or cultural sympathies overshadow glaring contradictions.

Whether it offends or not, the historical record stands. The expansions under the Rashidun caliphs, Umayyads, and Abbasids were rarely defensive alone. The repeated enforcement of tribute and the consistent reading of militant suras testifies to a religion that sanctioned conquest. Biblical faith, culminating in Christ, took a separate path. Even in the face of hostility, the apostles refused violence, seeing themselves as ambassadors of Christ's kingdom, not soldiers of an earthly domain (2 Corinthians 5:20). This difference in approach to outsiders—coercion or free invitation—profoundly affects how each religion advanced. The Christian must thus weigh whether jihad truly emerges from God's will, or if it belongs to a man-made or, at best, an Old Testament-like approach that ironically came centuries after Christ ended that system.

The Perceived Righteousness of Islamic Warfare

Many in Islam see jihad as a righteous cause, a means to defend or spread the truth of God. They reference the perceived moral decay of conquered societies, the oppression of older regimes, or the unity that Islam imposes by subduing tribal conflicts. Yet moral improvement alone does not justify forced conversion from the biblical viewpoint. Historical evidence shows that, in some areas, Islam did reduce idol worship or forbid destructive habits, but the same can be argued about many religious or secular movements that forcibly introduced new norms. The question remains whether the ends justify the means. Scripture stands on the principle that "righteousness exalts a nation" (Proverbs 14:34), but never endorses forcibly exporting that righteousness via religious armies under the new covenant. If an unbelieving land is truly wicked, believers are to rely on God's ultimate judgment or lawful secular intervention, not on crusades or jihads.

The biblical condemnation of child sacrifice, sexual perversion, or other atrocities never extended into a general call to conquer all similarly depraved peoples. In the special instance of Canaan, Jehovah's direct instructions to Israel had a unique covenant basis. Once that was fulfilled, no further indefinite expansions were authorized. Meanwhile, Islamic jihad claims indefinite application, lacking the miraculous evidence that accompanied the old covenant conquests, and continuing in the post-biblical era. The difference is stark.

The Contradiction of Conflating State and Faith

The earliest Christians, under Roman persecution, had no illusions of forging a theocratic state. Their instructions included paying taxes, praying for authorities, and leading quiet lives (Romans 13:6, 7; 1 Timothy 2:1, 2). They awaited Christ's return to establish a righteous heavenly kingdom, not a worldly empire. Islam, from its inception, blended religion and governance. Muhammad functioned as both prophet and head of state. The successors or caliphs inherited that model, forging an empire that expanded across continents. While some might see this as positive, bringing social order and monotheism, it nonetheless merges religion with the sword in ways that contradict Jesus' pronouncement: "My kingdom is no part of this world" (John 18:36).

Even the old covenant's theocracy did not revolve around indefinite expansion for God's glory. Israel had a distinct territory, genealogical inheritance, and a relationship to Jehovah that looked forward to the Messiah. By the time Jesus arrived, that old system was ready to pass away. The church was not given land ownership or instructions to conquer neighbors. Instead, it spread by preaching, culminating in a worldwide fellowship of believers from all nations (Matthew 28:19, 20; Revelation 7:9). The new covenant's global scope rests on free acceptance, not mandated subjection. Jihad's call for subduing entire populations to establish Islamic governance is irreconcilable with the new covenant's spiritual aims.

Supposed Defensive Jihad in Light of Offensive Conquests

Even if one tries to interpret jihad strictly as permissible only when Muslims are attacked, the historical expansions that marched thousands of miles from Arabia show a pattern of offense. The conquests of Spain, across the Pyrenees into France, or the repeated attempts to subdue Constantinople culminating in 1453, reflect no mere desire to repel aggression. They represent a determination, fueled by faith, to bring more lands under Islamic control. If the local

Christian kingdoms or other states had not taken up arms, the progress might have been even swifter. It was only the French victory under Charles Martel in 732 and later defeats such as the one at Vienna in 1683 that halted the tide. Many lands in between became Islamic dominions, with local populations eventually assimilating, converting, or existing as second-class citizens.

The entire phenomenon reveals that from the vantage point of adherents to the Quran, these expansions were the natural outworking of jihad: once an Islamic power is established, it is mandated to extend the domain of Islam. While some exceptions occurred, the impetus behind suras commanding warfare continued to justify these offensives. This stands in open conflict with Jesus' instructions: "Go, therefore, and make disciples of all the nations" (Matthew 28:19) by teaching them the gospel, not by compelling them at sword-point. The difference is so fundamental that attempts to conflate Christian missions with Islamic jihad are invalid. The early church never undertook expansions resembling the subjugation of foreign lands, further underscoring that Christ's kingdom is spiritual until he returns in power.

Jihadist Ideology Among Extremists in Modern Times

Even in the present day, radical groups like ISIS, Al-Qaeda, Al-Shabaab, Boko Haram, and others cite Quranic passages to justify violence, forced conversions, or extreme punishments. These movements see themselves as reviving the original militant spirit of the Medinan suras, implementing strict Sharia and purging unbelievers. While many mainstream Muslims denounce such extremism, the radicals find textual support in the same verses historically used to expand Islam. Their approach is arguably consistent with a literal reading of suras about fighting until all worship belongs to God. One cannot easily accuse them of inventing the warlike elements of the Quran—those elements remain integral to the text, especially in the abrogating suras.

A Christian observer might note that similarly, in the name of Christianity, crusaders in the medieval era waged wars. Yet they could not legitimately cite any new covenant text instructing them to do so. Their basis lay in corrupted traditions of Christendom, not in Christ's words. By contrast, jihadists quote suras plainly urging them to kill disbelievers unless they convert. This difference remains crucial: the crusades were an aberration from Christian teaching, whereas jihad is an integral concept historically embedded in the Quran. The violent jihad tradition, though disputed by modern reformers, is not foreign to canonical Islamic texts.

The Incoherence of "No Compulsion" With "Kill Them Wherever You Find Them"

Sura 2:256 states "There is no compulsion in religion." Surah 9:5 declares that after the sacred months, believers should "fight and slay the pagans wherever ye find them," letting them go only if they repent and observe Islamic worship. These two statements cannot both operate equally at face value. As discussed, the principle of abrogation typically resolves the conflict by granting supremacy to the suras that command warfare. Alternatively, a minority of Muslims interpret Sura 9:5 strictly as applying to a unique historical moment. But that reading runs against centuries of mainstream legal tradition in which Sura 9:5 is decisive for relations with idolaters.

Throughout Islamic legal commentary, the verse advocating no compulsion was seen either as overshadowed by later revelations or restricted to certain contexts. The end result in classical jurisprudence was that unrepentant idolaters had no recognized rights if they refused Islam or dhimmi status. The Christian view sees an irreconcilable contradiction: genuine freedom of religion cannot coincide with instructions to kill or forcibly convert worshipers of other gods. Biblical passages do not present such dissonance. Despite changes from the old to the new covenant, Scripture never instructs believers to forcibly convert. Jesus' own ministry, although empowered by miracles, never forced acceptance; many disciples walked away freely (John 6:66).

Critiquing the Claim That Jihad Merely Reflects Another Cultural Environment

Some might say the Quranic references to warfare reflect normal seventh-century Arabian culture, not necessarily God's universal will. Yet orthodox Islam regards the Quran as the direct speech of God, relevant for all times. The text itself claims to be the final revelation for humanity. If it were truly divine, it would reflect God's unchanging standard, not the violent ethos of a particular culture overshadowing the new covenant's ethic. The Christian sees continuity in God's dealings from Moses to Jesus, culminating in the cross. Scripture's moral law remains consistent, even while certain ceremonial aspects were superseded by Christ's sacrifice. The abrupt shift to forcibly converting or subjugating idolaters that the Quran promotes contravenes the final covenant established by Jesus.

Moreover, biblical teachings about personal defense or national defense do not legitimate an indefinite religious war to bring all corners of the earth under a single faith. The new covenant's global scope emerges from preaching, not conquests. If a text claims to finalize God's revelation but discards the central peace ethic taught by Jesus, it logically cannot derive from the same divine source. The so-called Christian crusades were not mandated by the New Testament, but jihad finds direct impetus in the Quran. That incongruity supports the conclusion that the Quranic stance on warfare does not continue but contradicts biblical revelation.

Biblical Counsel on Reasoning and Testing All Things

Scripture repeatedly encourages believers to employ discernment and reason, "making sure of all things," holding fast to what is fine, and discarding what is improper (1 Thessalonians 5:21). Proverbs 18:15 contains Jehovah's invitation: "The heart of the discerning acquires knowledge, for the ears of the wise seek it out." In John 8:32, Jesus states, "You will know the truth, and the truth will set you free." Adhering to these principles necessitates evaluating claims about jihad's nature. If Muslims or others disclaim the violent reality, ignoring explicit commands to kill idolaters, they evade an honest reading. If they attempt to equate jihad with purely defensive warfare, they disregard abundant historical evidence. The Christian, guided by biblical truth, must weigh the data objectively.

Some might feel offended at any suggestion that Islam endorses forced conversions, but ignoring the textual and historical facts out of courtesy or fear does not aid honest inquiry. True love for one's neighbor includes clarifying spiritual truths, even if that brings discomfort (Ephesians 4:15). The Christian apologist must emphasize that the God of Scripture never merges universal religious empire-building with the cross's message of redemption. No portion of the new covenant endorses a forced submission of unbelievers. Meanwhile, the Quran's repeated warlike instructions tie piety to waging armed struggle. Polite denials do not erase those texts or centuries of jihad. Genuine reasoning leads to the conclusion that the biblical and Quranic conceptions of "holy war" differ at the deepest level.

Does the Church's Abuse of Power Justify Jihad?

In certain debates, Muslims might point to the medieval crusades or inquisitions, claiming that Christians also used violence for religious ends. While it is true that elements within Christendom engaged in brutal campaigns, these actions stand contrary to the teachings of Jesus. The Catholic or state-driven crusades from the eleventh century onward did not reflect apostolic practice. They derived from a fusion of political power with ecclesiastical authority that Christ never instituted. Early Christianity grew under Roman oppression, never raising arms. By the time of the crusades, the Roman church had long deviated from biblical norms, endorsing forced conversions that the New Testament forbids.

Thus, the existence of Christian-based violence in the medieval era cannot nullify the difference in textual sources. The crusaders twisted Scripture or relied on church traditions, not on any direct statement from Jesus or the apostles to wage war. By contrast, jihad depends on explicit verses commanding believers to fight idolaters and subdue them until they accept Islam or pay tribute. Christian hypocrisy in the Middle Ages does not alter the biblical record's condemnation of forced conversions. Meanwhile, jihad has a direct lineage to the suras of the Quran. These distinct roots cannot be glossed over. Scripture's condemnation of unrighteous warfare stands unassailable, even if some claiming to be Christians flouted that principle.

Waiting on Christ's Return vs. Establishing an Islamic World Order

135

The new covenant's outlook is that believers await Christ's second coming, trusting him to resolve the world's rebellion and injustice. They do not stage violent campaigns to expedite that process. Passages like 2 Peter 3:9, 10 detail a future day of judgment orchestrated by God. Romans 12:19 says that Christians should not take vengeance but leave it to God. Such instructions steer the congregation away from establishing any earthly theocracy by force. The sense of mission in the gospel centers on personal transformation and voluntary acceptance of Christ as Savior, culminating in baptism and discipleship.

Islam, particularly in its classical jurisprudence, has often viewed the world as divided between the House of Islam and the House of War, implying that lands not under Islamic rule remain fair game for jihad. While not every Muslim community actively follows that approach, historically many did. The pursuit of a global caliphate reveals a fundamentally different method of achieving religious unity, one that lumps the spiritual and political into a single structure. This is not consistent with the biblical teaching of Christians as "resident aliens" in the present system, "no part of the world," longing for an everlasting kingdom from above (1 Peter 2:11; John 18:36). The final subjugation of wickedness awaits divine, not human, intervention (Revelation 19:11-21).

Summarizing the Christian Objection to Jihad

In reviewing the entire scope of Scripture, conservative believers see no place for indefinite expansions by armed force to impose worship. Jesus said that the greatest commandments are to love God and love neighbor (Matthew 22:37-39). Coercing neighbors under threat of violence to adhere to one's religion violates the spirit of love. The early church overcame hostility by patience, persuasion, and martyrdom, not by raising militias. Christ's kingdom grows by genuine conviction and rebirth, not by capturing territory or subduing populations (John 3:3-5). The new covenant disbands the old covenant's physical battles and transforms them into a spiritual struggle against sin and demonic influences, waged with truth, righteousness, and the gospel of peace (Ephesians 6:10-17).

Conversely, the Quran's jihad passages, especially those in the final Medinan suras, anchor a system that merges religion with government, sanctifies conquest, and tolerates violence to spread the faith. This approach, validated by history, is irreconcilable with the gospel's peaceful expansion. Attempts to equate the old covenant's Canaanite campaigns with jihad ignore the temporary, limited, and miraculously attested nature of those instructions. Moreover, those wars concluded centuries before Christ, who introduced a new command: "Put your sword back into its place. For all who take the sword will perish by the sword" (Matthew 26:52). Thus, jihad stands outside the trajectory of biblical revelation, demonstrating that Islam's final revelation claim cannot be reconciled with the framework God established in Scripture.

Concluding Thoughts

Examining Islamic jihads highlights the substantial gulf between the Quran's approach to religious warfare and the counsel of Scripture. On one side, the Quran transitions from an initial stance allowing for no compulsion to a militant stance endorsing violence until idolaters submit or are destroyed. On the other side, biblical faith transitions from old covenant wars confined to a promised land—accompanied by miracles and pointing to future judgment—to a new covenant that disavows carnal weapons and awaits divine intervention. Jihad's long history of offensive expansions reaffirms that the war verses in the Quran cannot be dismissed as strictly defensive or obsolete. They persist in shaping radical movements.

For the conservative Christian, the question is whether a religion that forcibly imposes itself could be the same faith taught by Jesus, who overcame evil by sacrifice, taught love for enemies, and refused to let his disciples use violence to protect him (Matthew 5:44; 26:52). The answer is no. Islamic jihad stands as a contradictory concept to the new covenant. A faith centered on the cross cannot be advanced by the sword. God's Word insists on free choice in worship. The biblical model of spiritual warfare is moral persuasion, abiding in Christ's love, not conquering or subjugating. Hence, Islamic jihads cannot be from Jehovah. Their emphasis on eradicating or forcibly converting unbelievers underscores that the spirit behind them diverges from the gospel's gracious invitation to "whoever wishes" (Revelation 22:17).

While acknowledging that many Muslims practice a more peaceful personal devotion, the textual foundation for jihad remains embedded in the Quran. Modern reformers who downplay or reinterpret it face the plain reading that shaped centuries of expansions. From a scriptural standpoint, the contradiction is too severe to ignore. Far from continuing or fulfilling biblical revelation, the calls for jihad defy it, further confirming that Islam, as a system, does not represent a legitimate sequel to the old and new covenants. Instead, it appears as an alternate religio-political framework that merges faith and force.

Believers in the Bible maintain that Christ's return, not jihad, will establish God's righteous rule. In the interim, Christian mission abides by love, reason, and free acceptance, exemplified by Jesus and the apostles. The existence of jihad underscores that Islam took a different course, one that may align with certain political successes but not with the redemptive plan culminating at the cross. The cause of Christ is vindicated by resurrection power, not by seizing territories and commanding forced conversions. To remain faithful to Scripture, Christians cannot condone or align with a theology that normalizes violence in the name of God. They must instead hold forth the gospel of peace and rely on God's ultimate judgment for final vindication of truth.

CHAPTER 7 Does Sharia Law Reflect Divine Righteousness or Merely Human Ambition?

The Islamic Sharia, sometimes called Sharia Law, stands as a defining feature of Muslim life, influencing spiritual, social, and political conduct among believers. Many describe it as a divine path meant to guide humankind into right living before God, regulating both public and private acts. In classical form, the Sharia is anchored in the Quran, the Hadith, and supplementary rulings or fatwas by legal scholars across the centuries. Since the earliest days of Islam, this legal system has claimed comprehensive authority over all spheres of life, promising blessings for those who obey and dire penalties for those who transgress. To outsiders, its scope can appear astonishingly invasive, stretching from worship, prayer, and dietary regulations to penal codes involving amputations, stonings, and floggings.

In contrast, the biblical record portrays God's dealings with man in a progression from the patriarchal era of Abraham (circa early second millennium B.C.E.) to the formation of the Mosaic Law at Sinai (1513 B.C.E.) and culminating in the new covenant through Jesus Christ (Matthew 26:28). Christians see the old covenant as a theocratic arrangement limited to ancient Israel, pointing forward to Christ's superior revelation (Galatians 3:24, 25; Hebrews 8:7-13). Unlike the Sharia, which seeks to govern all facets of Muslim life indefinitely, the Mosaic Law had a termination point once the Messiah arrived. The new covenant, as taught by Jesus, does not impose a broad civil or criminal code upon believers but emphasizes the transformation of the heart by faith and the Spirit-inspired Word (Romans 10:4; Ephesians 6:17). This distinction prompts questions: is the Sharia a final manifestation of divine righteousness, or does it reflect human tradition shaped by seventh-century Arabian contexts? And how does it align with or diverge from the truths taught in Scripture?

This chapter examines the origin, content, and application of Sharia Law, contrasting it with the biblical portrayal of God's moral standards. It also considers how Sharia, by prescribing legal, social, and even political frameworks, has shaped communities historically and continues to influence countries like Afghanistan, Iran, and Saudi Arabia. Throughout, we measure these developments against passages in Scripture, seeking to determine whether the Sharia's comprehensive intrusion truly reflects God's unchanging will, or if it is grounded in human ambition, local traditions, and a post-biblical ideology.

The Roots and Sources of Sharia

Islamic tradition defines Sharia as the totality of commands, prohibitions, and principles that guide every Muslim's life. The term itself can be rendered "the path leading to a watering place," symbolizing a route to spiritual nourishment and divine favor. Adherents regard it as the will of God expressed through:

1. The Quran, which devout Muslims believe to be God's uncreated Word revealed to Muhammad in the early seventh century C.E.

2. The Hadith, collections of traditions detailing Muhammad's words, actions, and tacit approvals. Early transmitters memorized or wrote these accounts, eventually producing voluminous compilations. The Hadith stands second in authority only to the Quran.

3. Scholarly rulings or fatwas, in which recognized jurists interpret or extend the Sharia's principles, creating a robust body of case law for diverse circumstances.

By the ninth century C.E., Islamic jurisprudence or fiqh had largely stabilized into recognized schools, each with comprehensive manuals explaining how to apply the Sharia in various realms. These schools—such as the Hanafi, Maliki, Shafi'i, and Hanbali—offer both consensus and disagreement in certain areas. Despite some differences, the premise uniting them is that Sharia rules were divinely mandated through the Quran and the Prophet's example, and that believers must comply wholeheartedly.

In this perspective, Sharia stands above secular or civil legislation. A devout Muslim sees man-made laws as inherently inferior, subject to the ultimate authority of God's revealed code. This mindset starkly contrasts with how Scripture depicts an evolving historical outworking of God's law, culminating in Christ. After Moses, many prophets of Israel contributed counsel and correction but never introduced a new all-encompassing code for every dimension of life. The Hebrew Scriptures presented moral and ceremonial directives for Israel alone, with a limited domain (Galatians 3:19). When Jesus instituted the new covenant, it transcended Mosaic forms, focusing on internal transformation (Hebrews 10:1). The Sharia, in contrast, envisions an enduring, unalterable set of statutes that remain binding upon the ummah, or Muslim community, irrespective of time and place.

The Five Categories of Action Under Sharia

Muslim authorities often mention five categories of action in the Sharia framework:

Fard (religious duty, obligatory). A fard action is commanded by God, such that neglecting it brings punishment in the hereafter. Canonical prayers five times a day exemplify a fard. Mustahabb (commendable, recommended). Actions that, while not mandatory, merit spiritual rewards. Failing them incurs no punishment. Examples might include greeting others with "Peace be upon you."

Jaiz (allowed or permissible). Also called mubah, these are morally neutral acts. Almost everything not explicitly forbidden or commanded falls into this category.

Makruh (detested, disliked). Acts that, while not haram, are morally frowned upon. Committing them does not bring immediate punishment, but avoiding them is believed to garner reward. Haram (forbidden, sinful). Engaging in a haram act is believed to incur divine wrath, demanding punishment. Drinking alcohol or committing adultery typifies haram behavior.

In some contexts, the Sharia extends these categories across everything from worship rituals to business dealings, from clothing standards to gender relations. This approach is far-reaching, not confining religious norms to places of worship. The biblical standpoint differs substantially. Under the old covenant, God gave Israel laws that dealt with moral, ceremonial, and civil matters (Exodus through Deuteronomy). Yet that arrangement served a prophetic function, foreshadowing Christ. Once Jesus arrived, the new covenant introduced freedom from the old ceremonial burdens (Galatians 5:1; Colossians 2:16, 17). The church did not maintain an exhaustive legal code enumerating permissible and forbidden acts for every daily scenario. Rather, believers received overarching principles—love God, love neighbor (Matthew 22:37-39)—along with moral imperatives. The impetus for Christian behavior arises from an inward transformation (Galatians 5:22, 23). Meanwhile, Sharia's classification system reasserts a rigid external ordering reminiscent of old covenant forms yet with additional layers introduced by post-Quranic jurists.

Intrusiveness and All-Encompassing Scope

Sharia's comprehensiveness extends far beyond the typical domain of Western law. It addresses personal piety, social transactions, and penal sanctions, offering instruction on everything from daily prayers, fasting in Ramadan, almsgiving, and pilgrimage to property contracts, family issues, inheritance, and even private moral conduct. Thus, the Sharia typically merges religious obligations with civil governance. Historically, Islamic states or caliphates organized themselves around Sharia, enforcing it upon Muslim populations (and sometimes upon non-Muslim subjects) with state power.

Modern critics note that such an intertwining of religion and law can severely limit personal freedom, especially for women, children, or religious minorities. Strict application of Sharia fosters punishments like amputation for theft, stoning for adultery, floggings for fornication, and even the death penalty for blasphemy or apostasy. Countries like Saudi Arabia, Iran, Sudan, and Afghanistan implement such measures, while other nations with Muslim majorities adopt partial Sharia codes. In everyday life, this legal system can hamper free speech, limit the roles of women, or curtail the rights of non-Muslim citizens to evangelize or publicly worship.

Biblically, no comprehensive system persists into the new covenant that merges state enforcement with religious commands.

Jesus explained: "My kingdom is no part of this world" (John 18:36). The apostolic writings do not instruct believers to set up a theocracy or enforce religious obligations via civil law. The old covenant did contain such features, but only for Israel's special arrangement up to the arrival of Christ (Galatians 3:24). That covenant never extended beyond the land's boundaries, nor did it remain once the Messiah came. The new covenant prescribes moral obligations for believers but not a universal civil code. The difference is stark. Sharia's imposition upon entire societies suggests a perpetual theocracy—despite the biblical narrative concluding that Christ fulfilled the old arrangement, leaving believers as "foreigners and temporary residents" in worldly nations (1 Peter 2:11).

The Advent of Sharia as Theocratic Rule

Islamic history records that with Muhammad's death in 632 C.E., revelation was deemed complete. The Quran and the Hadith then became the bedrock for constructing a system that regulated all life. By the eighth and ninth centuries C.E., schools of jurisprudence had codified Sharia. Because Islam considers the Quran uncreated and divinely perfect, it was not subject to reevaluation as society evolved. Muslims treat Muhammad's example in the Hadith as equally authoritative in day-to-day matters. The result has been a legal code considered timeless, overshadowing any notion of progressive or adaptive interpretation. This unchanging vantage point allowed the Sharia to become rigid and static, often resisting legal reform.

In many Western societies, laws evolve with societal changes, shaped by legislative processes and judicial precedents. In Sharia, the impetus for legal evolution is minimal because religious jurists claim the final word rests in the sealed revelation of the seventh century C.E. Once the "gate of ijtihad" (independent legal reasoning) was deemed closed by many classical scholars, the impetus for further changes waned. That stands in contrast to the biblical storyline: though moral principles remain stable, the old covenant's civil aspects were never intended to spread universally or last indefinitely. Instead, they guided a covenant people until the promised Messiah. Jesus introduced a new emphasis on grace, internal purity, and worship in spirit, not a new theocracy (John 4:21-24). Sharia's unbending approach to law suggests a worldview that sees no further revelation beyond Muhammad—unlike Christians who see the biblical record culminating in Jesus, the final spokesman of God (Hebrews 1:1, 2).

Sharia's Harshest Penalties

Critics frequently point to Sharia's penal or hudud laws, the severe punishments for offenses considered violations against God's boundaries. Common hudud penalties include:

Amputation of the hand for certain thefts.

Stoning or flogging for adultery.

Execution for blasphemy, apostasy (leaving Islam), or sometimes for repeated moral violations.

In some contexts, these penalties rest upon strict evidentiary thresholds. However, in practice, societies implementing Sharia penal codes often experience injustices against women or minorities. For instance, a woman who reports sexual assault might be charged with adultery if she fails to produce four credible male witnesses. From a biblical viewpoint, while the Mosaic Law did prescribe capital punishments for certain grave sins like adultery or blasphemy (Leviticus 20:10; 24:15, 16), that arrangement was specific to Israel's covenant (Deuteronomy 4:7, 8). Once Christ came, the new covenant never enforced stoning or amputation as a moral penalty within the Christian congregation. The church addressed sin through expulsion from fellowship if unrepented, leaving civil crimes to secular governments (1 Corinthians 5:11-13; Romans 13:1-4). The notion of God's final judgment at Christ's return supplanted any ongoing theocratic enforcement of old covenant punishments (Romans 12:19; Revelation 19:11-21). Meanwhile, Sharia states or communities continue to see these harsh measures as normative or even pious, further contrasting with the new covenant stance.

Gender Inequity in Sharia

A frequent critique of Sharia is its treatment of women. Under Sharia, a man can marry multiple wives (up to four), while a woman can have only one husband. A woman's testimony in court often counts for half that of a man. In inheritance, female heirs can receive half of what their male counterparts receive. Marital conduct sometimes allows a husband to administer physical discipline to a disobedient wife, citing Sura 4:34. Many argue that these rules reflect seventh-century Arabian customs, lacking parity with modern norms of gender equality. Even inside the older covenant, Scripture never mandated ongoing polygamy as a universal norm. While polygamy did appear historically among the patriarchs, it led to family strife (Genesis 16:4-6; 1 Samuel 1:4-7). Jesus reinforced God's original design that "they are no longer two, but one flesh" (Matthew 19:6). The Christian epistles advise overseers to be "a husband of one wife," implying monogamy (1 Timothy 3:2). Sharia's codification of polygamy and lesser rights for women diverges from this new covenant ethic. The biblical approach portrays men and women as spiritually equal heirs of life (Galatians 3:28; 1 Peter 3:7). Sharia, in practice, subordinates women within a legal structure that can hamper their liberty.

The Relevance of Taqiyya

A concept sometimes raised in discussing Sharia's infiltration into non-Muslim lands is Taqiyya, which references the allowance for Muslims to conceal or misrepresent certain beliefs under threat or in pursuit of the faith's protection. Although various Islamic sects differ on Taqiyya's scope, the principle has historically permitted deception to safeguard the Muslim community. Critics assert that Taqiyya can facilitate stealth expansion or covert agendas, particularly as Muslims seek acceptance in majority non-Muslim countries. Defenders counter that Taqiyya applies only when life or property is endangered, not as a broad license for duplicity. Yet the concept has fueled suspicions about whether Muslims in Western societies might feign moderation or align with liberal policies to gain political traction, only to later advocate Sharia once sufficiently numerous.

From a conservative biblical perspective, the ethic of Christian truthfulness stands in tension with any permissible falsehood (Ephesians 4:25). The new covenant exhorts believers to speak the truth, even under duress, trusting God. While the old covenant does record some cases of deception for righteous ends, such as the Hebrew midwives misdirecting Pharaoh (Exodus 1:19), these episodes never transformed into a codified principle that believers can lie for faith's advancement. In Sharia, Taqiyya appears as a recognized jurisprudential device. The difference can heighten mistrust among outsiders who worry that a publicly moderate stance might conceal a desire for Sharia compliance in the long run.

Sharia Implementation in History

Historically, as Islam spread from Arabia into Persia, North Africa, and beyond, various caliphates integrated Sharia into governance. Non-Muslims, called dhimmis, could keep their faith by paying a special tax (jizya) and accepting subordinate status. In some eras, these "people of the Book" (Jews and Christians) enjoyed relative autonomy, though under numerous restrictions. Others faced forced conversions or severe oppression, particularly in regions where radical rulers demanded uniform compliance with Islam. Over time, certain Muslim societies turned to secular codes or reformed versions of Sharia, especially in the modern era, in response to Western colonial influence or local movements for modernization. Yet in conservative strongholds like Saudi Arabia or post-revolution Iran, classical Sharia remains the official legal foundation.

Many see such states as the archetype of a Sharia-based society, replete with morality police, required veiling for women, and harsh punishments for violations. Public executions, amputations, and floggings sometimes occur, aiming to deter wrongdoing. Devout advocates hail this as a demonstration of moral seriousness. From a biblical vantage, one questions whether forcibly imposing outward conformity aligns with the kind of voluntary, heart-based worship Jesus called for (John 4:23, 24). Indeed, the new covenant uses spiritual discipline within the congregation, not a civil apparatus punishing private sins. As for nonbelievers, Paul taught that they stand outside the church's disciplinary framework. They face God's ultimate judgment, not immediate penal codes from Christian elders (1 Corinthians 5:12, 13). The distinction signals a fundamental difference in how biblical faith and Sharia define the role of religion in society.

Contrasts With Christian Ethics and Governance

Comparing Sharia with Christian teachings reveals a wide gulf in approach:

Sharia merges religion and state, aiming to structure all aspects of life under divine law. Christian writings under the new covenant see believers as spiritual sojourners in secular societies, not seeking to impose a theocracy (John 17:14-16).

Sharia imposes external legal codes with severe corporal or capital punishments for moral offenses. The new covenant fosters internal transformation and communal discipline that does not resort to lethal force (2 Corinthians 10:4; Matthew 18:15-17).

Sharia features polygamy, lesser inheritance for women, forced veiling, restrictions on female testimony, and other gender disparities. The Christian view frames men and women as coheirs of grace, encouraging monogamy and mutual respect (Galatians 3:28; 1 Timothy 3:2).

Sharia enforces punishments for leaving Islam, a capital offense in many interpretations. The Christian approach allows individuals to depart the faith if they choose, leaving final judgment to God (1 John 2:19; Hebrews 10:31).

These contrasts prompt reflection on whether Sharia truly represents a final revelation from God, continuing the line from Abraham and Moses, or whether it diverges from the message culminated in Christ. The new covenant that Jesus inaugurated is not a comprehensive civil code for states but an invitation to a spiritual kingdom transcending national boundaries (Acts 1:8; Ephesians 3:6). Meanwhile, Sharia's emphasis on worldly government is reminiscent of the old covenant, yet without the transitional role that Scripture ascribes to the Mosaic Law (Galatians 3:23-25). By forcibly binding entire societies to seventh-century Arabian norms, Sharia stands at odds with biblical teachings that emphasize a shift from external law to internal grace.

Western Nations and the Growth of Sharia Influence

In modern times, some Western countries have witnessed growing Muslim populations. Immigrants or refugees from predominantly Muslim regions often seek to maintain their religious identity. In places like Canada, the United Kingdom, and parts of Europe, attempts have been made to establish local Sharia councils or arbitration panels for family disputes among consenting Muslims. Advocates see this as a means of religious freedom, letting them resolve disputes in accordance with Islamic principles. Critics warn of parallel legal systems that can overshadow national laws, particularly in matters like divorce, child custody, or inheritance. They cite cases where women received unfair treatment from Sharia-based arbitration.

In some localities, pressure mounts to accommodate aspects of Sharia in public institutions, from Halal-certified meals in schools to permission for daily prayers. Meanwhile, extremist groups or radical preachers advocate for full Sharia enforcement, including hudud punishments, once Muslims constitute a critical mass. Critics highlight that while a minority might push for official Sharia implementation, many mainstream Muslims merely want freedom to practice their faith. Yet the possibility of incremental acceptance fosters concern among those who recall that devout Muslims see Sharia as an all-or-nothing imperative. The tension intensifies when Western liberal ideologies champion tolerance, inadvertently creating space for religious enclaves that enforce fundamentalist codes at odds with mainstream civil rights.

The Role of Political Correctness and Taqiyya in Sharia Ambitions

In the current climate, some politicians and media figures in Western lands downplay the potential ramifications of Sharia infiltration, branding as "Islamophobic" any critique of Islamic norms. This approach can hamper open debate about the real challenges posed by radical Islamic activism. Meanwhile, segments of the Muslim community might rely on Taqiyya, the principle allowing dissimulation under certain conditions, to allay suspicion. Publicly, they may emphasize benign aspects of Sharia or present it as purely a personal moral code. Behind the scenes, however, local leadership might work toward broader legal recognition of Sharia in family or criminal matters. Observers note that once demographic and political leverage grows, demands can escalate, culminating in attempts to supplant existing law entirely.

From a biblical perspective, Jesus never counseled believers to conceal or misrepresent truth for strategic gain. The apostles, though at times prudent in evangelism, consistently upheld transparency about the gospel's demands (Acts 4:19, 20). For instance, Paul wrote, "We have renounced the hidden things of shame, not walking in cunning" (2 Corinthians 4:2). The notion of cunning infiltration to impose Christian norms by stealth is foreign to the New Testament. Sharia-based activism that masks ultimate goals may thus appear suspect, especially in societies that historically prized open discourse. The question arises: if Sharia is truly from God, why rely on concealment or political correctness to advance it?

Sharia's Child Marriage and Female Mutilation Customs

In certain regions where Sharia holds sway, child marriages are permitted or at least tolerated, citing examples from the Hadith or early Islamic tradition. Some interpret the Prophet's marriage to Aisha, often described as consummated when she was around nine, as a precedent for permissible unions once a girl reaches puberty, even if she is under ten. Although many Muslim-majority countries have introduced higher marriage ages, conservative communities may resist, claiming that Sharia cannot be changed. Relatedly, female genital cutting, often justified by certain Hadith statements or local custom, persists in places like Somalia or parts of Egypt. Sharia-based rulings might condone or recommend such acts as part of modesty or purity.

From a biblical vantage point, child marriage or female genital mutilation is foreign to the moral guidelines taught by Jesus and the apostles. The new covenant underscores principles like love, honor, and respect for the vulnerable (Ephesians 5:25, 28). Such customs stand at odds with the biblical ethic that cherishes children as blessings from God, not as objects for early sexual union (Psalm 127:3). Meanwhile, Scripture never condones bodily mutilation as part of covenant identity, beyond the old covenant's male circumcision, which was itself superseded by the new covenant that no longer imposes circumcision as a religious requirement (Galatians 5:2). Thus, the presence of these harmful practices under Sharia challenges claims that it is the apex of God's revealed moral will.

The Apologetic Question: Is Sharia Truly a Divine Code?

Islamic tradition asserts that the Sharia represents God's final statement on how humankind should be governed. Yet measured by biblical standards—progressive revelation, the culminating sacrifice of Christ, freedom from an external legal yoke, spiritual worship in every land—Sharia does not extend the biblical storyline. Instead, it reverts to or expands upon a seventh-century Middle Eastern framework that lacks the robust theological continuity with Christ's teachings. The prophet Isaiah wrote that in Messiah's time, nations would "beat their swords into plowshares" (Isaiah 2:4). By imposing harsh punishments, legalistic regulations, and forcible expansion on entire societies, Sharia appears more reminiscent of a political empire safeguarding its power than a universal path of redemption.

One might ask: if God intended Sharia as the final revelation, why does it ignore or deny the central redemptive acts recounted in Scripture, particularly Christ's sacrificial death (Matthew 20:28)? Why does it cling to external codes while the new covenant reveals a transformation from within (2 Corinthians 3:6)? Why does it subjugate entire populations through legal intimidation, while the apostles never used compulsion to secure obedience? Far from confirming the biblical narrative, Sharia reconfigures moral law under a system shaped by local Arabian mores, imposing burdens that Christ lifted (Galatians 2:16). For these reasons, conservative interpreters of Scripture remain convinced that Sharia is a purely human construct with religious trappings, not an outworking of the new covenant or a legitimate continuation of what God gave through Moses and the prophets.

Modern Muslim Approaches: Secularization or Revival?

Today, across the Muslim world, there is a spectrum regarding Sharia's role. Some nations, like Turkey under secular influences, once restricted Sharia's public application. Others, including Saudi Arabia and Iran, fervently uphold it as state law. Fundamentalist groups—like the Taliban in Afghanistan or ISIS in its short-lived "caliphate"—seek to implement the strictest versions, including stonings, amputations, and child marriages. Moderates attempt to reconcile Sharia with global human-rights standards, selectively applying or reinterpreting older rulings. They face strong resistance from traditional scholars who argue that divine law cannot be revised.

In biblical comparison, the new covenant is not open to partial acceptance or adaptation either, yet it requires no legalistic civil code. The shift from old covenant to new was not a minor reinterpretation but a transformation of worship, based on the finished work of Christ (Hebrews 9:10-14). No further prophet is predicted to revise or reintroduce a worldly theocracy. Meanwhile, the Sharia endures as an unceasing legalistic system that, when fully enforced, ironically resembles aspects of the old covenant's theocratic structure but with significant differences—particularly its denial of the cross and attempt to universalize a local Arabian model. These tensions underscore that for those who accept Scripture, Sharia cannot be aligned with God's ultimate revelation in the gospel.

Immigration, Population Growth, and Potential Subversion

Observers note that in Western countries with liberal immigration policies, Muslim populations can grow swiftly. Some estimate that by having significantly higher birth rates and continued immigration, Muslims could become large minorities or even majorities in certain regions. That demographic shift, if accompanied by calls to adopt Sharia, poses a real question for liberal democracies. Are they prepared to resist or accommodate demands that entire neighborhoods or even entire cities abide by Islamic standards? Will multi-tiered legal systems arise, granting separate authority for Muslim communities? These concerns are not hypothetical. Nations like the United Kingdom have already permitted Sharia councils for family arbitration. Canada and the United States face sporadic attempts to introduce Sharia-based resolutions. Critics see this as foreshadowing a deeper subversion, aligning with historical patterns of incremental infiltration.

The biblical stance on how believers behave in a pluralistic society is quite different. Christians living among pagans did not strive to supplant local laws forcibly with the Mosaic code. They submitted to state authorities unless commanded to violate God's moral commands (Romans 13:1-7; Acts 5:29). Though Scripture expects the good news to spread globally, it never hints at imposing Christian law on entire societies prior to Christ's return. Meanwhile, Sharia sees itself as the final law for all humankind. If that law gains traction democratically or by subversion, its more radical aspects may gradually overshadow preexisting constitutional rights. This potential shift underscores the importance of clarifying biblical truth about man's free response to God's grace.

The Ultimate Issue: Spiritual Kingdom vs. Earthly Rule

Sharia's existence testifies to a religion that inherently weds spiritual practice to worldly government. By contrast, Jesus taught that his kingdom is not derived from the earthly sphere (John 18:36). The new covenant congregation is a fellowship of believers from every nation, living peacefully within or alongside secular governments, not forming its own civil dominion. Christians are to be separate from the world, shining as lights, not imposing top-down legal structures that punish unbelief (Matthew 5:14-16; Philippians 2:15). The biblical storyline reveals that once God concluded the old covenant, the epoch of a theocratic state implementing moral law ended, replaced by the church's universal mission. Only at Christ's second advent will he exercise global authority, judging the nations (Matthew 25:31-46).

Sharia, in effect, perpetuates or reinvents a theocratic approach, imposing penal codes for moral infractions, uniting religion with the state's power. Whether one sees that as righteous or oppressive often depends on whether one accepts the Quran as God's final revelation. Conservative Christian belief sees no basis in Scripture for reverting to a system akin to the old covenant. Indeed, Paul's writings emphasize that believers are "ministers of a new covenant," not of the letter that kills but of the spirit that gives life (2 Corinthians 3:6). Sharia's letter-based demands and earthly punishments do not align with the free invitation Christ extends. The central question thus becomes whether God, having provided redemption in Christ, would later institute a harsh legal code that denies the cross and merges religion with political dominance. The biblical testimony offers a clear "No."

Conclusion

Sharia Law, as a comprehensive legal-religious framework, draws its authority from the Quran, the Hadith, and subsequent juristic interpretations. It extends into every facet of life, imposing obligations that range from personal devotions to penal statutes for crimes. In nations where it holds sway, Sharia shapes political structures, family law, gender relations, and social norms. Meanwhile, some Western jurisdictions face pressure to accommodate Sharia elements for Muslim communities. Advocates portray it as God's unchanging code, but critics point to its oppressive aspects, especially regarding women's rights, religious freedom, and harsh punishments for moral offenses. Historically, states that fully implemented Sharia have shown authoritarian tendencies, often stifling dissent or punishing perceived blasphemy.

For Christians convinced of Scripture's final authority, the Sharia stands outside the trajectory established by God from creation through the old covenant to the new covenant in Christ. The old covenant was local to Israel and concluded at the Messiah's advent. Christ's covenant calls believers out of the world, forming a spiritual kingdom not enforced by swords or stonings. The new covenant rests on Christ's atoning sacrifice, extended freely to all. By reintroducing a worldly theocracy, Sharia departs from that ultimate gospel arrangement. Its legal codes ignore or deny the cross as central, presenting instead a system of external compulsion. The moral rigors of Sharia, while intended to reflect God's holiness, lack the redemptive basis found in Christ's righteousness imputed to believers. Given that biblical record, Sharia's alignment with unending legal demands, forced compliance, and the overshadowing of grace strongly suggests it originates from human tradition, not from the same God who authored the new covenant.

Time and again, attempts to harmonize Sharia's harsh penalties or polygamous norms with the biblical ethic fail under scrutiny. The gospel never instructs a church-state fusion nor endorses lethal force to punish doctrinal errors or personal sins. The law of Christ focuses on faith, hope, and love, with discipline restricted to excluding unrepentant wrongdoers from fellowship, not stoning them (1 Corinthians 5:13). The Sharia's call to unify spiritual and political spheres, culminating in a legal code that punishes apostasy with death, reveals a mismatch with the new covenant's spiritual foundation. Ultimately, the question remains: does a post-biblical seventh-century code that rejects the atoning cross, imposes theocratic rule, and denies personal religious freedom reflect God's final revelation or man's ambition? The biblical evidence compels the conclusion that it reflects

Edward D. Andrews

human initiative rooted in historical context, not the pattern of salvation orchestrated by Jehovah through Christ. Followers of Scripture, then, must stand firm, upholding the gospel's message of free acceptance and spiritual renewal, while recognizing that Sharia belongs to a different system.

CHAPTER 8 Does Islam's Modern Worldview and Radical Elements Align With Scriptural Truth?

Conversations about the worldview of Islam, including the manifestations of radical or fundamentalist elements, have intensified across the globe. Many wonder whether contemporary expressions of Islamic zeal, exemplified by extremist groups, reflect a perennial feature of historical Islam or a new phenomenon. However, a broad reading of early Islamic chronicles reveals that marauding campaigns and territorial expansions by force have marked Islam's development since the seventh century C.E. From Muhammad's earliest skirmishes in the Arabian Peninsula to far-reaching conquests that established large caliphates, warfare and doctrinal strictness were not innovations of modernity. Yet there remains a dynamic tension within Islam between those who champion the stricter "fundamental" or "radical" approach to implementing Sharia and those who prefer a more moderate path.

Radical Muslims, often called Islamists, advocate a literal reading of the Quran and the Hadith, striving to reestablish what they perceive as the purity of Islam during Muhammad's era. In their view, this objective can involve launching holy wars—or jihad—and forcibly implementing Sharia Law, a system that regulates worship, criminal codes, and personal conduct. Meanwhile, moderate Muslims, who sometimes adopt aspects of Western life, approach the Quran and the Hadith differently, seeking a more personal devotion that coexists with broader secular societies. The friction between these viewpoints deeply affects global politics, community stability, and religious coexistence.

From a conservative Christian perspective, questions arise about how these Islamic outlooks compare with Scripture's teachings on governance, the use of force, and the nature of true worship. Because biblical revelation culminates in Jesus Christ, the question stands: does the violent expansion of radical Islam and the sociopolitical regime it hopes to establish align with the final covenant in Christ? Are there parallels to the old covenant wars of ancient Israel, or do these modern calls to arms diverge from the biblical progression leading to a purely spiritual kingdom (John 18:36)? By examining the overarching worldview of Islam—particularly radical forms—Christians can more clearly discern whether these movements might reflect God's truth or conflict sharply with the gospel's message of free acceptance, heart transformation, and peaceful conduct among neighbors. This chapter explores that intersection, weighing fundamentalist and moderate Islamic beliefs against the biblical record.

The Historical Pattern of Islamic Expansion

No study of Islam's worldview can ignore its historical expansions. From the mid-seventh century onward, Islamic forces spread rapidly beyond Arabia. Under the first caliphs, armies conquered Syria, Persia, and large swaths of North Africa, eventually moving into Spain and pressing into southern France until stopped by Charles Martel in 732 C.E. In many of these campaigns, local populations faced a stark choice: embrace Islam, pay a special tax (if they were "people of the Book"), or face active hostilities. While modern minds might label some expansions "defensive," the historical record reveals numerous offensives that advanced far from Arabia.

Over the centuries, major caliphates (Umayyad, Abbasid, Ottoman) consolidated large territories under Muslim rule. These dominions often enforced aspects of Sharia, especially in penal codes and social norms. Non-Muslims who submitted could retain their religion but lived under varying restrictions. The impetus behind these expansions was not merely political; it was entwined with the religious conviction that Islam should reign supreme, consistent with passages in the Quran commanding the faithful to fight until only God is worshiped. Such calls shaped the worldview that the entire earth should eventually submit to the revealed law of Muhammad.

Even during the alleged "Golden Age" of Islamic civilization, the impetus of expansion, or at least the readiness to defend or propagate the faith by force, remained central to many devout Muslims. Though societies like medieval Baghdad embraced scholarship, that did not negate the underlying premise that Islam's future included dominion over unbelievers. For centuries, the tension between intellectual flourishing and militant zeal coexisted. From a Christian vantage point, the concept of forcibly spreading religious rule is distinct from the new covenant approach, which centers on peaceful evangelism, not conquest by arms (2 Corinthians 10:3-4). Instead of advocating political empire, Jesus commissioned believers to "make disciples of all the nations" (Matthew 28:19), persuading hearts rather than subduing them.

Radical Islam Today: A Continuation or a Novelty?

Modern media frequently speak of a "resurgence" or "new wave" of radical Islam. Groups like Al-Qaeda, ISIS, Boko Haram, and others stage terror attacks and proclaim the aim of a global caliphate. Yet to label this radicalization wholly new belies the continuum of militant interpretation. The impetus that led early armies to conquer large lands and subdue populations under Sharia did not vanish over time. While certain Islamic societies adopted more moderate or secular policies, the underlying call to reestablish the original fervor never disappeared among devout fundamentalists.

One might indeed call present-day jihadists "the latest rise" of radical Islam, fueled by modern technology and global interconnectedness. Transnational groups recruit disillusioned youth through online propaganda, praising the acts of self-martyrdom. Nevertheless, the textual basis for such radical acts remains the same seventh-century verses that commanded believers to fight unbelievers until they submitted (Sura 9:5; 2:193). Far from ignoring these passages, radicals cite them as final divine mandates. The biblical perspective sees a marked contrast: the old covenant wars ended with the arrival of the Messiah, who forbade violent expansion of his kingdom (Matthew 26:52). If the new covenant calls for spiritual warfare only (Ephesians 6:12), one cannot conflate biblical conquests with modern jihad.

Literalism and Interpretation in Islam

A crucial component of radical Islam is the literal reading of the Quran and the Hadith. Muslims who interpret these texts literally strive to live as Muhammad and his companions did—adopting seventh-century norms in dress, social relations, and governance. Their approach treats instructions about warfare, polygamy, punishments, and submission to the caliph as enduring commands. They also see no reason to filter these commands through modern ethical frameworks because, in their view, God's Word is final and unchangeable.

Of course, many moderate Muslims claim to read the Quran literally too, but interpret certain passages in a more symbolic or context-bound manner. They might label the warlike verses as historical instructions, relevant only to Muhammad's immediate context. Alternatively, they might argue that the instructions were purely defensive. Yet for radicals, such interpretive accommodations are tantamount to diluting God's will. They see the earliest Muslims as exemplars who forcibly expanded Islam, subjugated nonbelievers, and enforced strict codes on moral behavior. By returning to that lifestyle, they believe they honor God's law. Christian biblical interpretation, by contrast, holds that one must discern the historical context to differentiate descriptive from prescriptive passages (2 Timothy 2:15). Even in the old covenant, not every biblical event was a model for future conduct. The new covenant replaced the old, culminating in Christ who disarmed believers from the sword in matters of evangelism.

Differing Mindsets: Radical Versus Moderate Muslims

Among Muslims, the distinction between radical Islamists (who might become violent or support violence) and moderate Muslims is often stark. Radical Muslims, sometimes described as fundamentalists, believe the entire planet should be subjected to Sharia by any means, including terror if necessary. These individuals or groups may plan attacks against governments, secular institutions, or even fellow Muslims deemed insufficiently orthodox. Meanwhile, moderate Muslims embrace many Islamic devotions—praying, fasting, reading the Quran—but also coexist in Western societies, accepting at least partial separation of religion from governance. They might view stoning or amputation as archaic or situational, not mandated today.

However, scholars point out that many moderate Muslims still desire eventual recognition of Sharia as law or quietly uphold its moral supremacy. The difference is that they prefer peaceful propagation. While they might not forcibly impose Sharia or condone terror, they do not disclaim the ultimate goal of an Islamic society. A Christian might recall that the new covenant does not rely on incremental infiltration or the use of politics to overshadow civil laws. It champions persuasion by gospel truth, never resorting to subversion. That biblical stance stands in tension with radical expressions of Islam which push for infiltration into Western institutions, eventually seeking to rewrite legal codes to align with Sharia. Even moderate Muslims can exhibit solidarity with radical goals if they share the underlying theological premise that Islam must dominate.

Islam's Ideological Rift: Fundamentalists and the "Uncle Tom" Charge

Modern controversies sometimes pit fundamentalists against moderate Muslims, with accusations of treachery on both sides. Some fundamentalist clerics castigate moderates as betrayers who adopt Western ways and water down Islam to accommodate secular laws. In this vein, London's Muslim mayor, Sadiq Khan, once referred to moderate Muslim groups as "Uncle Toms," implying they were too subservient to non-Muslim powers. Similarly, Iranian Ayatollahs disparage moderate or "American Islam" as a distortion, labeling it a puppet of Western influences.

From the vantage point of radical clerics, moderation equates to ignoring divine commands. Passages in the Quran about fighting, punishing apostates, or subjugating women remain in effect, so to soft-pedal them is akin to heresy. The biblical record acknowledges that old covenant laws used harsh measures in ancient Israel, but those laws were never intended to become a permanent global system. By contrast, radical Islam sees no expiration on the seventh century blueprint. Indeed, fundamentalism defies any suggestion that the faith must "modernize" or "reform," interpreting such calls as direct challenges to the integrity of God's Word. For Christians, this highlights that radical Islam is not a misinterpretation so much as a literal application of certain Quranic passages, raising deeper questions

159

about whether the entire system aligns with or opposes Christ's law of love (John 13:34, 35).

Radical Islam's Goals: Reestablishing the Caliphate

Central to the radical worldview is the longing for a restored caliphate, a unified Islamic state under one supreme religious-political leader (the caliph). Historical caliphates ended, most notably the Ottoman Caliphate in the early twentieth century. Modern extremist groups like ISIS declared a short-lived "caliphate" over territories in Iraq and Syria, urging Muslims worldwide to pledge allegiance. Their harsh rule displayed draconian punishments, forced conversions, enslavement of minority women, and mass executions of perceived enemies.

While mainstream Muslim states might criticize the brutality of ISIS, the ideological desire for a caliphate extends beyond that group alone. Radical Islamists widely regard the absence of a caliphate as a humiliating loss for the Muslim world. Restoring it—through violent or subversive means—serves as a direct route to implementing Sharia globally. Scripture, however, presents a different vision for the people of God, culminating in Christ's return to establish a heavenly kingdom, not a mortal empire enforced by violence (Revelation 11:15). The new covenant depicts believers of all nations forming a spiritual body, awaiting the Lord's second advent to usher in genuine peace. No biblical mandate instructs them to form a theocratic monarchy or impose a binding set of penal codes upon the entire world.

Taqiyya and Subversive Approaches

As discussed in prior chapters, Taqiyya is a concept allowing Muslims to conceal or misrepresent beliefs when threatened, or to advance the cause. Radical Muslims sometimes use Taqiyya to mask extremist goals behind moderate rhetoric. This practice can sow confusion for outsiders, who see outwardly peaceful expressions from some Muslim communities while later discovering extremist activities or sympathies. Meanwhile, moderate Muslims may disclaim the broad usage of Taqiyya, limiting it to dire circumstances where life is at stake. The fact remains that fundamentalist traditions justify strategic deception if it safeguards the ummah or promotes jihad success.

Christian teaching in the new covenant forbids deception to promote the gospel. The apostle Paul wrote, "We have renounced underhanded ways," emphasizing transparency (2 Corinthians 4:2). Even under persecution, early Christians did not feign new allegiances or distort their aims. They endured suffering openly, trusting God to vindicate them (1 Peter 4:12-14). Taqiyya thus stands at odds with biblical ethics, revealing a deeper philosophical gap. If Sharia endorses deception in certain contexts, it confirms that the radical worldview invests a worldly conquest ethic with religious authority, a posture alien to the new covenant's spiritual nature.

The Complexities of Modern Muslim Communities in the West

In North America, Europe, and Australia, Muslim populations have grown significantly via immigration and high birth rates. Initially, newcomers often present themselves as no different from other immigrants. Over time, some communities press for Sharia-based arbitration in family matters or special accommodations in schools (like Halal meals or separate prayer spaces). Host societies, valuing religious freedom, often comply. Nonetheless, tension can arise if enclaves promote radical ideas or seek to supplant local laws with aspects of Sharia. Critics label these steps as stealth jihad, especially if radical clerics gain influence.

Moderate Muslims may genuinely assimilate or maintain a personal faith that respects the civic framework of their new country. However, fundamentalists view assimilation as capitulation, urging resistance and the ultimate transformation of the host society into an Islamic domain. Some observers voice concern that, once numbers permit, radicals shift from quiet persuasion to overt demands or even intimidation. The biblical position underscores that the Christian gospel never aimed to seize political power or remake societies through infiltration (John 15:19). Believers remain "aliens and sojourners," not forging an earthly dominion (1 Peter 2:11). The surreptitious effort to embed religious law in secular jurisdictions conflicts with that ethos. Thus, analyzing these developments helps Christians interpret whether they see a biblical continuity or an entirely foreign approach at work.

Examining the Reliance on Force in Radical Ideology

Radical Islam asserts that a show of force, or direct violence, can be a legitimate means of implementing God's will. Suicide bombings, hostage takings, hijackings, and mass killings become rationalized as forms of jihad. Leaders might also finance smaller cells or encourage lone-wolf attackers to strike Western targets in symbolic acts of defiance. While mainstream Muslim organizations condemn terrorism, radicals argue that these violent acts find justification in suras describing the Prophet's campaigns or in the principle of punishing those who resist God's law. The biblical record, however, teaches that the new covenant surpasses old covenant forms, substituting love for enemies in place of retribution (Matthew 5:44). The church never employed bombs or assassinations to spread the gospel among pagan Rome, even though Christians were persecuted. The mismatch reveals how the radical Islamist worldview diverges from the pattern established by Christ and the apostles, where no impetus exists for holy war or forced compliance.

Contrasting the Israelite Conquest With Radical Islam's Ambitions

Some radical Muslims assert that the conquest of Canaan by ancient Israel is analogous to Islam's call for conquest. Yet, the old covenant context was unique: Israel received direct commands from Jehovah, accompanied by miracles (Exodus 7-14; Joshua 10:11). The wars were geographically limited, intended to fulfill a specific promise to Abraham (Genesis 12:7). By the time Christ arrived, that arrangement had served its purpose (Galatians 3:24). Jesus never told his disciples to wage further conquests. Instead, he forbade using the sword for the kingdom's cause (Matthew 26:52). If the Islamic worldview attempts to universalize such warfare, pushing beyond the limited scope God gave Israel, it effectively disregards the biblical principle that these old covenant wars concluded once their function was complete. The radical notion that warlike expansions remain valid worldwide stands contrary to the new covenant approach, wherein spiritual transformation occurs one heart at a time.

Anthropological and Political Drivers of Radical Islam

While radical Muslims cite theology, observers note that economic, political, or social factors can contribute. Regions suffering from poor governance, oppression, or turmoil might breed fundamentalist resentment. Young men can be radicalized by a sense of alienation or perceived Western hostility. Online propaganda channels feed these grievances, linking them to a grand narrative that only the original form of Islam can save the world. In biblical terms, oppression can create a vacuum where false hopes flourish (Proverbs 29:2). Yet no worldly environment justifies terror in Scripture's view. Hardship or perceived injustice never legitimizes murdering civilians or forcibly imposing religion. The apostle Paul wrote: "Do not let yourselves be conquered by evil, but keep conquering evil with good" (Romans 12:21). Radical Islam, contending that social injustice warrants violence, starkly conflicts with that precept.

The "Moderates," Their Limitations, and Potential Alignments

Not all practicing Muslims in the West or globally want a caliphate or condone violent jihad. Many disclaim radical ideology, living side-by-side with unbelievers in peace. Some even identify with liberal democratic values. However, moderates often come under pressure from fundamentalists who accuse them of selling out. In nations like Iran or Saudi Arabia, official policies might hamper moderates from speaking freely. In Western lands, they face suspicion that they are practicing Taqiyya. Meanwhile, many moderates themselves may quietly accept the notion that Sharia is the ideal law or that apostasy deserves punishment, though they might not personally enforce it.

A Christian reflecting on this sees parallels to denominational differences. Yet crucial differences remain. The new covenant teaches that false teachers or heretics are disciplined by disfellowshipping them from the assembly (Titus 3:10), not beheading them. Christians do not rely on civil force to stifle unbelief or dissent. The presence of moderate and radical segments in Islam highlights an underlying tension: the Quran and the Hadith can be read to support either less intrusive social arrangements or a totalitarian theocracy. Ultimately, the question is whether the biblical template for how God's people should live in this final era is consistent with moderate or radical forms of Islam. The consistent answer is no. Biblical truths point to a spiritual kingdom, not a worldly empire.

A Christian Response: Discernment, Love, and Faithfulness

While acknowledging the complexities of Islam's worldview, particularly radical expressions, believers rooted in Scripture are called to maintain discernment (Philippians 1:9, 10). They reject the notion that jihad or forced subjugation reveals God's grace. They can, however, show compassion to individual Muslims, offering the gospel's invitation. They also remain vigilant about infiltration or coercive attempts that violate the freedom of worship central to biblical teaching. The Bible instructs that we speak truth with love (Ephesians 4:15), test every claim to see if it aligns with the gospel (1 John 4:1), and stand firm against destructive ideologies (2 Corinthians 10:5). Christians do not respond with hatred or counter-violence except in legitimate self-defense as permitted by civil law (Romans 13:4). Instead, they highlight that true peace arises only when hearts are transformed by Christ.

In contexts where radical Islam threatens public safety or fosters persecution, believers look to biblical examples of endurance under hostility (1 Peter 3:14, 15). They also pray for leaders to govern justly, punishing wrongdoers (1 Timothy 2:1, 2). Nonetheless, they refrain from demonizing all Muslims, remembering that many remain moderate or open to spiritual conversation. The key is balancing prudent awareness of radical infiltration with Christ-like compassion toward individuals. Scripture's main difference from radical Islam is that the cross overcame sin by self-sacrifice, not conquest. That hallmark sets the Christian worldview apart from any ideology contending that the sword can inaugurate divine rule.

Observing Modern Trends: Immigration and Birth Rates

Some radical theorists see a demographic strategy: with larger families and continuous immigration into Western countries, Muslim populations might eventually become dominant in certain regions. This is sometimes referred to as a silent jihad, leveraging liberal asylum policies or welfare systems. While moderate Muslims might be integrating peacefully, radicals celebrate the potential for incremental takeover without firing a shot. The biblical vantage point sees no parallel in Christian expansion. Indeed, the church expands by conversion, not fertility rates or infiltration. The new covenant fosters love in a local assembly, not a strategic push to overshadow the population. Still, it is not inherently wrong for families to be large. The question arises if the motivation is forcibly to reorient the host society under Sharia once numbers permit. That objective remains irreconcilable with the new covenant's ethic.

A Contrast: Scripture's Ending vs. Radical Islam's World Vision

Radical Islam's worldview typically envisions a final global domain, the ummah fully united under a restored caliph who implements Sharia in every land. Apostasy, blasphemy, or deviance from the prescribed norms face immediate penalty. This dream sets the stage for a nearly unstoppable dominion over the entire planet. By contrast, the new covenant outlines a future where Christ returns to gather believers from all nations, establishing an eternal kingdom not built by human hands (2 Peter 3:13; Revelation 21:1-4). The route to that kingdom is spiritual transformation, culminating in God's final judgment of the wicked. Believers do not take up arms to realize it. The biblical model shows that the meek inherit the earth, not by jihad, but by God's direct intervention (Matthew 5:5). This divergence underscores that the radical Islamic worldview does not continue the biblical storyline but rewrites the final act of salvation history.

The Ideological Core of Radical Islam: Denying the Cross

Beneath the focus on warfare and Sharia is the more profound theological rift: denial of Jesus as God's Son or the atoning death on the cross. Radical Muslims interpret Quranic passages that reject Christ's crucifixion (Sura 4:157) as central to their belief. The entire biblical message, from Genesis onward, points to redemption through the Messiah's sacrifice (John 1:29; Hebrews 9:28). By rejecting this, Islam positions itself outside the redeemed covenant community. Radical or moderate, the worldview that denies the cross and relies on outward law-keeping cannot align with the new covenant's plan of salvation. Paul wrote: "We proclaim Christ executed on the stake, to the Jews a cause for stumbling but to the nations foolishness" (1 Corinthians 1:23). The radical pursuit of an earthly empire stands in tension with the cross's humility and God's invitation to all through free grace (Ephesians 2:8, 9).

Hence, the underlying impetus for jihad, or Sharia enforcement, does not flow from the cross but from a works-based system. In such a system, moral or ritual compliance supplants redemption by Christ's blood. While moderate Islam might downplay violent expansions, it still upholds a theology that denies the gospel's core. If one understands that the cross is central to the biblical worldview, any system rejecting that atonement cannot be from God, whether it employs force or not. The radical approach simply accentuates the inherent conflict with biblical truth by actively persecuting believers or seeking to quell gospel preaching.

Conclusion

The worldview of Islam, including its radical expressions, reveals an inherent drive toward reestablishing the earliest form of the religion. Radical Muslim groups, referencing the Quran and the Prophet's example, interpret these sources literally, concluding that violent jihad, forced conversions, and strict enforcement of Sharia remain valid to unify the planet under God's law. Contrasting this militant ambition with the biblical storyline illuminates a fundamental incompatibility. Scripture culminates in Christ's revelation of a spiritual kingdom, advanced by preaching and rooted in sacrificial love, not by the sword. The old covenant's physical wars were never mandated as a global campaign to endure through all time. Rather, they served a temporary function until the Messiah. Jesus explicitly forbade using violence for his kingdom's cause, commanding love for enemies and teaching that his realm is "no part of this world" (John 18:36).

Radical Muslims, by intensifying the impetus to impose Sharia on entire societies, highlight the difference between Islam's prescriptive worldview and the new covenant's relational ethic of free acceptance. Even moderate Muslims, who disclaim violent methods, still share crucial doctrines that undermine the cross. Without affirming Christ's atoning sacrifice, they remain outside the new covenant, though they may coexist more peaceably. Radical expansions, infiltration strategies, or demographic takeovers underscore how deeply Islam's socio-political model diverges from the apostolic witness of purely spiritual warfare. Christians, guided by Scripture, can stand in truth and love—exposing violent ideologies, defending genuine religious freedom, and offering the gospel's invitation to all. The biblical hope remains that hearts can be changed by Christ, not forced into submission by human decrees or militant zeal. Where radical Islam seeks an earthly reign through compulsion, the new covenant points to a heavenly reign achieved by Jesus' resurrection power (Romans 1:4; 1 Peter 1:3, 4). In that sense, the modern push of radical Islam, though formidable, cannot supplant the saving grace accomplished at the cross.

Edward D. Andrews

CHAPTER 9 Does Radical Islamic Eschatology Clash With Scriptural End-Times Hope?

The eschatological ideas of radical and fundamentalist Islamists have long captured the attention of believers and secular observers alike. News outlets constantly highlight that some extremists invoke eschatology—an end-times vision—to fuel violence or to justify relentless expansion. Many recall that Islamic armies swept over vast territories from the seventh century onward, forging mighty caliphates. Later eras witnessed smaller revivals, but the modern resurgence of militant groups has provoked global concern. At the core is the question: do radical Islamists believe they can hasten the apocalypse through jihad? Are their doctrines truly grounded in the Quran and the Hadith, or are they innovative distortions? For Christians who hold to the new covenant scriptures, the question becomes whether these militant visions align with biblical teaching or contradict the final revelation found in Christ.

Christians know that the old covenant, given through Moses, eventually led to the new covenant sealed by Jesus' sacrifice (Matthew 26:28). By that new covenant, God's people stand distinct from the world, not forging theocratic empires or waging holy wars. Rather, they await the return of Christ and the final victory he secures (2 Thessalonians 1:6-10). In contrast, many radical Islamic groups foresee an earthly domain culminating in an ultimate clash where the "righteous" triumph, establishing a universal caliphate. Many also expect a Mahdi—a "guided one" who rules over an Islamic empire—and the return of Jesus (in the Arabic name ʿĪsa) to complete the conquest of infidels. In such a scenario, the entire planet is meant to submit to Sharia, from which no dissent is tolerated. This worldview can incite fervor, intensifying efforts for immediate expansion through terror or infiltration.

In exploring these themes, it is vital to consider that not all Muslims share the same eschatological outlook. Just as Christendom exhibits widely varied doctrinal stands, Islam too contains numerous sects and theological stances. Many ordinary Muslims do not dwell on end-time speculation, focusing instead on daily devotions. Still, fundamentalist Islamists derive impetus from a literal reading of the Quran and Hadith, convinced that reestablishing the early purity of Islam, culminating in a global caliphate, is the divinely decreed path. This chapter delves into these radical visions, highlighting how some groups see modern warfare—often in the form of terror—as a means to spark the chain of events leading to the Day of Judgment. It also compares these notions with Scripture's portrayal of how God's plan for the end of this age unfolds. Does the radical Islamist scenario find resonance in the Bible's revelation of eschatology, or does it stand in stark opposition to the new covenant's hope?

Varied Islamic End-Time Scenarios

Islamic eschatology, known in Arabic as "'Ilm al-Akhir," includes the broad notion that humankind proceeds toward a final reckoning, culminating in a Day of Resurrection. Though there are differences between Sunni and Shi'ite streams, certain core elements consistently appear: the coming of the Mahdi (for Shi'ites, he may be the Twelfth Imam who disappeared centuries ago), the return of 'Isa (Jesus) to assist him, the final conflict against an Antichrist-like figure called the Dajjal, and the subsequent establishing of an era of justice before Judgment arrives. Many devout Muslims hold these beliefs quietly, reading apocalyptic hadith that depict cosmic upheavals. However, radical groups do more than passively believe; they seek to expedite or facilitate this ultimate conflict.

A large portion of Islam sees the world as divided between the realm of Islam (Dar al-Islam) and the realm of war (Dar al-Harb). This dichotomy fosters the notion that it is not only permissible, but at times mandatory, to wage war against perceived infidels until they submit (Sura 9:5; Sura 2:193). For radicals, these suras are not relics of the seventh century but living mandates that must be obeyed today.

Hence, the path to the final era inevitably involves conquest or forced submission, culminating in the universal application of Sharia. From that vantage point, the Day of Judgment stands as the ultimate horizon, but it is ushered in by actively fighting those who resist. Meanwhile, moderate Muslims may interpret such texts figuratively or as contextual to Muhammad's era. Radical adherents, convinced of a plain reading, approach eschatology as a blueprint requiring immediate fulfillment.

Though some schools emphasize spiritual preparation—repentance, moral conduct—others interpret certain events as triggers for the end. This viewpoint leads them to see modern crises, whether political or environmental, as signs confirming that the hour is near. The impetus to reestablish the caliphate in Jerusalem, known in radical circles, resonates with hadith references to battles at "Dabiq" or "Ghuta," among others. The extremist group ISIS famously named its propaganda magazine "Dabiq," reflecting the prophecy that a final confrontation near that location in Syria preludes victory over nonbelievers. By naming it so, they signaled their conviction that eschatological events are not distant but imminent.

The Twelfth Imam or Mahdi

Of central significance is the figure known as the Mahdi. Within Sunni Islam, the Mahdi might be an awaited reformer or leader who appears near the last days, guiding Muslims to renewed piety and confronting the forces of evil. Shiʿite Islam, especially its largest branch known as the Twelvers, identifies the Mahdi as the Twelfth Imam, a hidden child purportedly born in 869 C.E. who vanished under mysterious circumstances. They hold that he remains in occultation, concealed by God, until the appointed time when he will reemerge to restore justice. In both traditions, the Mahdi is integral to the final fulfillment of Islam's global ascendancy.

Much of the modern Iranian regime's theology revolves around the Twelfth Imam's eventual unveiling, sometimes fueling grand or apocalyptic rhetoric. Radical factions such as certain elements in the Iranian Revolutionary Guard see themselves as catalysts for the Mahdi's return, believing they must prepare an environment conducive to his dominion. They will sabotage or attack perceived enemies of

Islam, hoping to provoke an end-time showdown that prompts the Mahdi's arrival. These convictions differ from the biblical approach, which never instructs believers to create conflagrations to hasten Christ's return. Instead, Scripture teaches that God alone fixes the times and seasons (Acts 1:7). The attempt to manipulate global events to provoke a final savior figure stands entirely outside the new covenant's teaching.

Across the broader Muslim world, this Mahdi concept retains widespread acceptance, though degrees of emphasis vary. Radical groups see the reappearance of the Mahdi as an immediate impetus. Meanwhile, moderate or secular-minded Muslims might relegate the idea to future providence, not something to be forcibly enacted. The stark difference is that the radicals interpret the hadith calling for an Islamic dominion, ironically reminiscent of old covenant expansions but extended globally. This impetus spurs them to stage lethal attacks, even courting global war, in the belief that if the conflict intensifies sufficiently, the prophesied redeemer will step in. The biblical vantage point on the Messiah's second coming refutes attempts to jumpstart the end times by mortal actions (Matthew 24:36). Jesus consistently taught watchfulness, not forced warfare, as the posture of those awaiting his return.

The Role of ʿĪsa (Jesus) in Islamic Eschatology

It surprises many Christians to learn that Jesus (ʿĪsa) occupies a pivotal place in Muslim end-time scenarios. Muslims widely affirm that ʿĪsa is a true prophet. According to certain hadith, he returns in the last days to support the Mahdi, break the cross (symbolically humiliating Christianity), kill the swine (often interpreted as outlawing forbidden foods or humiliating those who eat them), and abolish the jizya tax because all peoples will have embraced Islam. In these narratives, ʿĪsa is not the Son of God or the crucified Savior—those beliefs are rejected by the Quran (Sura 4:157). Instead, he becomes a subordinate figure, assisting the Mahdi to fully eradicate idolatry. The final stage is total Islamization of the globe.

This portrayal conflicts with biblical teaching on the second coming of Christ (Matthew 24:30). Scripture never depicts Jesus as returning to affirm a new prophet or to wage an earthly war that forcibly universalizes a single religion. Rather, he appears in glory to judge the living and the dead (2 Timothy 4:1). When Jesus spoke of signs of the end, he explained that lawlessness would increase, and the gospel would be preached in all nations (Matthew 24:12-14). The apostles, addressing Christ's return, insisted that believers anticipate a new heavens and new earth where righteousness dwells (2 Peter 3:13). No biblical text envisions Jesus as a second-tier champion under a Mahdi, nor does it suggest that all must convert or be slain. Instead, final judgment belongs to Christ, who separates sheep from goats based on faith and righteousness (Matthew 25:31-46). The violent, triumphant portrayal in Islamic eschatology denies the cross's atoning significance, reworking Jesus into a jihadist figure who assists in imposing Sharia. This redefinition underscores a theological chasm between radical Islam and new covenant Christianity.

Dajjal, the Islamic Antichrist

In radical Islamic traditions, a figure known as the Dajjal emerges as a false messiah or deceiver who leads many astray before the Mahdi and ʿĪsa defeat him. The Dajjal is often portrayed in hadith as a one-eyed charlatan performing wonders to trick people into worship. He spreads corruption and falsehood, only to be vanquished once the righteous forces unite. This narrative parallels biblical references to an Antichrist figure who exalts himself in the temple of God (2 Thessalonians 2:3-4). Christians identify a "man of lawlessness" or a "beast" described in Revelation 13, who performs deceptive signs. Yet the resolution of that rebellion belongs solely to Christ at his glorious coming (2 Thessalonians 2:8). The difference is that, in radical Islam, the immediate impetus includes mortal jihad as a catalyst for defeating the Dajjal, culminating in Sharia based rule. In Scripture, believers do not wage earthly war to overthrow the man of lawlessness. They remain steadfast, awaiting Christ's direct intervention. Thus, the radical Islamic approach to the Dajjal fosters an active, militant posture, whereas the new covenant fosters patient endurance in faith.

Contrasts with Biblical End-Times Teaching

The new covenant's eschatology revolves around Jesus' promised return, the resurrection of the dead, and the final judgment. It never hints that believers should attempt to bring about Armageddon by force or manipulate global conflicts to usher in the second coming. Jesus declared: "My kingdom is no part of this world" (John 18:36). He also taught that no one knows the day or hour but the Father (Matthew 24:36). The biblical role of believers is to remain watchful, proclaim the gospel, and exhibit love and holiness. By contrast, radical Islamic movements see an opportunity to hasten the final confrontation. Some groups, like ISIS, have openly boasted that they hope to provoke large-scale war with Western powers, anticipating that chaos will accelerate the final conflict. That is why ISIS rhetoric includes references to Dabiq, the location identified in hadith as a site of an epic battle between believers and "Rome" (often symbolizing Christian-led forces).

In the biblical record, the final cataclysm known as Armageddon is orchestrated by Jehovah and carried out by Christ leading heavenly armies (Revelation 16:14, 16; 19:11-21). Humans do not incite it, nor do they direct it. The Christian role is spiritual vigilance (1 Thessalonians 5:1-6). Meanwhile, radical Muslims interpret their eschatological texts as a call to arms, uniting believers in jihad. For them, the outcome is the subjugation or destruction of unbelievers, and the enthronement of the Mahdi. From a Christian standpoint, such a worldview subverts the cross's message of redemption and contravenes the new covenant's reliance on God's timing. The difference is stark: biblical revelation is forward-looking but passive concerning the final cosmic war's onset, trusting the Almighty's sovereignty. Radical Islamist ideology sees humanity, specifically devout Muslims, as the active agents who can accelerate or directly bring about that final confrontation.

Ties to Violent Jihad as an Eschatological Duty

When radical Islamist organizations engage in bombings or mass executions, they often label these acts as jihad fulfilling end-times prophecies. For instance, Al Qaeda sought to eliminate Western influences from Islamic lands, framing it as a step toward purifying the ummah so the Mahdi can appear. ISIS similarly declared its caliphate in parts of Iraq and Syria, imposing a harsh reading of Sharia, convinced this domain set the stage for the final battles. The group's propaganda recruited foreign fighters by appealing to apocalyptic fervor: "You can help realize the prophecy of the revived caliphate."

Such a viewpoint interprets the old expansions of Islam as a partial fulfillment that must be replicated on a global scale. Parallels to biblical prophecy—like the old covenant wars—are misleading, because Scripture never taught indefinite expansion culminating in forced conversions. Radical Islam's approach diverges from the new covenant approach of free acceptance into the body of believers by faith. The Christian sees no theological basis for forcibly building an empire to quicken the end times. Indeed, the notion of a theocratic empire was tied to ancient Israel, and even that was temporary, pointing forward to a spiritual kingdom in Christ. The jihad-centered approach attempts to restore a seventh-century Arabian template as if that pattern is timeless and universal. For new covenant believers, that directly contradicts the law of Christ, who taught, "Put your sword back into its place. For all who take the sword will perish by the sword" (Matthew 26:52).

Implications for Modern Geopolitics and Terrorism

Islamic radical eschatology has tangible ramifications. Groups that adopt these convictions might attempt to seize territories or commit terror attacks in the West, hoping to galvanize a broader conflict. They foresee a cosmic war that, from their vantage point, is beneficial in accelerating prophecy. Western societies, anchored in secular or pluralistic values, struggle to comprehend this worldview, often attributing extremist acts to mere socio-political grievances. Yet the theological underpinnings cannot be dismissed. The biblical perspective acknowledges that spiritual deception can motivate destructive behavior (1 Timothy 4:1). A robust Christian apologetic must recognize that radical Islam's impetus is not purely political or economic but also deeply religious, driven by the end-times narrative. Political solutions alone might not suffice if the underlying dogma remains unaddressed.

Additionally, moderate Muslims can be torn between rejecting terror as un-Islamic and acknowledging that classical texts do reference an ultimate victory over unbelievers. Many disclaim the radical methods but do not necessarily repudiate the concept of a future universal Sharia. The tension fosters ideological battles within the Muslim community. A Christian who reads Scripture might empathize with Muslims seeking to reform or interpret the violent hadith allegorically. Yet from a purely biblical vantage, no matter how moderate or radical, the entire system denies Christ's atoning death and the new covenant's final revelation (John 14:6; 1 John 5:11, 12). No measure of reformation can rectify that core theological conflict.

How Radical Islamist Eschatology Conflicts with the New Covenant

Christian theology presents a cohesive storyline from Genesis to Revelation. It culminates in Jesus' sacrificial victory, his commission to make disciples, and the promise of his personal return to judge. Nowhere does the new covenant propose that believers forcibly unify the globe. Instead, it warns of a final outbreak of rebellion that Jesus alone defeats (2 Thessalonians 2:8). The approach taught by radical Islam inverts that pattern, championing a final war orchestrated by believers to subdue unbelievers until the Mahdi or Twelfth Imam rules. Meanwhile, Jesus is relegated to a supportive figure, stripping him of his identity as the divine Son of God. The cross's significance is denied, replaced by a ritualistic and militant system.

Comparisons with the old covenant might mislead, since Israel's wars were historically confined and validated by miraculous signs, never intended for indefinite replication. Jesus insisted that with his coming, a new approach was instituted (Luke 16:16). The Great Commission bids disciples to preach the gospel of grace, not wage physical wars (Matthew 28:19, 20). Radicals, by blending eschatology with an archaic expansionism, produce a worldview irreconcilable with the cross's peace ethic. Paul wrote that believers "do not wage warfare according to what we are in the flesh" (2 Corinthians 10:3, 4). That principle thoroughly clashes with calls for terror bombings or forced conversions. Hence, from a conservative biblical stance, radical Islamic eschatology stands outside the realm of God's truth.

The Imam Mahdi, Armageddon, and Modern Conflict

Some radical Muslims equate the final confrontation between the Mahdi's forces and the unbelievers with an Armageddon-like scenario.

They believe the impetus lies with them, not with God, to initiate conflict. In Scripture, Armageddon belongs to Jehovah, who gathers the nations for a final display of his wrath (Revelation 16:14, 16). The Lamb of God descends with heavenly armies to judge the beast and the false prophet (Revelation 19:11-21). Humanity does not orchestrate these events. Meanwhile, radical Islam posits an entirely different chain of events—human-led jihad triggers the final cataclysm. This difference cannot be harmonized. The new covenant proclaims that the Lamb's victory is supernatural, not driven by an earthly caliph or a prophet.

Moreover, biblical Armageddon entails a universal unveiling of Christ's glory, after which a new heaven and new earth come forth (Revelation 21:1-4). Radical Islam imagines a future of strictly enforced Sharia over a worldly empire, with any remaining unbelievers subdued or executed. The final Day of Judgment follows once the Mahdi's era ends. The result is an outwardly uniform religious state. For believers abiding by the new covenant, the promise is that Christ returns to transform the creation, eradicating sin permanently from hearts, not by subjugation but by divine authority. The radical Islamic concept of forcibly unifying the world under a seventh-century code is neither the biblical new heavens and earth nor the kingdom of Christ, which is "righteousness and peace and joy" (Romans 14:17).

Radicalism, Terror, and the West's Responses

Western governments, confronted by terror or infiltration from radical cells, frequently fail to grasp that the violence stems from a coherent end-times worldview. Diplomacy or concessions will not satisfy those who see themselves as fulfilling prophecy. Their zeal, fueled by hadith illusions, interprets compromise as weakness, emboldening further aggression. The new covenant does not direct Christians to wage holy wars in retaliation. Romans 13:4 does allow governments to bear the sword for punishing evildoers. Thus, the state can justly respond to terror with force. Yet believers must remain vigilant that they do not confuse a biblical sense of moral order with adopting an anti-Muslim prejudice. They differentiate between legitimate self-defense under secular authorities and the gospel's call to love enemies individually (Matthew 5:44).

In the Christian worldview, the real struggle is not against flesh and blood but against principalities and spiritual forces that blind minds (Ephesians 6:12). Radical Islamist eschatology arises from a spiritual deception that exalts violence as piety. Christians can continue proclaiming Christ's redemptive message, knowing that some radicalized individuals have converted after encountering the truth of the gospel. Nonetheless, a society that cherishes freedom must stand firm against acts of terror. Meanwhile, believers trust that the final outcome rests in God's hands, not in stirring conflict. Where radicals see war as indispensable to usher in the last days, Christians see patient endurance and faithful witness until the appointed time (Matthew 24:13, 14).

The West's Liberal Progressive Culture as a Catalyst?

Some radical Muslims argue that Western liberalism—emphasizing permissiveness, secularism, and moral relativism—has inadvertently validated their condemnation of Western society as decadent. They exploit Western tolerance, ironically using it to operate freely. While moderate Muslims integrate into liberal democracies, radicals leverage freedom of speech and movement to recruit or raise funds. Then, extremist leaders portray the immorality of Western pop culture or moral laxness as proof that only Islam can restore virtue. For the radical eschatologist, the West stands as a domain ripe for infiltration and eventual overthrow, consistent with the prophecy that unbelieving societies must fall before the final triumph of Islam.

From the vantage point of biblical Christians, moral degradation is a genuine concern—Scripture warns that many will call evil good and good evil (Isaiah 5:20). However, the gospel solution is not imposing external strictures. Salvation arises from inward regeneration by faith in Christ (Ephesians 2:8). The radical Islamist approach conflates moral corruption with a license for violent subjugation. Biblical teachings maintain that a society's moral failings do not excuse terror or forced conversions. Indeed, even among morally compromised communities, the Christian approach is to preach the good news, aiming for repentance, not to unleash armies or bombs. Hence, while radical Islam claims that liberal culture necessitates jihad,

Scripture upholds that only God's grace can solve moral decline, not the scourge of militant theocracy.

Efficacy of Trying to Convert or "Deradicalize" Through Debate

Many Western observers propose that radical Muslims might be deradicalized through education or job opportunities. Others attempt theological arguments, hoping to reinterpret certain hadith to reduce militancy. Yet if radicals see themselves as fulfilling eschatological prophecy, rational appeals often fail. They believe God's Word stands supreme over any human treaties, empathy, or compromise. The biblical record suggests that hearts deeply entrenched in erroneous worship require divine intervention to be freed from deception (Acts 26:18). While believers can pray for miraculous transformations, the unyielding convictions of radical jihadists can remain unmoved. Some might indeed come to faith in Christ, forsaking violence. But many cling to a worldview in which violent jihad is not merely permissible but a form of ultimate devotion.

In the new covenant, the impetus is to love even enemies (Matthew 5:44). That does not equate to passive acceptance of terror. Societies can legitimately defend themselves (Romans 13:1-5). Christian outreach might focus on those less entrenched, or on families of radicals, shining a light on the new covenant's better promises. However, the success of such efforts depends on the Holy Spirit's convicting power. The purely rational or political approach often collides with the unwavering fervor radical Islamist eschatology instills. This scenario highlights that the conflict is not just about territory or politics; it is spiritual at root, as the new covenant consistently affirms (2 Corinthians 10:4).

The Future of Islamist Eschatology and Biblical Assurance

Examining the momentum behind radical Islamic eschatology, some foresee continued cycles of insurgency, terror, or attempts at establishing local caliphates. Even if certain groups like ISIS fade, the ideological seeds remain. From a biblical standpoint, none of these efforts can derail God's ultimate plan. Psalm 2:1-4 depicts nations raging in vain against Jehovah's anointed. The global stage might witness pockets of intense conflict, but believers stand assured that Christ's victory is unshakable. The day of the Lord will not be triggered by human war strategies but by God's fixed decree (2 Peter 3:9, 10).

Thus, while radical Islam exalts a vision of forcibly unifying the planet, culminating in an ephemeral Sharia-based regime, the new covenant invests hope in the resurrected Messiah returning in due season to judge and restore. Christians rest in that promise, refusing to mirror radical violence or to compromise the gospel. They show compassion to Muslims of all shades, radical or moderate, testifying that "there is no salvation in anyone else," but in Jesus (Acts 4:12). The love of Christ remains a powerful witness, even in regions overshadowed by extremist theology. Meanwhile, radical groups might continue to interpret every political event as a sign that final confrontation nears, but believers recall that Jesus forewarned of many false alarms, urging watchfulness and readiness (Matthew 24:23-27).

Concluding Thoughts

Radical and fundamentalist Islamists derive from an eschatological framework that envisions a last-days scenario culminating in the arrival or reemergence of the Mahdi, the supportive role of 'Īsa (Jesus), and the overthrow of unbelievers by means of jihad. This worldview contrasts pointedly with biblical prophecy, which hinges on Christ's personal return to consummate history in a spiritual manner, not on warfare executed by a caliphate. Where radical Islam sees mortal duty to spark apocalyptic chaos, the new covenant preaches patience until the appointed time. Where radical Islam denies Jesus' crucifixion and enthrones him merely as an assistant to the Mahdi, Scripture proclaims that Jesus alone is King of kings, who overcame sin and death through the cross, and who will return to judge (Revelation 19:11-16).

For Christians, the presence of these eschatological beliefs in radical Islam underscores the urgent need to ground themselves in biblical truth. The global turmoil fueled by extremist interpretations highlights the difference between a faith that labors for the gospel's spread by peaceful persuasion and a movement seeking dominance through terror. The new covenant grants no license to forcibly bring about God's kingdom. Instead, believers patiently proclaim the cross, trusting God's sovereign plan for the end of this age. If radical Islam attempts to accelerate its apocalyptic drama, Christians remain assured that "the word of Jehovah endures forever" (Isaiah 40:8). The Lamb's victory is certain, undeterred by human warfare. Therefore, in light of radical Islamist eschatology, the Church perseveres in its mission, mindful that no ideology can thwart the ultimate outworking of Christ's redemption and final vindication (Revelation 11:15).

CHAPTER 10 Does Archaeological Discovery Confirm the Inspired Record?

Many sincere readers have asked whether archaeological findings in Bible lands really prove that the Bible is more than just an ancient text. Archaeological efforts, especially from the mid-nineteenth century onward, have yielded an abundance of evidence: coins bearing the names of biblical rulers, engraved stelae referencing events described in Scripture, and entire ancient cities whose ruins correspond precisely with the biblical narratives. While our faith as believers rests on the Word of God rather than on human excavations, these archaeological discoveries often strengthen our conviction that the Bible is historically reliable and truly inspired. The fact that many secular archaeologists, sometimes with no sympathy for conservative theology, have uncovered data that align with the biblical account intensifies the sense that the events recorded in Scripture genuinely happened. Further, it reveals how the people, places, and cultures described in the pages of the Bible fit seamlessly within the historical and geographical realities of the Middle East.

Archaeology itself remains a field of exploration, uncovering artifacts such as pottery, inscriptions, clay tablets, coins, and building remains. Interpreting these relics can be subjective, and at times earlier conclusions have been revised by subsequent findings. Yet far from undermining the Bible, archaeology has repeatedly converged with it, illustrating that the references to kings, battles, social customs, and city gates presented in Scripture are anchored in concrete realities. Archaeology does not create faith, since faith is "the assured expectation of things hoped for" (Hebrews 11:1). Even so, sincere researchers appreciate how archaeological evidence clarifies local practices in biblical times, illuminates the reliability of chronological statements, and shows that scriptural narratives reflect accurate knowledge of events and places. The Hebrew Scriptures and the

Christian Greek Scriptures alike have benefited from these external confirmations. This chapter surveys some notable examples in which archaeology intersects with biblical texts, strengthening our understanding that God's Word stands unshaken despite centuries of debate.

Archaeology and the Hebrew Scriptures

The opening books of the Bible describe pivotal events such as the creation of mankind, the global Flood, the dispersion at Babel, and the call of Abraham. Although some of these events predate the earliest known civilizations that have left written records, archaeologists focusing on Genesis onward have found a wealth of data showing the advanced culture and intercity trade of Mesopotamia and the broader region, consistent with the environment described in the patriarchal accounts. Excavations at cities like Ur, Mari, Nuzi, and Haran have revealed libraries of cuneiform tablets, inscriptions detailing legal customs resembling those in Genesis, and extensive trade routes that confirm how Abraham and his family could have migrated northward, then south into Canaan. While one must read these data carefully, the cumulative evidence supports that the patriarchal era is not mythic but stands in line with known Bronze Age norms.

The Tower of Babel and the Rise of Cities

Genesis chapter 11 describes the Tower of Babel as a grand construction project in the land of Shinar, culminating in a sudden confusion of language that scattered humankind. For centuries, scholars dismissed this as myth, but archaeological excavations in and around Babylon revealed ziggurats, stepped temple-towers that soared high above flat Mesopotamian plains. Inscribed records from Babylonia sometimes use language reminiscent of "its top in the heavens." One ancient text says of such a tower: "Its top shall rival the heavens." Another surviving fragment alludes to a tower's partial collapse, describing how "in a single night they threw down what had been built" and forcibly scattered those who labored there. Though not precisely paralleling the biblical event, these references confirm that massive temple-towers existed in Mesopotamia. The memory of a catastrophic disruption resonates with the biblical depiction of

Jehovah thwarting that monument to human self-glorification (Genesis 11:1-9). While archaeologists do not produce direct inscriptions reading "This is the Tower of Babel," the existence of enormous ziggurats, famously including Etemenanki within Babylon's walls, highlights that the biblical tradition of an ambitious tower in Shinar corresponds to known Mesopotamian building practices.

The Water Tunnels at the Spring of Gihon

The Hebrew Scriptures often mention Jerusalem's water supply, key to the city's survival. Second Samuel 5:6-10 depicts how David's men penetrated the fortress of Zion, apparently through a water conduit. In 1867, the British engineer and archaeologist Charles Warren discovered a vertical shaft carved into rock near the Gihon spring, connecting a subterranean water channel to higher ground within the city. Later, further excavations uncovered a labyrinth of tunnels and a massive channel more than 1,700 feet in length, cut through solid stone. Scholars identify this as Hezekiah's tunnel, constructed to bring water from Gihon inside the city walls, thus shielding the supply from enemy siege (2 Kings 20:20; 2 Chronicles 32:30; Isaiah 22:9, 11). Workers found a Hebrew inscription in that tunnel, describing how two teams of quarrymen cut from opposite ends until they heard each other's picks, uniting the passage to guide water to the Pool of Siloam. This discovery dramatically verifies the scriptural narrative of Hezekiah's waterworks, attesting to the skill and resilience of Judah's engineers in the face of Assyrian invasion.

The Military Campaigns of Shishak

The Old Testament records that King Shishak (Sheshonk I) of Egypt invaded Judah in Rehoboam's time because the king and the people abandoned Jehovah (1 Kings 14:25, 26; 2 Chronicles 12:1-12). Shishak is said to have captured many fortified cities, though Jerusalem itself was spared full devastation. For a while, only the Bible mentioned this event, but modern archaeology has uncovered inscriptions in the Karnak temple near Thebes showing King Sheshonk's conquests in Canaan, listing around 150 localities, many of which the Bible references (such as Beth-shean, Taanach, Rehob, Gibeon, and Megiddo). These hieroglyphic records depict bound prisoners representing conquered cities, each labeled with the city's name.

Although Egyptian scribes do not detail Jerusalem's tribute payment or the humiliating capitulation, the biblical account of Shishak's invasion stands independently confirmed, reinforcing that the scriptural references to a massive Egyptian incursion into Judah are authentic (2 Chronicles 12:2-9).

The Moabite Stone and King Mesha

Second Kings 3:4-27 recounts how King Mesha of Moab rebelled against Israel after Ahab's death, provoking conflict with Jehoram. This story was once known solely from Scripture. Then, in 1868, a missionary in Dhiban (biblical Dibon) in Moab discovered a large black basalt stone inscribed with ancient Semitic writing. Known as the Moabite Stone or Mesha Stele, it recounted Mesha's version of his revolt, mentioning Omri and citing the God of Moab, Chemosh, who supposedly gave him victory over Israel. The text states: "I, Mesha, son of Chemosh-[...], king of Moab from Dibon... Omri, king of Israel, oppressed Moab many days... His son followed him, and he too said, 'I will oppress Moab,' but I triumphed over him." Notably, the Tetragrammaton (the divine name Jehovah in Hebrew letters) appears in line 18, referencing vessels of "YHWH" captured by Moab. This historically significant artifact directly corroborates the existence of the Moabite revolt and the interplay between Moab and Israel in the ninth century B.C.E. It even references multiple towns likewise named in Joshua, Isaiah, and Jeremiah (Numbers 21:29, 2 Kings 3:4, 5, 21-27).

Sennacherib's Prism

Second Kings 18:13 through 19:37 describes the invasion of Judah by Assyrian King Sennacherib in 732 B.C.E., culminating in the siege of Jerusalem. The prophet Isaiah was present, and Scripture details how the angel of Jehovah destroyed 185,000 Assyrian soldiers in one night, forcing Sennacherib's retreat (2 Kings 19:35, 36). Modern excavations at Nineveh, led by Sir Austen Henry Layard in the mid-nineteenth century, revealed Sennacherib's palace with tens of thousands of inscribed clay tablets. Among them is the Taylor Prism (or Sennacherib's Prism), in which the Assyrian king records his third campaign, claiming he laid siege to 46 of Hezekiah's fortified cities. He omits mention of his disastrous defeat at Jerusalem, but he does say, "Hezekiah himself I locked up like a caged bird in Jerusalem." This partial testimony from the enemy side, though silent about the catastrophic loss, confirms essential details: Sennacherib's invasion of Judah, Hezekiah's rebellion, and the tribute extracted before that final confrontation. Once more, archaeology buttresses the biblical account, this time from the vantage point of the conquering empire.

The Lachish Letters

Lachish, located southwest of Jerusalem, was a major fortress city in Judah. Jeremiah 34:7 states that Lachish and Azekah were among the last strongholds before the Babylonian conquest. In 1935, archaeologists found 18 inscribed pottery fragments (plus 3 more in 1938) at the gate of ancient Lachish. Written in ancient Hebrew, these ostraca are dispatches from an outpost to a commanding officer named Yaosh at Lachish, dated around 609 to 607 B.C.E. They mention watchers looking for signal fires from Lachish and Azekah, apparently discovering that Azekah had fallen. One letter reads, "We cannot see the signals of Azekah." The biblical detail that Azekah survived almost until Jerusalem's downfall is thus corroborated. Another letter references the name Elnathan, also found in Jeremiah 36:12, and the name Hoshaiah, paralleling references in Jeremiah 42:1. The repeated appearances of biblical names and the presence of the Tetragrammaton in these letters show that everyday correspondence in Judah used Jehovah's name and reflect the tense final days before Babylon triumphed.

Babylon's Fall and the Nabonidus Chronicle

Daniel 5 recounts Belshazzar's feast, the handwriting on the wall, and the city's downfall to the Medes and Persians. Critics once doubted Belshazzar's existence, but cuneiform tablets verified he was co-regent with his father Nabonidus. The Nabonidus Chronicle, discovered in Mesopotamian ruins, logs how Nabonidus fled as Persian forces advanced, culminating in Babylon's capture without major battle in 539 B.C.E. The Chronicle indicates the city fell in Tishri (October), consistent with Daniel 5:30, 31, where Belshazzar was killed. The text also mentions Gobryas (Ugbaru) as the Persian general who entered Babylon ahead of Cyrus. Though it omits Darius the Mede (mentioned at Daniel 5:31), many surmise he might be either an alternate name for Gobryas or a subsequent figure. Regardless, the documents from

---

Babylon's final days confirm the timeframe Daniel gives and match the biblical depiction of an abrupt change of rule. Further tablets, like the Cyrus Cylinder, reveal Cyrus' policy of repatriating exiled peoples, aligning with the biblical account of his decree allowing Jews to return to rebuild the temple (2 Chronicles 36:22, 23).

Archaeology and the Christian Greek Scriptures

The second section of the Bible, from Matthew to Revelation, frequently references Roman officials, local magistrates, and city designations across the eastern Mediterranean. Scholars once disparaged Luke's mention of obscure political terms or out-of-the-way towns, suspecting errors. Archaeology reversed these suspicions, showing that the author of Luke and Acts was a remarkably precise historian.

Coins and Inscriptions in the Gospels

In Mark 12:13-17, the Pharisees tested Jesus about paying taxes to Caesar. Jesus requested a denarius coin, noting Caesar's image on it. Archaeologists have identified a silver denarius minted by Tiberius Caesar, used in that period after 14 C.E. The question of whose image was upon the coin is thus historically plausible, since Tiberius' effigy circulated widely. This small artifact underscores how the Gospels reflect genuine first-century monetary systems. Elsewhere, a partial inscription from a building dedicated by Roman prefect Pontius Pilate was found at Caesarea, reading "Pontius Pilate...prefect of Judea." This find anchors Pilate as a real historical figure, as described in the Gospels (Matthew 27:2, 11-26).

The Areopagus Where Paul Spoke

Acts 17:19-34 recounts Paul's sermon at the Areopagus, or Mars' Hill, in Athens around 50 C.E. The Areopagus is an outcropping of rock northwest of the Acropolis, still visible today. Steps hewn into the rock lead up to a flat area with seats carved into stone, presumably used by the council. This feature is consistent with Luke's statement that certain philosophers brought Paul to the Areopagus to hear his new teaching. Visitors to Athens can stand on that hill, further verifying the accuracy of Luke's geographical references.

The Arch of Titus and Jerusalem's Fall

Jesus in Matthew 24:2 prophesied the destruction of the Jerusalem temple: "By no means will a stone be left here upon a stone." That prophecy was fulfilled in 70 C.E. when Roman armies under Titus razed Jerusalem. The Arch of Titus in Rome, built after Titus' death, commemorates his triumph. The bas-reliefs along the arch's passage show Roman soldiers carrying the menorah (seven-branched lampstand) and other sacred vessels from the Jewish temple. This silent witness, standing in Rome's Forum, confirms the biblical mention of the city's downfall and the temple's spoils. It remains an iconic piece of art that depicts Roman victory over the Jews, consistent with Jesus' predictions that not one stone would be left upon another (Matthew 24:1-2).

The Relevance of Lysanias, Politarchs, and the Proconsuls

An underlying theme in Luke-Acts is the writer's knowledge of precise political structures. Luke mentions Lysanias as tetrarch of Abilene (Luke 3:1). Critics once alleged no tetrarch named Lysanias existed. Archaeological inscriptions now confirm the existence of a Lysanias as tetrarch in that region near Damascus at the correct time. Similarly, in Acts 17:6, local authorities in Thessalonica are called "city rulers," literally politarchs. Ancient Greek literature never used that term, so skeptics claimed an error—until inscriptions were discovered in Thessalonica's arches referencing the politarch title. Acts 13:7 calls Sergius Paulus the "proconsul" of Cyprus, aligning with the fact that at that date, Cyprus had been returned to Senate administration. That historical nuance changed frequently, so Luke's mention of proconsul indicates a narrow window when such a title was correct. Over and over, archaeology has validated Luke's painstaking fidelity to official designations.

Archaeology's Limitations and the Believer's Faith

Though archaeology repeatedly supports biblical authenticity, believers acknowledge that faith rests on Scripture, not on external artifacts. Archaeological interpretations can change as new layers of strata are uncovered or reevaluated. Some findings remain ambiguous or incomplete, generating multiple theories. Sincere Christians do not hinge their devotion on whether each site is definitively identified. Instead, they see in the repeated confirmations a pattern of remarkable accuracy, consistent with the conviction that "every saying of God is refined" (Proverbs 30:5). Moreover, the Bible's message of redemption, love, and hope extends far beyond historical details. It forms a cohesive revelation of God's dealings with humankind, culminating in the Christ. In that sense, archaeology merely provides ancillary evidence that the biblical narratives are not fables but trustworthy records of real events.

An honest approach recognizes that archaeology, like any science, has an interpretative dimension. For instance, certain researchers might claim a discovered city conflicts with a biblical date, yet subsequent reanalysis of pottery styles or carbon dating can lead to adjusted chronologies. Repeatedly, the biblical text emerges unsullied from earlier accusations. Thus, faithful students of Scripture do not become anxious when archaeologists or historians propose that some narrative "did not happen." They recall that "God cannot lie" (Titus 1:2), and they watch as new data frequently vindicate Scripture's reliability. Such was the case for Belshazzar in Daniel 5, dismissed as mythical until cuneiform inscriptions surfaced. Similarly, the existence of the Hittite empire, once regarded as a biblical invention, is now widely recognized, the fruit of numerous tablets and city excavations across modern Turkey.

Why the Bible Remains Supreme Over Other Texts

Amid all these confirmations of biblical authenticity, one might compare them with the relative lack of archaeological or textual verification for the Quran's historical references. While the Quran alludes to biblical figures, it does not consistently place them within known chronological frameworks, sometimes merging or confusing them. The archaeological record typically references the biblical accounts, especially concerning ancient Israel, Babylon, Persia, and the Roman world, not bridging a separate tradition akin to the Quran's recasting. This underscores that the biblical text stands in unique continuity with verifiable ancient civilizations. The same is true for other religious texts from the ancient Near East or the Greco-Roman realm: none replicate the scope or detail that the biblical record demonstrates. The prophecy in Isaiah 44:28 naming Cyrus about two centuries before his conquest of Babylon is unmatched. The synergy between the Moabite Stone, Sennacherib's annals, the Lachish ostraca, and the biblical story reveals a uniform authenticity.

Those who approach the Bible from a faith perspective see God's sovereign hand not merely in preserving the text but also in orchestrating the unearthing of data that highlight Scripture's fidelity. The extended genealogies, topographical descriptions, and historical asides that once seemed superfluous now provide a wealth of points for cross-checking. The more we dig, the more we see that Scripture's references to kings, roads, rivers, and local customs were penned by individuals intimately familiar with these realities. This approach resonates with Jesus' words at John 17:17: "Your word is truth."

Conclusion

Archaeology, though never the foundation of faith, has repeatedly shown that the biblical record reflects tangible realities in Palestine, Mesopotamia, Egypt, and the broader Mediterranean world. Excavations since the nineteenth century have uncovered city gates, stone inscriptions, and entire archives of cuneiform tablets that confirm the existence of biblical characters, the sequence of conquests, and the daily life of God's people across many centuries. From the Tower of Babel illusions in Mesopotamian temple-tower texts, to the Moabite Stone's corroboration of King Mesha's revolt, to the Taylor Prism's proud boasting from Sennacherib about besieging Jerusalem, the overlap with Scripture stands plain for those who would see it. Even as new archaeological insights occasionally prompt reevaluations, the underlying synergy between the Bible and the ancient record abides.

In the Christian Greek Scriptures, the Gospels and Acts are validated by local references, coinage, administrative titles, and place-names accurate to the mid-first century C.E. These are not the marks of a text contrived after the fact. They reveal eyewitness detail, consistent with Peter's statement, "We did not follow artfully contrived false stories" (2 Peter 1:16). Indeed, the arch of Titus in Rome still displays the captured Jewish menorah from Jerusalem's temple, fulfilling Jesus' prophecy about the city's downfall. The father of the faithful stands in contrast to the ephemeral nature of humanity's attempts to revise or ignore biblical reality. Over millennia, God's Word remains. Uncovered artifacts and inscriptions that confirm the existence of biblical towns, kings, and events highlight the deeper truth: that Scripture is not an abstract moral or philosophical essay but the "word of the living God" (Hebrews 10:31).

In summation, archaeology cannot replace faith, nor did God design it to. Instead, it functions as an external witness that time and again upholds the Bible's precise recollection of historical developments. The significance is twofold. First, believers see these findings as further proof that the divine author superintended Scripture's composition, ensuring that it is not a cunningly devised fable but verifiable truth. Second, for critics claiming that the Bible is mythological or contradictory, the artifacts in museums across the globe bear silent testimony that Scripture's accounts align with actual events. In that sense, archaeology stands as a friend to the biblical record, revealing, in so many ways, that "the word of Jehovah endures forever" (1 Peter 1:25). Thus, the results of careful, scientific excavations do not undermine but reinforce the reliability of the inspired record, pointing to the abiding worth of the Bible as God's message for all who seek truth.

CHAPTER 11 Can the Bible Alone Be Trusted as the One Complete Revelation?

When examining which spiritual writings truly speak with divine authority, both the Quran and the Bible come to the forefront. Although Muslims revere the Quran as God's final word, this same sacred text repeatedly alludes to earlier scriptures—the Torah (the law of Moses), the Zabur or Psalms (given to David), and the Injil or Gospel (proclaimed by Jesus)—as God's inspired Word. Surah 2:4 acknowledges those who "trust what has been revealed to you [Muhammad] and to others before you, and firmly believe in the life to come." Surah 5:43-47 references the Torah and the Gospel as containing "guidance and light," urging their followers to judge in accord with what Allah revealed. Numerous other passages affirm that the Torah, the Psalms, and the Gospel were the Word of God, which true believers should respect and obey. Nevertheless, among devout Muslims—whether fundamentalists or moderates—the question remains: does the Bible still stand intact and reliable, or has it been corrupted?

From a conservative biblical perspective, Scripture claims to be "inspired of God" (2 Timothy 3:16). Internal evidence and external confirmations reinforce that the Torah, Psalms, and Gospels remain valid, preserving God's message despite centuries of transmission. Indeed, the new covenant scriptures rely on and quote the Hebrew canon extensively, and the church from the first century onward recognized the Greek apostolic writings as equally authoritative. If the Quran itself alludes to these earlier books as God's word, the next question arises: do the biblical writings demonstrate authenticity, historical accuracy, and prophetic fulfillment beyond any rival text, including the Quran? This chapter explores that contention, revealing multiple lines of evidence that the Bible truly is "the word of Jehovah" (Isaiah 40:8), culminating in the gospel of Christ. The final inquiry becomes: can the Quran overshadow a text it acknowledges as God's revelation, or does the biblical record stand supreme as the complete, enduring Word of God?

Why the Quran Alludes to the Torah, Psalms, and Gospel

Anyone reading the Quran encounters references to Moses, David, and Jesus. In Surah 5:44-46, we find explicit statements that the Torah and the Gospel are from God, enshrining His judgments. Surah 2:136 instructs believers to say they trust in what was revealed to Abraham, Ishmael, Isaac, Jacob, the Tribes, and Moses, as well as what was given to Jesus. Surah 29:46 enjoins speaking with "the people of the Book"—commonly meaning Jews and Christians—without hostility. These texts confirm that Islam, in theory, venerates earlier scriptures. However, many Muslims today assert that the Bible has been tampered with, questioning its modern reliability.

Yet the Quran does not provide specific evidence of widespread textual corruption. In Surah 10:94, Muslims in doubt are told to consult those who read the earlier Book. That advice presupposes that the earlier scriptures remain extant. While some passages accuse Jews or Christians of hiding or misquoting verses, there is no blanket teaching in the Quran that the entire text of the Bible was lost or altered. Historically, thousands of manuscripts, including the Dead Sea Scroll of Isaiah from about the second century B.C.E., confirm that the Hebrew canon's essential content stands intact. Early Greek manuscripts of the Gospels and letters attest to the faithful transmission of the Christian Greek Scriptures. If these predate the Quran by centuries and remain consistent, the argument of total corruption fails. Instead, the biblical record emerges as an unbroken testimony, recognized by the Quran's repeated mention yet surpassing it in historical depth and prophetic scope.

The Unity and Authority Claimed by the Bible

Long before Muhammad's era, the Hebrew Scriptures were widely circulated, and Jesus endorsed them as God's Word (Matthew 5:17, 18). In the first century C.E., the apostles penned additional inspired writings. Each recognized the canonical authority of the other epistles (2 Peter 3:15, 16). By the close of the first century, the Christian congregations, spread across diverse regions, already recognized an authoritative collection of apostolic Gospels and letters. This body of Scripture, combined with the Hebrew canon, forms a cohesive narrative. Luke 24:44 quotes Jesus highlighting the Law of Moses, the Prophets, and the Psalms, placing them under God's direct inspiration. When the new covenant authors quote the Torah or the Prophets, they assume divine authorship. They also speak of their own writings as authoritative, claiming that "All Scripture is inspired of God" (2 Timothy 3:16). If the Quran endorses the same tradition, acknowledging these earlier revelations, we have at least a theoretical synergy: each tradition states that the Torah, Psalms, and Gospel have divine backing. But does the textual record prove that the Bible retains reliability? Yes, it does—and to an astonishing degree surpassing any other ancient text.

Historical and Archaeological Confirmation

Skeptics for centuries assailed the Pentateuch, attributing it to later redactors. But as archaeological discoveries multiplied in the nineteenth and twentieth centuries, evidence consistently affirmed biblical place-names, customs, and political realities that align with Moses' era. The Dead Sea Scrolls, found in the mid-twentieth century, include large sections of Isaiah, confirming a stable textual tradition from the second century B.C.E. This undermines claims that scribes rewrote the text during the Christian era. Meanwhile, the genealogical details, the lists of nations, the descriptions of kingdoms like Babylonia, Persia, and Rome, all match secular discoveries. The city states and laws described in Genesis match what archaeologists found in Mesopotamia. The conquests recorded in Joshua and Judges correspond with topographical realities in Canaan. King David, once doubted by some, has supporting references in the Tel Dan Stele from the ninth century B.C.E. The synergy between biblical accounts and extrabiblical finds intensifies confidence that the text remains historically grounded.

Likewise, the Gospels and Acts mention Roman governors, obscure local titles, and cultural details that historians consistently verify. Luke, for instance, calls Sergius Paulus a "proconsul" in Acts 13:7. In that era, Cyprus was indeed a senatorial province, requiring a proconsul. At Thessalonica, the city officials are called "politarchs" (Acts 17:6), matching inscriptions discovered on local arches. These incidental details are so consistently accurate that classical scholars like William Ramsay, initially skeptical, concluded Luke ranks among the great historians for ancient times. The notion that the Christian Greek Scriptures are late forgeries collapses when confronted with these verifiable data points. If authenticity so thoroughly characterizes the biblical text, it stands as "God's Word," consistently validated. By contrast, no parallel archaeological or historical backing elevates the Quran's references beyond the seventh century C.E. context of Arabia.

Geographical and Cultural Fidelity

Another hallmark of the Bible's authenticity is its precise depiction of Middle Eastern geography. From the layout of the Sinai wilderness to the territorial descriptions of Israel, from references to major rivers (Euphrates, Tigris, Nile) to minute local topography, the biblical record never betrays ignorance or anachronism. Moses' mentions of desert springs in Exodus align with actual wadis. The distinctive vegetation and climate details (in references to tamarisk trees or seasonal floods) fit the environment. Meanwhile, the narratives about Egyptian life reflect correct knowledge of crops, building practices, and the significance of the Nile's inundation. In the Gospels, the movement between Galilee, Samaria, and Judea matches first-century reality. The mention of local customs, such as how the synagogues functioned or how the Pharisees tithed small herbs (Matthew 23:23), resonates with known Jewish practice of the era.

This authenticity extends to how each biblical writer reflects his own time. Moses uses Egyptian terms, while Daniel references Persian or Babylonian expressions. The Christian apostles reflect Greek or Roman influences. This consistent cultural fidelity over the 1,600-year writing period underscores that the Bible's authors were eyewitnesses or close to the events, culminating in a library that never contradicts itself. That unity defies the notion of random compilation. By contrast, the Quran references biblical characters but does not always align them in correct historical sequences or contexts. For instance, it sometimes merges Mary the mother of Jesus with Miriam, the sister of Moses (Surah 19:27, 28). Such confusion suggests that while the Quran points to biblical heroes, it lacks the precise chronological or genealogical knowledge that the Bible preserves.

Candor of the Biblical Record

One of the Bible's most striking features is its unabashed honesty about its central figures. Far from whitewashing Israel's sins, the text includes humiliating national failures, repeated rebukes by the prophets, and the condemnation of revered kings like David or Solomon when they fell into serious wrongdoing (2 Samuel 11, 12; 1 Kings 11:1-13). The Psalms record David's remorseful prayers, revealing no attempt to hide moral lapses. Similarly, the Gospels reveal the apostles' cowardice at Jesus' arrest, Peter's denial, and the disciples' repeated misunderstanding of Jesus' teachings (Matthew 26:56, 69-75; Mark 9:32). Paul admitted his prior persecution of Christians (Galatians 1:13). This candor is rare in ancient texts, where national epics typically glorify heroes and omit defeats or moral failings. The biblical willingness to record the authors' own sins or humiliations strongly supports its reliability. If the Quran acknowledges the Torah and the Gospels as legitimate revelations, one must accept these frank narratives as part of God's truth. Contrariwise, the Quran's portrayal sometimes glosses over certain details or reinterprets them. The biblical principle of entire truthfulness stands as a prime reason to trust Scripture's genuineness.

Predictive Prophecy as Evidence of Divine Authorship

Perhaps the strongest hallmark of the Bible's divine authorship is fulfilled prophecy. Over centuries, biblical prophets declared future events in remarkable detail. Examples include Isaiah's naming of Cyrus around 200 years in advance (Isaiah 44:28; 45:1-7), Jeremiah's seventy-year forecast of Babylonian captivity (Jeremiah 25:11), Daniel's predictions of successive empires (Babylon, Medo-Persia, Greece, Rome) in Daniel chapter 2. The New Testament Gospels highlight how Jesus fulfilled numerous messianic prophecies, from being born in Bethlehem (Micah 5:2; Matthew 2:1-6) to being betrayed for thirty pieces of silver (Zechariah 11:12; Matthew 26:14, 15). No other ancient text, including the Quran, demonstrates a similar breadth of validated predictions. The Quran acknowledges some biblical prophets but does not supply comparably specific prophecies that span centuries and come true. While the Quran references the Day of Judgment and general conditions, it lacks the detailed foretelling that characterizes biblical prophecy. This distinct feature cements the Bible's status as God's Word, which God alone can authenticate via foreknowledge (Isaiah 46:9, 10).

Practical Guidance and Moral Superiority

Though often overshadowed by theological controversies, the Bible's moral code and practical counsel stand unrivaled in comprehensiveness, fairness, and compassion. From the Mosaic laws on justice and charity to Jesus' Sermon on the Mount calling for love of enemies (Matthew 5:44), Scripture's teachings shape ethical behavior in a way unmatched by typical ancient codes. The Law's emphasis on caring for widows, orphans, and foreigners (Deuteronomy 24:19-21) outstrips many pagan systems. The Christian instructions to "continue putting up with one another" and "forgiving one another freely" (Colossians 3:13) reflect a radical standard of compassion. Surah-based morality might incorporate some noble tenets, but it often merges legal restrictions with social punishments typical of seventh-century Arabia. Meanwhile, the biblical approach moves beyond externals, focusing on heart transformation (Romans 12:2). The impetus to measure oneself by God's holiness (1 Peter 1:15, 16) yields a moral high ground that fosters sincere love, not forced submission. This ethic resonates with the entire storyline of the Bible, from creation to Christ's ransom, culminating in the law of love that goes beyond mere legal obligations.

Transmission and Preservation of the Biblical Text

If the Bible is indeed God's Word, we might expect He would preserve it accurately. Over the centuries, scribes meticulously copied manuscripts in Hebrew, Aramaic, and Greek. By the time Muhammad arrived in the seventh century C.E., multiple translations and manuscript traditions already existed across vast regions. The Dead Sea Scroll of Isaiah, dating from approximately 150 to 100 B.C.E., reveals a text strikingly similar to the Masoretic Text from a millennium later. Meanwhile, the new covenant writings are attested by about 5,800 Greek manuscripts, plus early versions in Latin, Syriac, and Coptic, many from the second and third centuries C.E. This dwarfs the textual foundation for any classical work or for the Quran. The Quran was compiled within decades after Muhammad's death, with conflicting versions reportedly burned under Caliph Uthman. Meanwhile, the biblical text never required an official purge, since the abundance of manuscripts allowed cross-comparison, ensuring stable preservation. This strong textual foundation underscores God's providence in guarding Scripture from corruption.

The Quran's Silence on Alleged Biblical Corruption

Though modern Muslim polemic often insists that the Bible was irreparably altered, the Quran itself references no such sweeping textual corruption. Instead, it criticizes some Jews or Christians for misquoting, hiding, or forgetting parts, yet implicitly affirms the scriptures' continuing existence. Jewish and Christian communities venerated their texts centuries before and after Muhammad, leaving no evidence of a systematic rewriting. If such an unprecedented corruption had occurred, the Quran would presumably detail it. Instead, Surah 5:48 calls the Quran a "guardian" over previous revelations, not their replacement. Coupled with the historical evidence, we see that biblical content was widely dispersed in multiple languages by the seventh century, making total corruption impossible to coordinate. The presence of uniform theology in extant manuscripts from far-flung regions—Antioch, Rome, Alexandria—demonstrates the text's continuity. The biblical narrative thereby stands beyond the claims of Muslim revisionism.

The Test of Unity and Fulfillment

As a final point, the Bible's unifying theme from Genesis to Revelation has no parallel in religious literature. Roughly forty writers, spanning 1,600 years, contributed to a narrative that unfolds God's plan: the creation, mankind's fall, the promise of a messianic seed (Genesis 3:15), the calling of Abraham, the deliverance of Israel, the establishing of David's dynasty, the prophetic hope of a new covenant, the arrival of Jesus the Messiah, his sacrificial death and resurrection, and the promise of a restored creation (Romans 8:19-21). Each stage builds on the previous, culminating in Christ's mandate to preach salvation to all nations (Matthew 28:19, 20). This unwavering thread of redemption and the kingdom of God surpasses any claim of confusion or editorial patchwork. Where the Quran references biblical stories in truncated or rearranged ways, it does not replicate the integrated storyline that the biblical record reveals. Indeed, the difference is so profound that even moderate Muslim readers who study Scripture often marvel at its depth and coherence.

Reconciling the Quran's Affirmations of Earlier Scripture With Reality

If the Quran declares that the Torah, Psalms, and Gospel are from God, the logical conclusion is that these earlier revelations remain accessible, accurate, and necessary. A consistent Muslim might examine the actual biblical text and discover a comprehensive revelation culminating in Christ's atonement—doctrines the Quran denies. The tension is inescapable: the Quran acknowledges biblical authority but then rejects core biblical truths, such as Jesus being the unique Son of God or that he actually died on the cross (Sura 4:157). That contradiction suggests that either the Quran is inconsistent or it relies on partial knowledge of Scripture. By contrast, the Bible does not rely on external texts to validate itself. Its prophecies, historical confirmations, and unified theology stand self-sufficient. For those who revere the Quran's endorsement of earlier books, the rational step is to investigate the Bible thoroughly. A sincere heart might see that the biblical message is complete, overshadowing the contradictory claims made in the seventh century C.E.

Is the Bible the One Book of Truth?

When measuring divine revelation, the question arises: is there truly only one complete Book of Truth, or can multiple texts stand equally? The biblical record never cedes that there is a second or final text after the apostolic era. The closing warnings in Revelation 22:18, 19 condemn adding to or subtracting from the prophecy. Jude 3 affirms that the faith was "once for all time delivered to the holy ones." Meanwhile, if the Quran were truly from the same God, it would fully corroborate the cross, the resurrection, and the new covenant. Instead, it dismisses or reinterprets these foundational events. Contrarily, the Bible thoroughly testifies to Christ's sacrificial role, explaining that "without the shedding of blood there is no forgiveness" (Hebrews 9:22). The real tension is whether to trust the Bible, validated by manifold evidence, or to allow a latter-day text that partially endorses but also negates the biblical storyline.

Scripture calls itself "God's word" (1 Thessalonians 2:13), and Jesus identifies the Hebrew canon as "the word of God" (Mark 7:13). The new covenant expansions were also recognized as Scripture in Peter's and Paul's generation. Summing up the question, the biblical data confirm that these collected books—66 in total—comprise the complete revelation. If the Quran or any other text claims to supplant or correct them, that claim must be tested. The biblical principle stands: "Even if we or an angel out of heaven were to declare to you as good news something beyond what we declared to you as good news, let him be accursed" (Galatians 1:8). For that reason, devout Christians trust that the Bible alone is fully authoritative, while the Quran's partial endorsements do not override the final, fully realized new covenant. The Bible emerges as the single Book of Truth, verified by history, prophecy, moral excellence, and God's preserving power.

Conclusion

As the Quran itself acknowledges the Torah, the Psalms, and the Gospel as revelations from God, the question naturally follows: does that testimony lead one to revere the Bible as the one complete Book of Truth? Examining the biblical text reveals overwhelming evidence of authenticity: it presents an unbroken narrative from creation through Israel's covenant to Christ's final revelation, anchored in historical and archaeological confirmations, enriched by consistent cultural accuracy, validated by fulfilled prophecy, and infused with moral integrity. Jesus and the apostles repeatedly affirmed the inspiration of the Hebrew Scriptures, themselves adding a harmonious cluster of new covenant writings. Over the ages, these 66 canonical books stood unrefuted, forging the foundation of Christian faith.

While the Quran venerates those earlier writings, it also denies core biblical teachings about Christ's death and sonship. This discrepancy undercuts the notion that both can represent final, equal revelations from the same God. Conversely, the Bible holds that revelation concluded with Christ's apostolic circle. Indeed, Jesus' sacrifice and resurrection epitomize the pinnacle of God's saving purpose, beyond which no subsequent revelation can add or subtract.

If the Quran's references to the Torah and the Gospel are sincere, they imply that those prior books remain vital, yet the actual biblical content stands in contradiction to the Quran's altered claims about Jesus. Hence, the Bible remains the one consistent Book of Truth, overshadowing contradictory texts. For earnest hearts seeking God's Word, the Bible alone provides the entire counsel, validated by prophecy, historical candor, textual preservation, and a moral ethos that points to spiritual redemption through Christ. Embracing it in full leads to a faith not reliant on partial glimpses or latter reinterpretations, but on the unchangeable Word of Jehovah, culminating in salvation for those who respond in obedience and trust.

CHAPTER 12 How Should We Share Our Faith in Christ With Muslims?

Understanding the Task

Speaking with Muslims about the truths of Scripture requires thoughtful preparation, patience, and a firm grasp of Christian beliefs. The Quran upholds a reverence for God, whom Muslims call Allah, and presents Muhammad as the preeminent prophet. It references many biblical figures—Noah (Nūḥ), Abraham (Ibrāhīm), Moses (Mūsā), and Jesus ('Īsa)—but it recasts certain details, denying essential Christian doctrines such as Jesus' sacrificial death and sonship. Despite these differences, many Muslims show a strong zeal for worship and for what they perceive as the only true revelation. A Christian seeking to witness must remember that biblical evangelism calls for gentleness, discernment, and unwavering reliance on Scripture. As Peter wrote, "Always be ready to make a defense before everyone who demands of you a reason for the hope in you, but doing so with a mild temper and deep respect" (1 Peter 3:15). If we reflect on Paul's words, "I have become all things to people of all sorts, so that I might save some" (1 Corinthians 9:22), we realize the need to adapt our approach without compromising the truth.

Many Muslims believe that the Bible was once the Word of God but has since been corrupted, with the Quran alone remaining pure. This stance prompts them to resist biblical arguments as invalid. Yet the Quran also praises the Torah, the Psalms, and the Gospels as originally sent down by God. A Christian witness who acknowledges these earlier revelations in conversation can find an opening, given that the Torah, Psalms, and Gospel stand recognized in Surah 5:46, 47 and Surah 2:4. The key is to avoid immediate debate, instead building rapport and establishing the principle that one pursues truth wherever it leads (John 17:17). A witness can encourage the Muslim to examine the older Scriptures, trusting that God's Word remains incorruptible. Paul wrote, "Every saying of God is refined" (Proverbs 30:5), an assurance that leads us to treat the Hebrew and Greek Scriptures as a faithful record of God's revelation. Only by humble patience and scriptural reasoning can we guide a Muslim to see that Jesus is more than a prophet: he is the unique Savior and the culminating focus of all prior revelation (Luke 24:44).

Recognizing Muslim Beliefs

Christians who evangelize often meet Muslims who present a heartfelt conviction that Islam is the only valid religion and that the Quran is God's final message. They assert that "There is no God but Allah, and Muhammad is his Messenger," summing up the Islamic creed. Many hold to certain distinctive tenets: daily ritual prayers, obligatory charity, fasting in the month of Ramadan, and possibly aspirations to undertake the pilgrimage to Mecca. They maintain that Jesus was a true prophet but deny his crucifixion or the concept of his divine sonship, in conflict with fundamental Christian teachings (Matthew 16:16). They also see the Trinity as polytheism, considering it an insult to pure monotheism. Additionally, they claim that the biblical text was altered, while the Quran remained pristine. A Christian witness may learn that a devout Muslim condemns idol worship, immorality, and falsehood—points that can serve as areas of agreement, since Scripture likewise condemns these (1 Thessalonians 4:3; 1 Corinthians 6:9, 10).

Talking with Muslims about God's name, Jehovah, might be an interesting path: the Tetragrammaton in Hebrew can highlight how the God of the patriarchs is a personal deity, not an unnamed force. Nonetheless, many Muslims find "Son of God" offensive, interpreting it as if Christians claim God had a literal child. Careful explanation, grounded in Scripture, clarifies that "Son of God" is a title reflecting Jesus' unique position, not physical procreation. Still, wise evangelists wait until they have built trust to address such a sensitive topic directly. They might reference Surah 2:4's acceptance of earlier revelations, noting that these revelations show Jesus' role in a manner that completes, rather than contradicts, the lineage of prophets. Ultimately, the goal is to show that Christ alone mediates between God and mankind (1 Timothy 2:5), far surpassing the function assigned to him in Islam.

Cultivating Empathy and Patience

The apostle Paul wrote, "To the Jews I became as a Jew so that I might win Jews; to those under law I became as under law... to those without law I became as without law... to the weak I became weak" (1 Corinthians 9:20-22). Paul's example encourages adopting an empathic stance, without endorsing errors, in order to relate more effectively. Muslims, especially devout ones, want to see sincerity rather than combative argument. If a Christian's approach is adversarial, insisting from the outset that the Quran is false, the conversation will likely end in frustration. Instead, mild speech can break down barriers (Proverbs 25:15). The Christian can be transparent about personal devotion, trust in the Word of God, and a deep respect for moral living. This resonates with a Muslim perspective that cherishes outward piety. If the Muslim sees that a Christian leads a righteous life, upholds God's holiness, and defends the high moral standards of Scripture, that may open a pathway for earnest dialogue.

Many Muslims seldom read the Bible, relying on hearsay from Islamic teachers who claim it is corrupted. The Christian can gently ask if the friend has ever personally examined the Torah or the Gospels. He might add how Scripture overcame centuries of opposition, surviving with an unbroken chain of manuscripts (such as the Dead Sea Scroll of Isaiah or extensive Greek papyri). Over time, if the Muslim is open, references to textual evidence can show that no global corruption of the text could have occurred. The Christian then suggests reading certain passages from the Gospels. Surah 5:47 states, "Let the people of the Gospel judge by what God has revealed." Affirming that we still have that Gospel intact can help. Simple reading of John 3:16, John 14:6, or Jesus' own statements about the Father might spark reflection that the new covenant message remains unaltered.

Avoiding Needless Offense

Paul reminded believers, "Whether you are eating or drinking or doing anything else, do all things for God's glory. Keep from becoming causes for stumbling" (1 Corinthians 10:31, 32). In Muslim evangelism, a few guidelines preserve peace. A Christian sister might dress more modestly than usual, even wearing a head covering when engaging a Muslim woman, thus showing respect for local custom. A Christian man should ordinarily not attempt to teach a group of Muslim women in a formal setting, as this can raise eyebrows or offend. Similarly, one should not brandish pictures of Jesus or crosses, which Muslims associate with idolatrous imagery. The Christian can instead emphasize that worship is spiritual, not reliant on icons (John 4:24). If the Muslim friend calls Jesus only a "prophet," the Christian can graciously use that term for a time, waiting for the right moment to discuss the full identity of Christ as the Messiah, "the beginning of the creation by God" (Revelation 3:14). When the conversation later turns to atonement, the Christian can reference the willingness of God to provide redemption. But pushing these truths too soon can cause shutdown.

A Christian must also be cautious about how to handle the Quran. Some Muslims are extremely sensitive regarding its sanctity. Ridiculing the text or flippantly quoting from it might provoke hostility. Quoting it briefly to highlight how it mentions Abraham or Moses can be constructive, yet that tactic might also backfire if done condescendingly. The Christian stands on the Bible's authority, not the Quran's. The apostle Peter wrote that we are "keeping a good conscience, so that in the thing in which you are spoken against, those who speak against you may be put to shame" (1 Peter 3:16). Calmness in the face of potential tensions upholds the Christian's dignity and love.

Pointing to Early Revelations: The Torah, Psalms, and Gospels

Surah 2:4 highlights "what was revealed to you [Muhammad] and what was revealed before you," acknowledging that earlier scriptures came from God. Surah 10:94 suggests that one can consult the people who read the Book if in doubt. Based on this, the Christian can gently note that many essential truths appear first in the Torah, such as the covenant with Abraham, the moral laws for Israel, and prophecies pointing to a greater Deliverer (Genesis 22:15-18; Deuteronomy 18:15). The Christian might show how these relate to Jesus, who told the Jews, "If you believed Moses you would believe me, for that one wrote about me" (John 5:46). The psalms that Muslims theoretically accept, for instance David's Psalm 110:1, show Jehovah saying to David's Lord, "Sit at my right hand." The Christian can explain how Jesus employed that text to reveal himself as David's greater Lord (Matthew 22:44). Bit by bit, the Christian reveals that these older writings consistently foretell the Messiah's role, culminating in the Gospels.

Once the conversation moves to the Gospels, the Christian can highlight how they present a carefully preserved account of Jesus' life, consistent with the apostles' eyewitness testimonies (Luke 1:1-4; John 21:24). The Christian might ask, "If the Quran says the Torah and the Gospels are from God, how could God allow them to be corrupted everywhere, with no uncorrupted copies left?" The mention of thousands of manuscripts preceding the seventh century (like partial papyri from the second century C.E.) might plant a seed that the biblical text was stable long before the Quran's writing. If a Muslim insists that corruption occurred anyway, the Christian could gently ask for a plausible historical scenario that would unify all Christian or Jewish communities worldwide in rewriting every biblical manuscript. Absent such an explanation, the Christian can calmly suggest that God's Word remains intact, just as He promised (Isaiah 40:8). Over time, such reasoning might reduce the Muslim's assumption of a corrupted Bible.

Emphasizing God's Plan for Redemption

At some juncture, the Christian must convey that the entire Bible, from Genesis onward, leads to Christ's sacrificial role. Muslims, taught that Jesus did not die on the cross, need to see scriptural proof of atonement. The Christian can mention how the Torah set up a system of sacrifices for sin (Leviticus 17:11), foreshadowing a greater sacrifice. The prophet Isaiah (Isaiah 53:5) wrote that one servant would be wounded for our transgressions. The Gospels identify Jesus as that "Lamb of God" (John 1:29). The Christian can note that the new covenant revelation surpasses prior limited ceremonies, fulfilling them completely. Not that God established new truths that contradict earlier prophets but that He carried out His original purpose. Jesus said, "I came, not to destroy, but to fulfill" (Matthew 5:17).

As the Christian shares these insights, he or she might highlight how this plan to ransom mankind underscores God's love and holiness—attributes Muslims also believe in but do not link to the cross. For instance, the Christian might read Romans 5:8: "God recommends his own love to us, in that, while we were yet sinners, Christ died for us." This stands at the heart of the Christian message, clarifying that "the wages sin pays is death, but the gift God gives is everlasting life by Christ" (Romans 6:23). Gently contrasting that with the idea that men must earn acceptance through Islamic works can open the Muslim's mind to the biblical principle of grace.

Responding to Typical Objections

Muslims often raise certain objections. One is that "God has no son." The Christian can clarify that we do not teach God had a literal child but that "Son of God" expresses a profound relationship and a role in creation (Colossians 1:15, 16). Another is "How can God be three?" The Christian might respond that Scripture never depicts three gods but that God manifests Father, Son, and Holy Spirit in harmonious oneness. Indeed, we do not want to articulate erroneous Trinity theology, but we clarify that Jesus is subordinate to the Father (John 14:28), consistent with biblical monotheism. Muslims also question the cross, claiming a substitute died in Jesus' place. The Christian can read from John 19:33-35, describing eyewitness testimony of Jesus' death, and note that the earliest followers, many of whom died for their faith, believed unwaveringly that Christ truly died and rose. They never taught a body double or any such notion. The Christian can also point out that "without shedding of blood there is no forgiveness" (Hebrews 9:22). Another question might arise about unclean foods or daily prayers. The Christian can gently explain that under the new covenant, believers are not bound by Mosaic dietary laws but follow Christ's instructions. Refraining from forcing complex discussions, the Christian aims to show the essential unity of God's plan in Scripture. Over time, these seeds can bear fruit if the Muslim allows the spirit of truth to work in his heart.

The Vital Importance of Personal Conduct

Muslims watch carefully how Christians behave. Many harbor stereotypes that Westerners and nominal Christians champion immorality or irreverence. A sincere Christian witness who models humility, chastity, honesty, and devotion can break down these preconceived ideas. James wrote, "Show me your faith without works, and I will show you my faith by my works" (James 2:18). If the Muslim sees consistent prayer habits, moral purity, and a generous spirit, that might speak more loudly than theological arguments alone. The Christian must avoid hypocrisy. If the Christian rails against drunkenness but engages in shady conduct, the Muslim sees contradiction. The apostle Paul emphasized that we strive not to place an obstacle. Our integrity can powerfully attest to the transforming power of Christ's message.

This also means being slow to take offense if the Muslim friend criticizes. We can respond with mildness, as Jesus taught. Muslims respect self-control and dignity. If a Christian uses God's name in vain or shows ignorance of biblical teachings, the Muslim might suspect we do not truly value our faith. So, the Christian invests time in personal study, knows the biblical texts well, and prays for God's wisdom. As Paul told Timothy, "Be diligent to present yourself approved to God, a workman with nothing to be ashamed of, handling the word of truth aright" (2 Timothy 2:15).

Practical Methods of Engagement

Since the earliest Christians spread the gospel by personal visits, traveling from house to house or conversing in marketplaces (Acts 20:20; 17:17), we can do likewise in modern contexts. Meeting Muslims in daily life—perhaps at a store, a bus stop, a park—can lead to a simple friendly conversation. If the region allows public witnessing, we might politely greet passersby, being prepared for either acceptance or refusal. Online interactions also arise. Social media can become a place to share scriptural truths with Muslims abroad. The Christian who does so must carefully maintain respect, clarity, and gentle speech, aware that typed words might be more easily misunderstood.

It helps to use the approach Jesus modeled with Nicodemus (John 3:1-21). He engaged him at night, in a personal conversation, addressing questions about spiritual rebirth. Similarly, the Christian might find it best to speak one-on-one with a Muslim, not challenging him in front of others. This fosters a less defensive environment. If the Muslim invites you to a further talk, you can accept, ensuring you have enough knowledge about their beliefs. Keep lines of communication open, perhaps with phone or email, to address follow-up questions. Remember that conversion to Christ for a devout Muslim is a huge step. Family or community repercussions can be severe. The Christian must remain supportive, guiding the new believer so that fear does not derail his spiritual growth (Mark 8:34-38). The apostle Paul "planted, Apollos watered, but God kept making it grow" (1 Corinthians 3:6). We must do our part and let God's Spirit handle the rest.

Concluding Confidence in God's Word

Witnessing to Muslims can be an occasion both to defend biblical truth and to demonstrate Christlike love. It demands a thorough knowledge of Scripture, an awareness of basic Islamic doctrine, a readiness to adopt modest approaches, and a heart of compassion. The gospel is "God's power for salvation to everyone having faith" (Romans 1:16). That includes Muslims. If we remain calm, polite, and reliant on God's Word rather than on belligerent argument, we can be used by Jehovah to touch hearts. Though not all will respond, seeds of truth planted may later sprout. Our role is to proclaim the good news faithfully, not to force acceptance. Jesus said: "No one can come to me unless the Father, who sent me, draws him" (John 6:44). We trust in that divine drawing.

In sum, approaching Muslims with scriptural knowledge, considerate conversation, and genuine humility allows for pre-evangelism that may, in due time, open their hearts to the fullness of redemption in Christ. The unified thread of revelation from the Torah to the Gospels—and the subsequent apostolic writings presents a powerful, coherent testimony that stands uncorrupted, consistent with the principle that "the saying of Jehovah endures forever" (1 Peter 1:25). If a Muslim is willing to examine that testimony, searching with honest intent, the Holy Spirit can bring conviction. The Christian's task is to remove stumbling blocks, present the truths of Scripture with clarity, and manifest the character of Christ in daily life. By doing so, we honor God's call "that all sorts of men should be saved and come to an accurate knowledge of truth" (1 Timothy 2:4), including those who once fervently adhered to Islam.

Bibliography

Anderson, K. (2017). *UNDERSTANDING ISLAM AND TERRORISM: A Biblical Point of View*. Cambridge, OH: Christian Publishing House.

Andrews, E. (2018). *THE EARLY CHRISTIAN COPYISTS OF THE NEW TESTAMENT: The Making and Copying of the New Testament Books*. Cambridge: Christian Publishing House.

Andrews, E. (2020). *FROM SPOKEN WORDS TO SACRED TEXTS: Introduction-Intermediate New Testament Textual Studies*. Cambridge: Christian Publishing House.

Andrews, E. D. (2012). *DIFFICULTIES IN THE BIBLE UPDATED: Updated and Expanded*. Cambridge, OH: Christian Publishing House.

Andrews, E. D. (2016). *THE COMPLETE GUIDE to BIBLE TRANSLATION: Bible Translation Choices and Translation Principles [Second Edition]* . Cambridge: Christian Publishing House.

Andrews, E. D. (2016). *YOUR GUIDE FOR DEFENDING THE BIBLE: Self-Education of the Bible Made Easy*. Cambridge, OH: Christian Publishing House.

Andrews, E. D. (2017). *EARLY CHRISTIANITY IN THE FIRST CENTURY: Jesus' Witnesses to the Ends of the Earth*. Cambridge, OH: Christian Publishing House.

Andrews, E. D. (2017). *IS THE BIBLE REALLY THE WORD OF GOD?: Is Christianity the One True Faith?* Cambridge, Ohio: Christian Publishing House.

Andrews, E. D. (2019). *INTRODUCTION TO THE TEXT OF THE NEW TESTAMENT: From The Authors and Scribe to the Modern Critical Text*. Cambridge, Ohio: Christian Publishing House.

Andrews, E. D. (2019). *THE READING CULTURE OF EARLY CHRISTIANITY: The Production, Publication, Circulation, and Use of Books in the Early Christian Church.* Cambridge, OH: Christian Publishing House.

Andrews, E. D. (2020). *INERRANCY OF SCRIPTURE: How Can We Believe Inerrancy of Scripture In the Originals When We Don't Have the Originals?* Cambridge, OH: Christian Publishing House.

Andrews, E. D. (2020). *THE NEW TESTAMENT DOCUMENTS: Can They Be Trusted?* Cambridge, OH: Christian Publishing House.

Andrews, E. D. (2023). *CHRISTIAN APOLOGETICS: Answering the Tough Questions: Evidence and Reason in Defense of the Faith.* Cambridge, Ohio: Christian Publishing House.

Andrews, E. D. (2023). *INTRODUCTION TO OLD TESTAMENT TEXTUAL CRITICISM.* Cambridge, OH: Christian Publishing House.

Andrews, E. D. (2023). *INTRODUCTION TO THE TEXT OF THE OLD TESTAMENT: From the Authors and Scribes to the Modern Critical Text.* Cambridge, OH: Christian Publishing House.

Andrews, E. D. (2023). *ISLAM & THE QURAN: Examining the Quran & Islamic Teachings.* Cambridge, OH: Christian Publishing House.

Andrews, E. D. (2023). *ISLAMIC ESCHATOLOGY: Awaiting Al-Mahdi—The Twelfth Imam and the Future of Islam.* Cambridge, OH: Christian Publishing House.

Andrews, E. D. (2023). *THE BIBLE ON TRIAL: Examining the Evidence for Being Inspired, Inerrant, Authentic, and True.* Cambridge, Ohio: Christian Publishing House.

Andrews, E. D. (2023). *THE OLD TESTAMENT: Commentary, Background, & Bible Difficulties (Introduction to the Old Testament).* Cambridge, OH: Christian Publishing House.

Andrews, E. D. (2023). *THE SCRIBE AND THE TEXT OF THE NEW TESTAMENT: Scribal Activities in the Transmission of the Text of the New Testament.* Cambridge, Ohio: Christian Publishing House.

Andrews, E. D. (2023). *THE TEXT OF THE NEW TESTAMENT: A Beginners Handbook to New Testament Textual Studies.* Cambridge, OH: Christian Publishing House.

Andrews, E. D. (2024). *DO WE STILL NEED A LITERAL BIBLE?: Discover the Truth about Literal Bibles.* Cambridge, OH: Christian Publishing House.

Andrews, E. D. (2024). *FAITH UNDER FIRE: Refuting the Top 30 Arguments Atheists Make Against Christianity.* Cambridge, OH: Christian Publishing House.

Andrews, E. D. (2024). *THE ENCYCLOPEDIA OF CHRISTIAN APOLOGETICS: The Resource for Pastors, Teachers, and Believers.* Cambridge: Christan Publishing House.

Andrews, E. D. (2025). *BIBLE DIFFICULTIES: How to Approach Difficulties In the Bible.* Cambridge, OH: Christian Publishing House.

Andrews, E. D. (2025). *BIBLICAL WORDS AND THEIR MEANING: An Introduction to Lexical Semantics.* Cambridge, OH: Christian Publishing House.

Andrews, E. D. (2025). *CAN WE TRUST THE BIBLE?* Cambridge, OH: Christian Publishing House.

Andrews, E. D. (2025). *EARLY CHRISTIANITY: Exploring Backgrounds, Historical Settings, and Cultures.* Cambridge, OH: Christian Publishing House.

Andrews, E. D. (2025). *LINGUISTICS AND THE BIBLICAL TEXT: Unlocking Scripture Through the Science of Language.* Cambridge, OH: Christian Publishing House.

Andrews, E. D. (2025). *OVERCOMING BIBLE DIFFICULTIES: Answers to the So-Called Errors and Contradictions [Second Edition].* Cambridge: Christian Publishing House.

Andrews, E. D. (2025). *THE EARLY VERSIONS OF THE NEW TESTAMENT: Their Origins, Transmission, and Reliability.* Cambridge, OH: Christian Publishing House.

Andrews, E. D. (2025). *THE ENCYCLOPEDIA OF THE TEXT OF THE NEW TESTAMENT: The Resource for Pastors, Teachers, and Believers.* Cambridge, OH: Christian Publishing House.

Andrews, E. D. (2025). *THE FACES OF ISLAM: Faith or Facade: Decoding Islam's Strategies.* Cambridge, OH: Christian Publishing House.

Andrews, E. D. (2025). *UNDERSTANDING BIBLICAL WORDS: A Guide to Sound Interpretation.* Cambridge, OH: Christian Publishing House.

Brand, C., Draper, C., & Archie, E. (2003). *Holman Illustrated Bible Dictionary: Revised, Updated and Expanded.* Nashville, TN: Holman.

Bromiley, G. W. (1986). *The International Standard Bible Encyclopedia (Vol. 1-4).* Grand Rapids, MI: William B. Eerdmans Publishing Co.

Bukay, D. (2016). *Islam and the Infidels: The Politics of Jihad, Dawah, and Hijrah.* New Jersey: Transaction Publishers.

Clayton, J. (2006). *Luther and His Work.* Whitefish: Kessinger Publishing.

Cyril, G. (2013). *The New Encyclopedia of Islam (4th Edition).* Walnut Creek, CA: Rowman & Littlefield Publishers.

Dashti, A. (1985). *23 Years: A Study of the Prophetic Career of Mohammed.* London: George Allen & Unwin.

Dodge, C. H. (2003). *The Everything Understanding Islam Book: A Complete and Easy to Read Guide to Muslim Beliefs, Practices, Traditions, and Culture .* New York: Simon and Schuster.

Elwell, W. A. (1988). *Baker Encyclopedia of the Bible.* Grand Rapids: Baker Book House.

Elwell, W. A. (2001). *Evangelical Dictionary of Theology (Second Edition).* Grand Rapids: Baker Academic.

Erickson, M. J. (2001). *The Concise Dictionary of Christian Theology.* Wheaton: Crossway Books.

Esposito, J. L. (2016). *Islam: The Straight Path.* New York: Oxford University Press.

Geisler, N. L. (1999). *Baker Encyclopedia of Christian Apologetics.* Grand Rapids: Baker Books.

Geisler, N. L., & Saleeb, A. (2006). *Answering Islam: The Crescent in Light of the Cross.* Grand Rapids, MI: Baker Books.

Gibb, H. A., & Kramers, J. H. (1953). *Shorter Encyclopedia of Islam.* Ithaca: Cornell University Press.

Green, J. B., McKnight, S., & Marshall, H. (1992). *Dictionary of Jesus and the Gospels.* Downers Grove, IL: InterVarsity Press.

Hitti, P. K. (2002). *History of The Arabs, 10 Revised Edition.* New York: Palgrave Macmillan.

Is the Qur'an Written in Pure Arabic? - Study to Answer. (2017, May 22). Retrieved May 29, 2017, from http://www.studytoanswer.net/islam/purearabic.html

Janosik, D. (2019). *THE GUIDE TO ANSWERING ISLAM: What Every Christian Needs to Know About Islam and the Rise of Radical Islam.* Reynoldsburg, OH: Christian Publishing House.

Jeffery, A. (1952). *Materials for the History of the Text of the Quran.* New York: Russell F. Moore.

Jeffery, A. (2009). *The Foreign Vocabulary of the Quran.* Piscataway: Gorgias Press.

Lenski, R. C. (1942, 2008). *The Interpretation of St. John's Gospel.* Minneapolis: Augsburg Fortress.

Levy, R. (1957). *The Social Structure of Islam.* Cambridge: Cambridge University Press.

Morris, C. (1916). *Winston's Cumulative Loose-Leaf Encyclopedia: A Comprehensive Reference Work.* Chicago: The John C. Winston Company.

Mounce, W. D. (2006). *Mounce's Complete Expository Dictionary of Old & New Testament Words.* Grand Rapids, MI: Zondervan.

Newby, G. (2002). *A Concise Encyclopedia of Islam.* London: Oneworld Publications.

Pratt Jr, R. L. (2000). *Holman New Testament Commentary: I & II Corinthians, vol. 7.* Nashville: Broadman & Holman Publishers.

Ryken, L. (2009). *Understanding English Bible Translation: The Case for an Essentially Literal Approach.* Wheaton: Crossway Books.

Sookhdeo, P. (2001). *A Christian's Pocket Guide to Islam.* Pewsey, Wiltshire: Isaac Publishing.

Sproul, R. C. (2016). *KOWING SCRIPTURE (Expanded ed.).* Downers Groves: InterVarsity Press.

Stewart, D. (1967). *Great Ages of Man Early Islam.* Des Moines: Time/life Books.

Tennent, T. (2017). *Essentials of Islam - Student's Guide.* Seattle: CreateSpace Independent Publishing.

Wayne, G., & J. I., P. (2005). *Translating Truth: The Case for Essentially Literal Bible Translation.* Wheaton, IL: Good News Publishers/Crossway Books.

Wherry, E. (1973). *A Comprehensive Commentary on the Quran.* Otto Zeller Verlag: Osnabruck.

Williams, J. A. (1994). *The Word of Islam (Avebury Studies in Green Research).* Austin: University of Texas Press.

Wood, D. R. (1996). *New Bible Dictionary (Third Edition).* Downers Grove: InterVarsity Press.